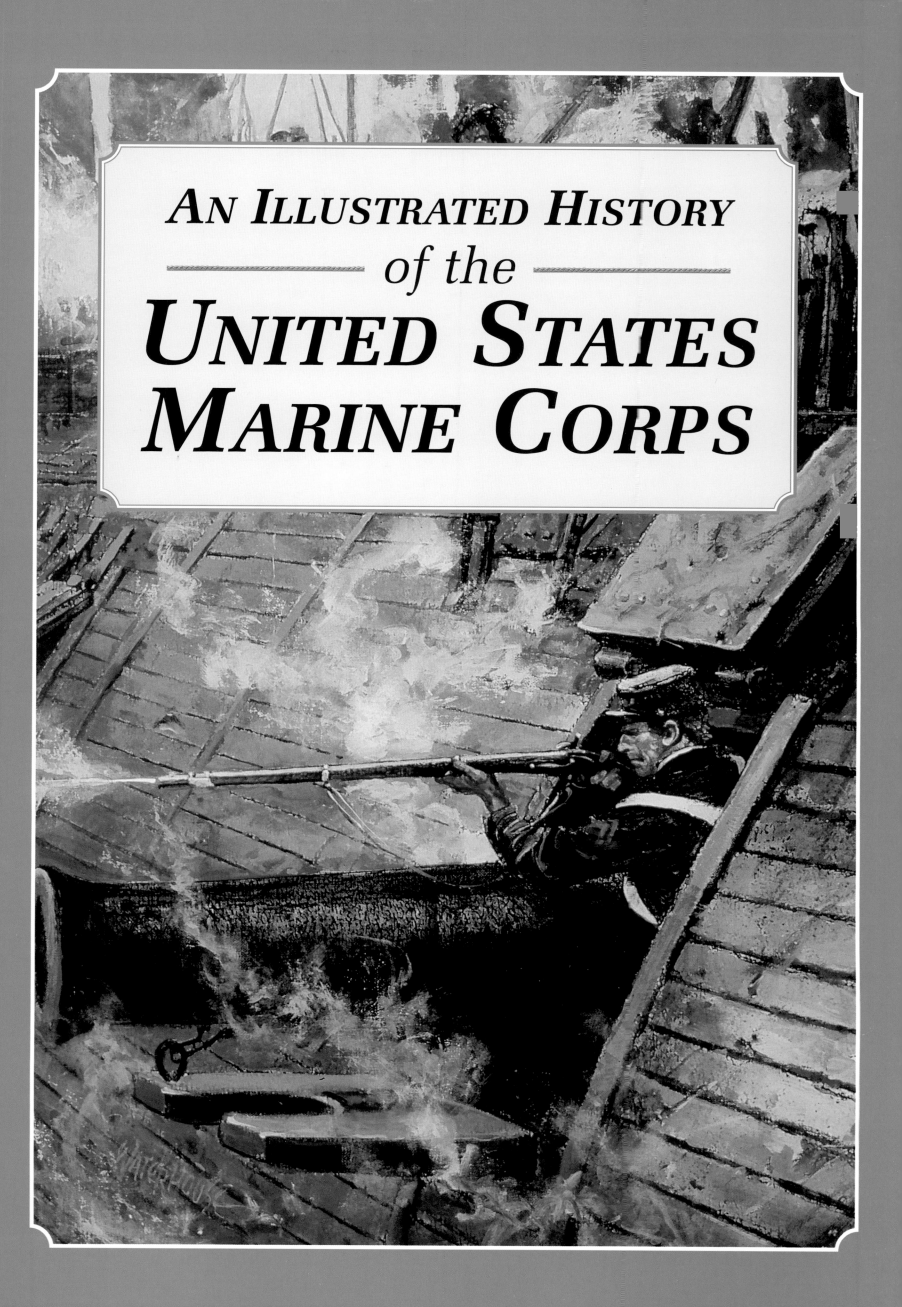

AN ILLUSTRATED HISTORY
of the
UNITED STATES MARINE CORPS

An Illustrated History
of the
United States
Marine Corps

Chester G. Hearn

SALAMANDER

A Salamander Book

Published by
Salamander Books Ltd.
8 Blenheim Court
Brewery Road
London N7 9NT
United Kingdom

© Salamander Books Ltd., 2002

A member of **Chrysalis** Books plc

ISBN 1 84065 396 5

Credits

Project Manager:
Ray Bonds

Designer:
Mark Holt

Picture Research:
Anne and Rolf Lang

Commissioned photography:
Don Eiler

Color reproduction:
Anorax Imaging Ltd.

Printed in China

The Author

Chester ("Chet") G. Hearn is a former member of the United States armed forces. He has written more than a dozen books on U.S. military history, including *An Illustrated History of the United States Navy*, *Naval Battles of the Civil War* (published by Salamander), and *George Washington's Schooners: The First American Navy*, *Admiral David Glasgow Farragut*, and *Admiral David Dixon Porter* (published by the U.S. Naval Institute Press). Three of his titles have been "alternate selections" for the History Book Club of America. He graduated from Allegheny College with a B.A. in Economics and a minor in History, and spent much of a civilian career as an executive in industry. He now spends all his time writing and researching – when he is not afloat on Lake Erie, Pennsylvania, or at a local pool keeping in shape for competitive swimming.

Acknowledgments

The publishers are grateful to the U.S. Department of Defense, the U.S.National Archives, and the Library of Congress for contributing many photographs and copies of valuable paintings for inclusion in this book. In addition, special thanks go to the private individuals and organizations who made available many rare artifacts and fascinating images for photography by Don Eiler. It would not have been possible to publish this work without their efforts and generosity. They include: Gunnery Sergeant Tom Williams of the United States Marine Corps Headquarters and Headquarters Detachment, Marine Corps Historical Company, Fredrick, Md, who provided artifacts that appear on pages 14, 17, 20-21, 30-31, 35, 36, 38, 39 (headgear), 50, 60 (jacket and trousers), 63, 65 (artifacts at top right), and 149; Major Richard Spooner, USMC (ret), The Globe & Laurel, Triangle, Va, who provided artifacts that appear on pages 27, 39 (epaulets), 46, 48 (top), 56, 75 (bottom left), 84 (top left and six emblem plates), and 111 (bottom); and also, in particular, Jim LaPine who not only made his own artifacts and other materials available but also arranged for other collectors (including Sgt Major Charles J. Austin, USMC Ret., Peter Killie, Howard Wulforst and Brian Benedict) to bring some of their artifacts to his home for photography and reproduction on the following pages: La Pine 45 top, 47, 48 bottom, 49 bottom left and right, 57, 59 bottom, 66 bottom left, 68-69 bottom, 75 bottom right, 79 bottom, 81 artifacts, 82-83 artifacts, 84 top right, 85, 100 center, 104 left; Austin 60, 79 top; Killie 65 bottom, 74 center; Benedict 66 bottom right; combined collections of LaPine and Austin 49 bottom right; combined collections of LaPine, Austin and Killie 69 top, 72 top.

Contents

INTRODUCTION

The history of the United States Marine Corps is a remarkable account of how a small, nondescript group of ships' guards evolved into a multi-functional organization that combines ground, air, and sea combat units. From a primitive, underpaid, and often-abused force of 1,000 men, the Marines have survived numerous political and inter-service attempts to emasculate the Corps. Yet the Corps prevailed with a tenacious fortitude and during times of crisis grew to six divisions with more than 475,000 men and women. Through all these scuffles during peace and war, the Marines continued to adapt, filling voids in the United States' defense structure while developing the unique capability of amphibious assault.

After more than two hundred and twenty-five years, the Marine Corps has never relinquished a major function or suffered one being stripped away by inter-service rivalry, despite the efforts at various times of such contemporary notables as Theodore Roosevelt, Harry Truman, and Dwight Eisenhower. Marines still serve as detachments on capital ships and act as security guards at naval shore installations, but they also serve as specially trained, highly mobile attack units operating from uniquely dedicated vessels carrying Harrier jets, helicopters, and the very latest in laser-guided weaponry. The evolution of the airplane and the helicopter brought an end to the primitive ideology that all Marines were basically infantrymen, and the evolution of the short-platform aircraft carrier made today's Marine Corps the multi-purpose, always ready, amphibious component of America's land, sea, and air forces.

From its birth swathed in organizational simplicity to its growth in military complexity, a Corps of proud men led by determined commandants weathered four abrupt changes in their doctrine of warfare. The first phase began with Continental Marines serving on ships during the American Revolution. Not much changed until the Spanish-American War when Marines went ashore at Guantanamo Bay, Cuba, and routed the defenders.

The second phase began a year later when the Navy put men ashore on the Philippines and soon learned that their Marines were among the fiercest and most determined fighters in the world. For more than forty years (1899-1941), from Mindanao to Belleau Wood to Shanghai, the Marines evolved into an expeditionary force using infantry, artillery, and eventually aircraft to fight the Germans in World War I and mount military interventions into trouble spots in Latin America. During this phase the Navy asked the Marine Corps to create units capable of seizing advanced naval bases by amphibious assault, giving birth to the Fleet Marine Force and new doctrinal guidelines. Without this action, there would have been no Marine Corps in 1942 to lead the fighting in the South and Central Pacific and no amphibian vehicles to breach the enemy's beach defenses.

During the third phase, the Corps established itself as a veritable "force in readiness." During World War II Marines became more than a Fleet Marine Force, leading the first amphibious assault of the war on Guadalcanal, stopping the advance of the Japanese in its tracks, and turning the war around in the Pacific while the U.S. Army concentrated its efforts on defeating Germany. The Corps proved to all detractors that it was America's principal readiness force, particularly outside the European continent and, compared to all other ground forces, the "first to fight." World War II provided the Corps with a first-time opportunity to perform a major offensive role in an offensive war. Marines tested their amphibious warfare doctrine, learned to use amphibian tractors, perfected naval support gunfire, and developed the world's best close air support, all of which paid enormous dividends in future campaigns. In 1945 the bitter fight for Iwo Jima elevated the public's image of the Marine Corps to heights surpassing all the campaigns that went before. And after the war with Japan ended victoriously, the Marines were the first provisional brigade to respond to the call during the Korean War, and the first tactical ground brigade to land in South Vietnam. From these wars came new traditions for the Marine Corps.

The changing technology of warfare brought the Marine Corps into a fourth phase. The U.S. Air Force operated the strategic bombers, the new stealth fighters, and munitions that could destroy the world or any part of it. The Navy possessed submarines armed with intercontinental strategic missiles, carriers with jet aircraft armed with surgical-strike weapons, missile ships with Tomahawks, and targeting devices beamed off satellites, AWAC coordinates, and even unmanned drones. The U.S. Army had its ground forces with Special Operations units, Rangers, Green Berets, airborne divisions, and mountain troops.

Once again the Marine Corps had to re-evolve, to modify its doctrine, and become an all-purpose force, ready to do the work of the other three services on an instant's notice. If the nation needed men to perform air missions for attack, rescue, or reconnaissance, the Marines were ready. If the Department of Defense needed a rapid deployment force in Kuwait, Somalia, or Afghanistan, Marines now had the ships to get them there in a matter of days, and sometimes a matter of hours. They became a mini-force in readiness, a Marine Expeditionary Unit with aircraft and artillery fully capable of performing any task for any emergency where an instant response became critical, whether the call required fighting or the performance of humanitarian tasks.

Afghanistan provided a new and different testing ground for the Marine Corps of the twenty-first century. The Middle East has never been a perfect place for Marines to match their capabilities against an enemy, and Afghanistan must rank among the worst geographically. The enemy wears no uniforms. He, and sometimes she, may smile at you one day and shoot or truck-bomb you the next.

Muslim terrorists fly jetliners into tall buildings occupied by civilians. Palestinians prefer strapping charges to their bodies and blowing themselves up among groups of Israeli civilians – all of which suggests that new countermeasures are required to deal with terrorists willing to commit suicide to take the lives of those of a different faith.

To keep pace with the changing times, in recent years the Marine Corps has made their expeditionary units Special Operations Capable (SOC). In a new century where the enemy, supported by radical Muslim leaders, has established terrorist cells throughout the world, the Marine Corps must continue to adapt to changing conditions, which is exactly what they have done since their formation in 1775.

The troublesome outbursts of fighting in Afghanistan may not end for years, and while it lasts the Marine Corps must stand ready to respond. If the Muslim nations of the Middle East do not curb terrorism, MEU(SOC) units will be asked to respond to every emergency – be it a firefight, a mass invasion, or peacekeeping – and they must and will be prepared to answer any call.

Today Marines are spread around the world. They train Filipinos to fight Muslim cells controlled by Moros in the southern islands of the Philippines. They train recruits who joined the army of Afghanistan's coalition government. Throughout the world they guard U.S. embassies and protect American interests at home and abroad, while also participating in humanitarian missions. The Corps continues to expand and perfect its technology, weaponry, and warfighting capabilities.

Some tacticians say that if the Marines had been turned loose on Afghanistan's Taliban and al-Qaida during the early phase of Operation Enduring Freedom, Osama bin Laden and his henchmen would have either been captured or killed right along with their ragged army of mercenaries. In warfare, Marines like to have a free hand, and they understand that casualties may be suffered to get the job done. But to get the job done is why many men and women who joined the armed services chose to be Marines.

Born on 10 November 1775, the Marine Corps is as old as the history of the U.S. Navy, and the two forces have been inseparably bound together since their births. Unlike the Navy, whose paternalism and long career has also been beset by the vagaries of politics, the Corps' history has been especially turbulent. Like a runt among the bigger boys, Marines have fought domestic enemies as well as foreign forces, using words instead of bullets. On some occasions they fought among themselves, yet always remaining faithful to the "Marine tradition." They are a proud force, wanting neither charity nor unearned respect. They live by their motto: *Semper Fidelis* – always faithful. Lieutenant General Victor H. Krulak, one of the Corps' great leaders, said it best when he wrote "...the Corps is less of the flesh than of the spirit."

And so it is.

CHESTER G. HEARN,
Erie, Pennsylvamia

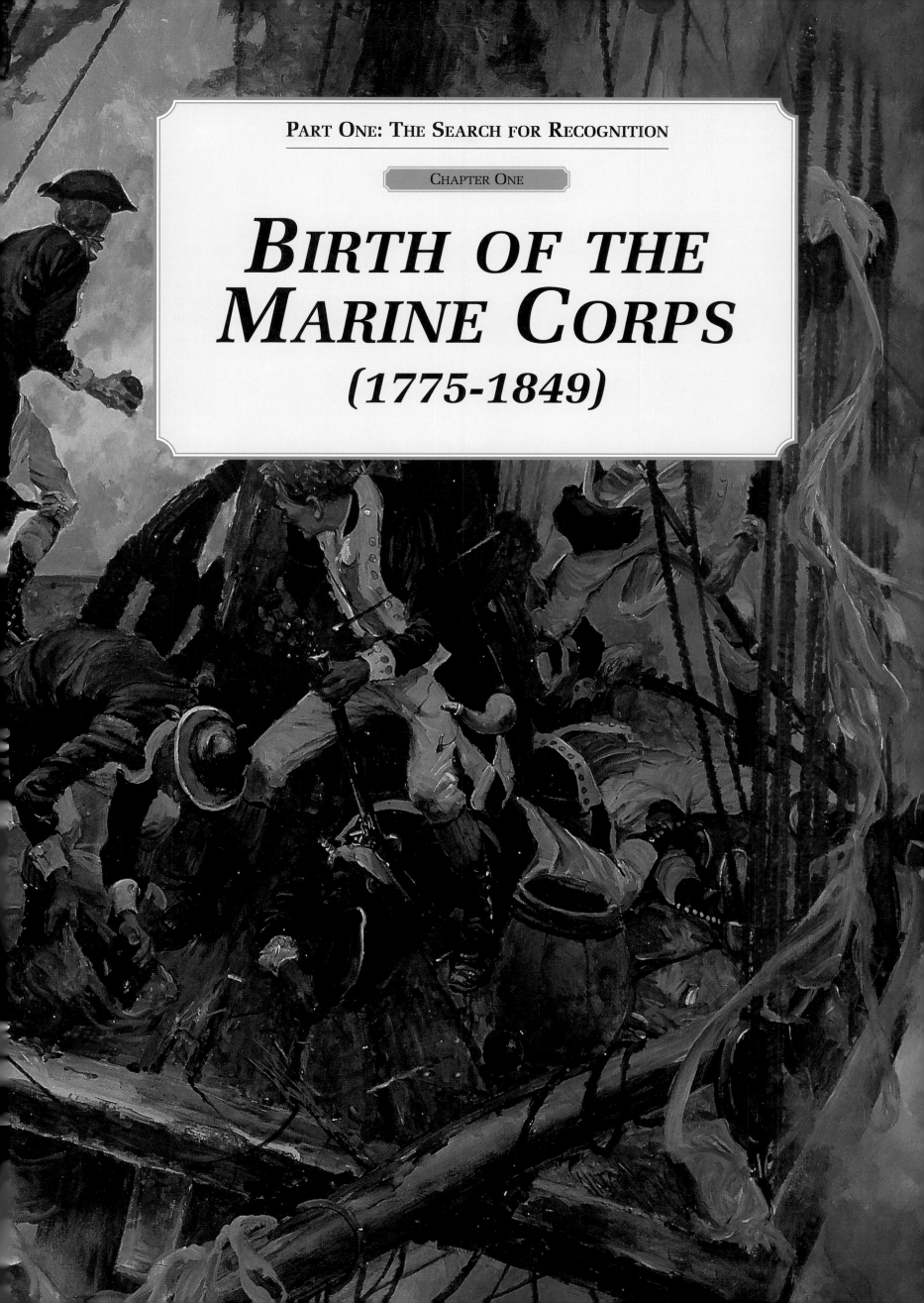

CHAPTER ONE

BIRTH OF THE MARINE CORPS

(1775-1849)

Previous page: *When the Continental frigate* Alliance *attacked the British sloops-of-war* Atalanta *and* Trespassey, *Marines took positions in the tops and sprayed the decks of the enemy with musket fire.*

Above right: *After his first fight, the typical Continental Marine fortunate enough to have a uniform soon found his clothes in tatters. He took good care of his rifle, but after a few battles wore whatever clothing he could find in the slop chest.*

Right: *In May 1775, a rag-tag mixture of Continental Marines wearing odd uniforms joined volunteers from the Green Mountain Boys to capture and garrison Fort Ticonderoga on Lake Champlain.*

arines are as old as warfare at sea. England adopted the concept in 1664, calling it a "Maritime Regiment of Foot" when the country went to war against the Dutch. In 1740 the idea spread to America when the British, during the war with Spain, raised a regiment of 3,000 colonists. Colonel William Gooch took command of the unit, and the men became known as "Gooch's Marines." In April 1741 the colonel led the regiment into battle at Cartagena, Colombia. A few months later Gooch's Marines captured Guantanamo Bay, Cuba, and secured it as a base for Great Britain.

Then came the Seven Years' War in 1754, and Americans serving as marines on British fighting ships performed new roles. They hardened sailors to their duties and enforced ship discipline. When doing battle at sea, marines formed in the tops as sharpshooters and grenadiers, and when the fighting closed, they led the boarding parties. Then as now, it was marines that spearheaded the attack.

Colonists were still under British rule when the first clashes for American independence occurred. On 19 April 1775 British foot soldiers skirmished with angry citizens at Lexington and Concord. Four weeks later Americans captured Fort Ticonderoga and Crown Point on Lake Champlain. The rag-tag garrison complained that "men and money" were desperately needed to hold the fort. Hartford, Connecticut, sent "money escorted by eight Marines," and Albany, New York, chipped in a unit of state marines to garrison the fort and serve on boats. Benedict Arnold, commanding the Colonial forces on Lake Champlain, took one look at the motley group and described them as "the refuse of every regiment."

In August 1775 General George Washington took the next step in organizing a force of marines when he fitted out two armed schooners for operations along the coast of New England. To man the schooners he selected infantrymen from his Army and made them marines. By the end of October three types of marines were fighting for independence: regular marines under Washington, marines recruited by state navies, and marines serving on privateers.

In November 1775 the Marine Committee, sipping ale in Tun Tavern on King Street in Philadelphia, wrote "Rules for the Regulation of the Navy of the United Colonies." They established a "Navy Pay List," and drafted a resolution creating the Continental Marines. On 10 November the Continental Congress, mightily pressed by John Adams and his Marine Committee, authorized:

"That two Battalions of Marines be raised consisting of one Colonel, two lieutenant Colonels, two Majors & Officers as usual in other regiments, that they consist of an equal number of privates with other battalions... and are good seamen, or so acquainted with maritime affairs to be able to serve to advantage by sea, when required."

THE FIRST AMPHIBIOUS ASSAULT

The Marine attack on New Providence Island could have been a huge success had Commodore Esek Hopkins not made his intentions so obvious. Instead of landing his Marines swiftly and capturing the island, he lay offshore in sight of Fort Nassau and put the British garrison on alert. Having missed his chance for a direct surprise attack, Hopkins sailed around to the other side of the island. At 2:00 p.m. on 3 March, Marines and sailors stormed ashore through the surf. *Providence* and *Wasp* covered the landing but never fired a shot.

After forming his men on the beach, Captain Nicholas moved rapidly along the coastal road towards Fort Montague, alarming inhabitants as the column passed. Before the battalion reached the first of two forts, Nicholas received a message from Governor Montford Browne asking the purpose of the raid. The captain replied, "to take possession of all the warlike stores on the Island belonging to the Crown…" He promised that no harm would come to Bahamians if the forts surrendered.

As the battalion approached from the rear, Fort Montague fired three 12-pound shot, which caused Nicholas to stop and reconsider his plan. He sent a message under a flag of truce demanding surrender. The garrison spiked the fort's guns and withdrew to the town, leaving seventeen cannon. Marines entered the fort, relaxed for the night, and removed the spikes from the cannon.

While Nicholas dallied in the fort, Governor Browne tried to mobilize the islanders but without much success. Fort Nassau could not

Right: *On 3 March 1776 Continental Marines and Navy bluejackets land on eastern New Providence Island in the first amphibious assault of the war.*

Below: *At the age of thirty-one, Captain Samuel Nicholas became the first commandant of the Marine Corps, serving for six years.*

be defended with so few men, so the governor ordered the fort's 160 barrels of powder loaded on a small sloop lying in the harbor. Hopkins had not thought to blockade the channel, and the sloop took to sea after dark, thereby depriving the commodore of the purpose that brought him to New Providence in the first place.

In the morning Marines under Nicholas entered Nassau, captured Governor Browne, and without firing a shot took possession of the fort. Marines collected another 71 cannon, 15 mortars, thousands of round-shot, and 24 barrels of powder that the British had failed to carry away. Loading the booty on Hopkins's ships took two weeks, and the commodore had to commandeer an island schooner to carry the surplus.

The first American amphibious landing ended in success, such as it was, and Nicholas became the first major and first commandant of the Continental Marines.

Instead of commissioning a colonel to head the Marines, the committee chose innkeeper Samuel Nicholas of Philadelphia and on 28 November 1775 made him a captain. Tun Tavern, owned by Robert Mullan, became the recruiting rendezvous, and the patriotic tune "Drum, Fife, and Colours" mixed with liberal servings of intoxicating beverages filled the ranks. Because Mullen proved to be an effective recruiter, he became the second captain of Marines.

A Marine private received six and two-thirds dollars a month and the Navy ration: a pound of bread, a pound of beef or pork, a pound of potatoes or turnips or a half pint of peas, and a half pint of rum. On some days of the week Marines also received butter, cheese, and pudding. Marines wore green and white uniforms, which were not always made with the best material and were not always readily available.

In early 1776 Captain Nicholas prepared 268 Marines for their first expedition, the capture of New Providence Island where the British stored what Washington's Army dearly needed – a large cache of arms and gunpowder. On 17 February

1776 Nicholas put his battalion on board Commodore Esek Hopkins's Continental squadron and sailed for the Bahamas. In a spirited landing on 3 March, Captain Nicholas attacked two British forts from the rear and took the British governor prisoner. The loot fell short of expectations. The Marines captured tons of shot, shell, and cannon, but the British had spirited away most of the powder.

Below: *When Commodore Esek Hopkins could not force an entrance to Nassau Harbor, he sent the Continental Marines around to the eastern end of New Providence Island, where they quickly secured a beachhead.*

The adventure of Nicholas and his Marines did not end at New Providence. On the voyage home Commodore Hopkins's squadron fell in with the 20-gun HMS *Glasgow* off Block Island. In the lubberly night action that followed, Nicholas's ship *Alfred* lost her second lieutenant of Marines, John Fitzpatrick, who became the first U.S. Marine officer killed in action. Six more Marines lost their lives and four more suffered wounds during Hopkins' inept management of the fight. *Glasgow* reported four killed, all by musketry from the Continental Marines.

NICHOLAS WITH WASHINGTON

On 25 December 1776, 300 Marines under Major Nicholas joined General Washington's Army prior to the first Battle of Trenton. Nicolas's battalion never made it across the Delaware River, remaining on the Pennsylvania side as reserves. The Marine unit rejoined Washington on the following day and on 3 January 1777, serving for the first time with the Army, fell on the British flank and rear at Princeton and scored a major victory. Nicholas and his Marines stayed with Washington throughout the winter, bivouacking at Morristown. When spring came, part of the battalion joined the Army as artillerymen. Most of the men returned to duty with the Navy. In their last action ashore, they defended Fort Mifflin, pro-

tected the Delaware, and helped to repulse the British fleet under Admiral Lord Richard Howe.

In January 1778 a small force of Marines, commanded by Captain James Willing, saw action in the West when they sailed down the Mississippi in a vessel appropriately named *Rattletrap*. Willing and his force spent twelve months around New Orleans harassing British traders before returning upriver to fight hostile Indians.

In European waters, Captain John Paul Jones favored Marines because of their value as fighting men. Captain Matthew Parke and Lieutenant Samuel Wallingford served as Marine officers on *Ranger* during two raids on British soil – one at Whitehaven and the other at St. Mary's Isle. On 22 April 1778, after terrorizing the British in their homeland, Jones attacked the British sloop *Drake*. In a sharp action, Wallingford lost his life – the only American officer killed in this hard-fought battle.

While the Marines proved their worth in a series of engagements, the Navy continued to have problems with its officers – Commodore Dudley Saltonstall for one. In July 1779 a force of 300 Continental Marines under Captain John Welsch joined Saltonstall's squadron and 900 militiamen in the war's last organized amphibious attack – on the British fort in Penobscot Bay (now Castine, Maine). The Marines executed two successful landings, capturing Banks Island on 26 July and storming Bagaduce Heights on 28 July. Despite an arduous climb up steep cliffs, the

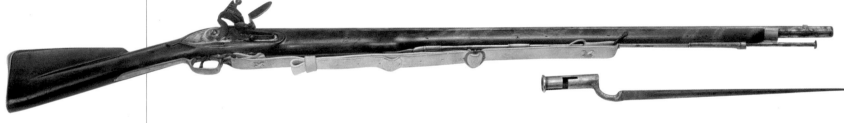

Above: During the Revolution, Marines used the British Army's "Brown Bess" flintlock musket and bayonet. Having no industrial base to produce weapons, the Marines used the arms of the enemy.

Right: During the Battle of Princeton, Marines under the command of Captain Samuel Nicholas fall on the British flank and, with bayonets fixed, score a major victory to the beat of drums emblazoned with the words "Don't Tread on Me."

Marines took the heights but not the fort. Captain Welsch and seventy Marines lost their lives in the assault, but the battalion held the position and waited for reinforcements from Saltonstall. The commodore failed to support the landing, trembled in his boots when a British squadron arrived eighteen days later, and fled, leaving the Marines and the militia on the beach in what one member described as "a most disheartening affair."

On 11 April 1783 the Treaty of Paris brought an end to the American Revolutionary War. Congress authorized the Board of Treasury to sell *Alliance*, the Continental Navy's last armed frigate. After the sale, Congress dissolved the Continental Navy and Marines, and Samuel Nicholas returned to his Philadelphia inn. Such shortsightedness would soon be rewarded by more expensive problems.

In 1789 the first Congress assembled in New York to take up the business of governing. Because Britain's Navy no longer protected American commerce in the Mediterranean, trouble with the Barbary pirates erupted over the payment of tribute. Yet five years passed before the legislature gave much thought to creating a navy. In March 1794 they finally agreed to build six frigates but failed to provide funds for doing so. Two years later Congress authorized enough money to build three of the frigates – *United States, Constellation,* and *Constitution* – each of which would carry Marines. The congressional act of 1 July 1797 provided for 167 Marines – 5 lieutenants, 8 sergeants, 8 corporals, 3 drummers, 3 fifers, and 140 privates. A Marine Corps had not been officially organized, so the men were con-

Left: In the spring of 1779, a company of Marines under the command of Captain John Welsch, fiercely attack a position occupied by the British on the tip of Bagaduce Peninsula in Maine's Penobscot Bay.

"I HAVE NOT YET BEGUN TO FIGHT"

If John Paul Jones had had his way when he took command of the *Bonhomme Richard* – a tired old East Indiaman of 900 tons – he would have sailed with more Marines and fewer Frenchmen. Being in France, Jones had little choice in the matter. He recruited three Irish officers to make American Marines out of 137 Frenchmen borrowed from King Louis XVI's *Corps Royaux d'Infanterie et d'Artillerie de Marine*. Jones preferred Marines because they understood military discipline. The typical officer in the Continental Navy had been an ex-shipmaster or mate who knew nothing about tactics.

On 23 September 1779, after a successful cruise along the east coast of Scotland, Jones fell in with a British convoy off Flamborough Head led by the powerful 44-gun frigate HMS *Serapis*. Though he commanded a sluggish ship armed with 40 old guns, Jones attacked the *Serapis* and would have been badly whipped if the two vessels had not collided and become entangled. At this critical point, Captain Richard Pearson of *Serapis* shouted, "Has your ship struck?" Jones replied, "I have not yet begun to fight," and the Marines began to take over the battle, throwing grappling hooks on board *Serapis* to bring the vessel abeam.

"Well done, my brave lads," Jones shouted. "We have got her now!"

Captain Pearson struggled to break away from *Richard*'s deadly embrace, but every time a British sailor showed himself Marine sharpshooters stationed in the tops greeted him with a hail of musket fire. They cut down British crews serving *Serapis*'s 18-pounders,

which had been knocking out *Richard*'s main batteries. As Nathan Miller, who chronicled the Continental Navy in *Sea of Glory,* said, "Jones's sole advantage outside his own courage was the marksmanship of the French marines and seamen in the tops."

One frantic Marine ran up to Jones and said, "For God's sake, Captain, strike!" Jones replied angrily, "No, I will sink, I will never strike!"

While Marines in the tops maintained a deadly fire on *Serapis*, other sharpshooters concealed on *Richard*'s gun deck fired through shot holes and ports, picking off British gunners. Jones had a difficult time keeping his officers from surrendering, but in the end the Marines played a decisive role in saving the day but not the ship. *Bonhomme Richard* eventually sank, but not until after Jones had captured *Serapis* and transferred his men to the prize.

Above: John Paul Jones, having accepted the surrender of the HMS Serapis, disembarks two boatloads of Marines and bluejackets from the Bonhomme Richard to take possession of the prize.

Above right: On 12 July 1798, the day President John Adams signed the act creating the U.S. Marine Corps, he appointed Major William Ward Burrows of Charleston, South Carolina, the second commandant of the Corps. In 1800 Burrows moved Marine headquarters from Philadelphia to the new District of Columbia and encamped them near the site of today's Washington Monument.

sidered part of a ship's crew and therefore part of the Navy.

On 9 April 1798, Secretary of War James McHenry wrote Congressman Samuel Sewall of Massachusetts recommending that an organization of Marines be formally established. Sewall put the wheels of lawmaking in motion, and the House passed a bill calling for the creation of "a battalion to be called the Marine Corps." Not to be overshadowed by forward thinking in the House, the Senate increased the size of the Corps to a regiment. On 11 July 1798, with the concurrence of the House, "An Act for Establishing and Organizing a Marine Corps" landed on President John Adams's desk for signature. The bill placed the Corps directly under the orders of the chief executive and thus became known as the "Presidential Troops," giving Adams the freedom to decide their disposition "according to the nature of the service (Army or Navy) in which they shall be employed." Samuel Sewall, having energetically steered the bill through Congress, earned rightful ownership to the title "Father of the Marine Corps."

The Corps of 1798 consisted of 33 officers and 848 noncommissioned officers, musicians, and privates. Its mission, according to the recently appointed first Secretary of the Navy, Benjamin Stoddert, were to be "of amphibious nature," including duty at sea, duty in the forts, and "any duty on shore, as the President, at his discretion shall direct." Within twenty-four hours of signing the bill into law, President Adams appointed William Ward Burrows as Major Commandant of the Marine Corps.

THE MARINE BAND

Major Burrows, a Charleston businessman and veteran of the Revolutionary War, wasted no time handpicking a group of outstanding officers. Within six months he brought the Corps up to strength, even though Marine privates received four dollars less pay per month than the ten dollars received by ordinary sailors. Before Christmas 1798, Burrows took another step that would have a major influence on the future Corps. He organized the U.S. Marine Band by the simple expedient of assessing every officer ten dollars. When the seat of government moved from Philadelphia to Washington, D.C., Burrows and his musicians moved with it, ensuring that, come what may, the president would always have his band. In the fall of 1800 Thomas Jefferson defeated John Adams for the presidency, and on 4 March 1801 the Marine Band played for Jefferson's inauguration. Early in 1804 ill health forced Burrows to resign. By then the band had become the "President's Own." In less than a year Burrows died. Had he lived until 1806, he would have seen the new Marine barracks finished in Wash-

Ranks and Monthly Pay for the Marine Corps – 1798	
Major	$50 and 4 rations
Captain	$40 and 3 rations
First lieutenant	$30 and 3 rations
Second lieutenant	$25 and 2 rations
Sergeant major	$10
Drum major: fife major	$ 9
Sergeant	$ 9
Corporal	$ 8
Fifers and drummers	$ 7
Private	$ 6

ington, and it was on 8th and I Streets, S.E., that the commandant of the Corps made his home.

Congress could enact laws providing for the Marine Corps but could not generate the funds for such extravagances as uniforms. Marines assigned to the USS *Boston* went on board in their street clothes. One early clothing requisition read:

On Board the Boston   April 11th 1778

Wanted, for the use and service of the Marines belonging to this ship:

40 green coats faced with white
40 white waistcoats, and 40 white breeches
The buttons of the whole to be plain white.
Coats to be open-sleeved, and a belt for every waistcoat.

In behalf of the Captain of Marines,

William Jennison
Lieutenant of Marines

Lieutenant Jennison's requisition failed to include other items. Continental Marines wore short black gaiters (spatterdashes), round hats (for officers, tricornes), and leather stocks. The leather neckpiece gave rise to the Marine nickname "Leatherneck." Marines wore the leather stock until Jacob Zeilin, the seventh commandant of the Marine Corps, abolished the encumbrance in 1875 because, he said, "it was out of fashion".

During Burrows's administration, French privateers began harassing American commerce on the high seas. Between the Barbary pirates and

> '*I presume you will have heard before this reaches you that a French privateer has made captures at the mouth of our harbor. This is too much humiliation after all that has passed – Our merchants are very indignant – Our government very prostrate in the view of every man of energy.*'
>
> ALEXANDER HAMILTON TO
> SECRETARY OF WAR JAMES MCHENRY, 17 MAY 1798.

Above left: *The Continental Marine uniform contained many variations but standardized on a green coat with buff facings, a tri-corn hat looped on one side, shoes like those worn by civilians, and a black-tarred canvas gaiter to keep dirt out of the shoes.*

Above: *Marine "small cloths," or underclothing, consisted of a linen shirt, white heavy linen breeches, a buff-colored waist-coat, white or buff wool or cotton socks, and a cloth cravat, which was later replaced by the leather stock on a Marine uniform.*

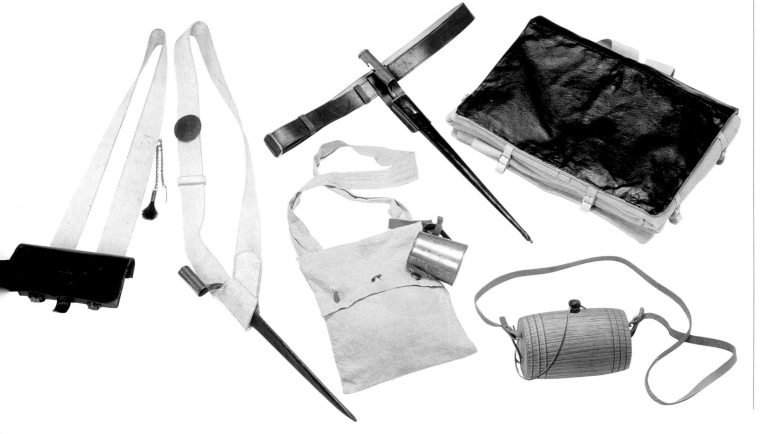
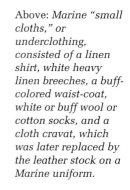

Left: *Marine accouterments included a cartridge box with sling, a bayonet or baldric, a pack to carry supplies, a haversack with a tin cup, a leather waist belt with bayonet frog, and a barrel-shaped canteen made of wood.*

▶ 1812

18 June: President Madison declares war on Great Britain.

1813

March: 1st Lt. John Gamble commands the first Marines in the Pacific and the first ship of the U.S. Navy to be commanded by a Marine.

'Congress will break-up on Monday, without a declaration of war against France. We shall not on that account be the less at war, against their armed vessels.'

Secretary of the Navy Stoddert to Captain John Barry, USN, 13 July 1798.

Below: *During the naval war with France, Marines from the USS* Constitution, *under the command of Captain Daniel Carmick, use the sloop* Sally, *commanded by Lieutenant Isaac Hull, to capture the French privateer* Sandwich *off Puerta Plata harbor, Santo Domingo.*

French raiders, the puny American Navy became outmatched and over-extended. Without a strong fleet the United States could neither go to war nor protect the nation's growing merchant fleet. By 28 May 1798 persistent disregard of neutrality forced the United States into an undeclared naval war – the Quasi-War with France.

During the undeclared war with France, Marines served aboard federal vessels and participated in every engagement afloat and ashore, including the guarding of French prisoners incarcerated at Philadelphia. Lieutenant Bartholomew Clinch, commanding Marines on the USS *Constellation*, played a prominent role in 1799 during the capture of the French frigate *Insurgente*. A year later the same Marines participated in a five-hour night battle that led to the destruction of the French ship *Vengeance*. In between actions against the French, Marines on the USS *Norfolk* and *Boston* smashed

attacks by armed barges operated by Haitian leader "General" Rigaud and his picaroons.

One of the noteworthy escapades during the turn of the century occurred on 11 May 1800 when Captain Daniel Carmick, commanding a Marine detachment from the USS *Constitution*, joined forces with a group of sailors on the sloop *Sally* and recaptured the British ship *Sandwich* from the French. Using *Sandwich* as a "Trojan Horse," Carmick and his crew sailed into Puerto Plata on the north coast of Santo Domingo and captured the local fort, spiked the cannon, and sailed away.

Also during 1800 the USS *Enterprise*, perhaps the most successful of all American ships, used its detachment of sixteen Marines to capture ten French vessels and liberate eleven American ships that the enemy held at sea.

Navy and Marines Reduced

When the Quasi-War ended in 1810, the new government under Jefferson failed to take notice of the mistakes made in the previous decade and all but banished the Navy and the Marine Corps. To reduce the national debt Jefferson ordered naval vessels sold, construction of new ships stopped, naval constructors discharged, remaining frigates dismantled, and the Marine Corps reduced to 450 men.

As the president launched his cost cutting spree, the Bey of Tripoli, annoyed because Americans were paying too little tribute, disrupted Jefferson's revelry in May 1801 by declaring war on the United States. By then the Barbary States had extorted two million dollars, quite enough for America to have built a formidable navy. Stoddert hurriedly mobilized a squadron of four ships under Commodore Richard Dale and in June sent them with 180 Marines to the Mediterranean.

Dale's paltry force – *President, Essex, Philadelphia,* and *Enterprise* – could do little to disrupt the depredations of the Barbary corsairs sailing out of Morocco, Tunis, Algiers, and Tripoli, so the commodore sent messages home asking for reinforcements. Meanwhile, on 31 October 1803, Captain William Bainbridge allowed the USS *Philadelphia* to be swept onto a reef off Tripoli. Yusef Caramanli's Tripolitans captured the frigate, refloated the vessel, towed her into port, and imprisoned Bainbridge, his sailors, and 44 Marines. Yusef intended to add *Philadelphia* to the Tripolitan Navy, but Lieutenant Stephen Decatur stole into the harbor on the night of 16 February 1804 and, with a small complement of men that included eight Marines, set fire to the frigate. The heroic endeavor kept *Philadelphia* out of Yusef's navy, but the night attack neither ended the war nor freed Bainbridge and his crew. That task fell to an unlikely combination: American consul William H. Eaton, Lieutenant Presley N. O'Bannon of the Marines, and Hamet Bey, Yusuf's jealous brother.

Until the so-called Patriot's War erupted in 1811, a peaceful knell had settled over the Marine Corps. The government feared that Great Britain had designs on Florida, a colony of Spain, and rushed a detachment of Marines under Captain John Williams to aid the Army, Navy, and Georgia volunteers in an effort to keep the British out of East Florida. Instead, the mixed force ended up fighting Spanish soldiers and bands of Indians.

Williams drew the assignment of transporting supplies to Army outposts. Indians attacked his wagon train, killing and scalping one Marine and wounding seven others. Williams suffered eight wounds and died on 29 September 1812. Words engraved on his tombstone said his men fought "as long as they had a cartridge left." By then the War of 1812 had begun. Lieutenant Alexander Sevier assumed command of the Marines and remained in East Florida until 13 May 1813, at which time he withdrew by sea and returned to Washington in time to participate in the defense of the capital.

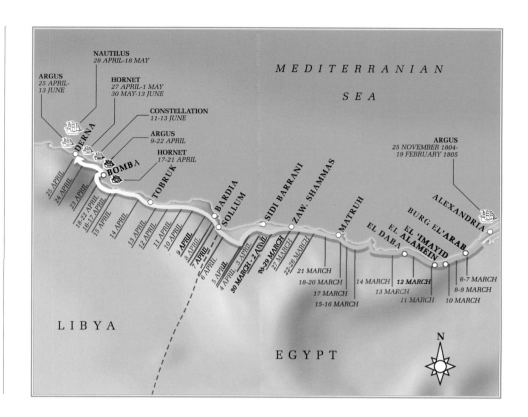

TO THE SHORES OF TRIPOLI

The overland campaign against Derna, spearheaded by a squad of Marines commanded by Lieutenant Presley N. O'Bannon, compares in rugged adventure to the exploits of Lawrence of Arabia. A brainchild of American diplomatic agent William H. Eaton, the scheme entailed a 600-mile overland march from Alexandria, Egypt, to Yusef's capital at Derna. The purpose – to install Hamet Bey on his brother's throne.

Eaton borrowed from the Navy Lieutenant O'Bannon one midshipman, and seven Marines. After receiving them, he recruited 67 "Christian" (Greeks and Turks) mercenaries, 100 Arabs, and 200 camel drivers and bearers. During an epic seven-week march across the Sahara with 107 camels and assorted combatants of conflicting religious persuasions, Eaton, O'Bannon, and Hamet fought thievery, mutiny, and thirst. On 25 April 1805 this strife-torn group of Marines and grumbling adventurers deployed before the walls of Derna. Eaton dispatched a demand for surrender, to which Yusef replied, "My head or yours."

Eaton and O'Bannon accepted Yusef's challenge and contacted the Navy for support. On the morning of 26 April, the USS *Argus, Hornet,* and *Nautilus* arrived offshore and opened fire on Yusef's fort. Eaton posted Hamet and the Arabs on the shoreward side of Derna, and O'Bannon formed his Marines and the Christians – some fifty in all – for an assault on the fort. At 2:00 p.m. the cannonade ceased and O'Bannon's force rushed through a shower of musketry, took possession of the fort, planted the American flag on its ramparts, and turned the batteries on the demoralized Tripolitans. The sudden rout enabled Hamet's Arabs to get possession of Yusef's palace, and a little after four o'clock the threadbare desert force took

possession of the town. Most of the stunned inhabitants promptly declared their allegiance to Hamet.

O'Bannon lost two Marines killed and one wounded in a thoroughly lopsided affair. He became the first American to raise the Stars and Stripes over a captured fortress in the Old World. The Marmaduke sword, carried by future Marine officers, takes its pattern – an ivory hilt topped with a golden eagle's head – from the Arab sword presented to O'Bannon by Hamet. In one of the ironical twists that often occur during war, Hamet's sword became O'Bannon's only reward. Though he and Eaton broke a four-year stalemate that led to a favorable treaty with Tripoli, the United States government did nothing. Virginia, his native state, rewarded O'Bannon with another sword, but when no brevet or promotion came after two years of waiting, he left the Corps and spent the rest of his life in Kentucky.

Above: On 6 March 1805 General William H. Eaton, supported by Lieutenant Presley O'Bannon and a squad of Marines, began their epic march across the North African desert to capture Derna. The map depicts their daily progress.

Below: General Eaton's 600-mile trek across the desert culminated with the attack on Derna by Lieutenant O'Bannon's Marines. The small force overwhelmed the defenders of the city and planted the American flag on the ramparts.

▶ **10 SEPTEMBER:** Lieutenant John Brooks is the first Marine officer killed, during the Battle of Lake Erie.

1814

24 AUGUST: During the Battle of Bladensburg, 114 Marines are killed defending the capital.

24 DECEMBER: The U.S. and Britain sign a treaty of peace.

On 18 June 1812 President James Madison had ventured into a war he should have avoided, but he had a problem. The great European belligerents fighting the Napoleonic Wars – Britain, France, and Spain – continued to treat American maritime commerce as a reservoir for manpower. Of the three warring combatants, the Royal Navy's impressment of seamen became the most arrogant and infuriating.

> '*British cruisers have been in the practice of violating the rights and peace of our coasts. They hover over and harass our entering and departing commerce. To the most insulting pretensions, they have added the most lawless proceedings in our very harbors, and have wantonly spilt American blood within the sanctuary of our territorial jurisdiction...*'
>
> PRESIDENT JAMES MADISON TO CONGRESS, 1 JUNE 1812.

When Madison declared war on Great Britain, half of the under-strength Marine Corps were at sea. U.S. military personnel totaled 12,631, but the Marine Corps consisted of only 10 officers and 483 enlisted men. Madison gambled that by forcing Britain to fight a war on two fronts, the United States stood a reasonable chance of absorbing British territory in Canada.

Although the U.S. Navy operated only three first-class warships – *President, United States,* and *Constitution* – Madison believed that the merchant fleet could be converted into enough warships or privateers to drive the British from American shores. He expected the war to be fought mainly at sea, and it was not long before *Constitution* destroyed the HMS *Guerri re* off Nova Scotia, *United States* seized *Macedonia* off Madeira, and *Constitution* sank *Java* off Brazil, where she earned the sobriquet "Old Ironsides." Marines participated in all the actions, leading boarding parties and sharpshooting from the tops.

The land war became a more troublesome issue for Madison when General William Henry Harrison failed to win a significant battle in the west. The military defeats were caused by Britain's domination of Detroit and the Great Lakes. During the fall of 1812 the Navy sent Commodore Isaac Chauncey to the eastern end of Lake Ontario to establish a base at Sackett's Harbor, and Captain Oliver Hazard Perry to Pennsylvania to build a fleet for service on Lake Erie. During the winter and spring of 1813, Perry struggled with wilderness conditions to create his squadron, and because of a shortage of Marines, he augmented his crew with volunteers from the Army and used his

Below: *The first U.S. enlisted Marines wore a hat banded with yellow wool and with the left side looped. They carried a blackened buff baldric and a cartridge box on a blackened buff sling.*

Right: *During the Battle of Lake Erie in the summer of 1813, Captain Oliver Hazard Perry is forced to abandon his flagship, the USS* Lawrence. *Marines and bluejackets row him to USS* Niagara, *where he transfers his flag, rallies his fresh-water squadron, and secures the surrender of the British fleet.*

Marines to train the men as sharpshooters. On 10 September 1813 Perry's fleet defeated the British squadron during the Battle of Lake Erie, and the victory opened the way for General Harrison to drive the British out of Detroit and into Canada.

While Perry and Harrison regained control of the Michigan Territory, Captain David Porter, commanding the USS *Essex*, began one of the war's most dramatic adventures at the other end of the world. With him went twenty-three-year-old Lieutenant John Marshall Gamble and thirty-one Marines. The cruise did not get off to a good start. Having sailed late, Porter could not find the squadron's flagship at the prescribed rendezvous. He decided to take *Essex* around Cape Horn and into the South Pacific, where he hoped to smash the British whaling fleet. Porter's odyssey, which began on 22 October 1812, did not end for Lieutenant Gamble until August 1815.

GAMBLE'S ADVENTURES

Soon after the USS *Essex* sailed into the South Pacific, Captain David Porter captured three British whalers. Among his prizes he found one vessel that would sail well. In April 1813 he commissioned the ship USS *Greenwich* and put Lieutenant John Marshall Gamble in charge of her. With a crew of fourteen men, Gamble became the only Marine to ever captain a ship of the U.S. Navy.

While cruising in the Galapagos during July, Gamble engaged *Seringapatam*, an armed British whaler and the terror of American whalers in the Pacific. He maneuvered *Greenwich* according to the best principles of naval tactics, frustrated all the enemy's efforts to escape, and after delivering effective broadsides, forced *Seringapatam* to strike. Porter watched the fight and decided that he had chosen the right man to command the ship.

Essex and *Greenwich* next stopped at Nukuhiva in the Marquesa Islands. Porter established a base

> '*No Marine officer in the service ever had such strong claims as Captain Gamble, and none have been placed in such conspicuous and critical situations, and none could have extricated themselves from them more to their honor.*'
>
> DAVID PORTER TO
> SECRETARY OF THE NAVY BENJAMIN CROWNINSHIELD.

on the island, built Fort Madison, and then sailed away, leaving Gamble behind with three vessels and orders to hold the island. Porter never returned, losing *Essex* in a battle with the HMS *Cherub* and *Phoebe* off Valparaiso.

Soon after Porter departed, tattooed Nukuhiva natives threatened to attack Fort Madison. Gamble landed thirty-five men, including amiable British prisoners, and under covering fire from his ships attacked the natives' stronghold. After a brisk fight, Gamble imposed an uneasy peace. Though faced with desertions and hostile natives, he held out, waiting for the return of Porter. British prisoners mutinied, wounded Gamble, and set him adrift in the ocean with two midshipmen, a single pair of oars, some powder, and three old muskets. Despite his wound, Gamble brought the boat back to Nukuhiva, boarded *Greenwich*, gathered together a few loyal Marines and sailors, and transferred all hands to the *Sir Andrew Hammond,* a seaworthy prize. He put the vessel underway with no charts and a seven-man crew barely strong enough to sail the ship.

Now a captain, though Gamble would not know this for another year, he ran before the trade winds, hoping they would blow him to the Sandwich Islands (Hawaii). Using dead reckoning, Gamble reached one of the islands, only to fall into the hands of the HMS *Cherub*, the same ship that had sunk *Essex*. While he was imprisoned by the British at Rio de Janeiro, the war ended. Though penniless and five thousand miles from home, he found a ship to carry him back to the United States. In August 1815, and still suffering from his wound, he limped ashore with his men at New York. For gallantry, leadership, and seamanship, Gamble was brevetted major; he died a lieutenant colonel in 1834.

BRITAIN ATTACKS AMERICA

In April 1814 the war at sea quickly shifted to land operations after Napoleon abdicated and Britain's Peninsular War veterans became available for service in America. The British mounted three geographically separate campaigns against their former colonists: one against the nation's capital; one against New York, using Lake Champlain for access to the Hudson River; and the other against New Orleans.

On 19 August 1814, 5,400 battle-tested troops under Major General Robert Ross landed unopposed on Maryland's Patuxent River. They

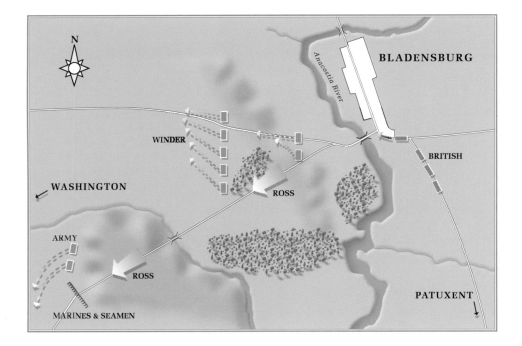

lake lasting two hours and twenty minutes, Prevost lost his principal vessels and beat a hasty retreat back to Canada.

The British campaign to capture New Orleans proved to be even more bizarre, partly because it continued beyond the 24 December 1814 signing of the Treaty of Ghent, which ended the war. The British campaign began on 8 December when 7,500 battle-hardened veterans under Major General Sir Edward M. Pakenham anchored at Chandeleur Island off the mouth of the Mississippi River. Well positioned to challenge Pakenham's attack, General Andrew Jackson waited with a command composed of militia, Jean Lafitte's pirates, and 300 Marines under the command of Major Daniel Carmick.

On 8 January, after skirmishing with the Marines for a month, Pakenham decided to attack in force. The British soldiers, weighted down with equipment and carrying scaling ladders, assaulted Jackson's defensive position in heavy columns. The Marines seemed to be everywhere. They fought beside the Creoles; others served with the artillery on the left; and some mixed together with U.S. Army regulars. Despite brave assaults by the British, by noon the battlefield grew silent. Pakenham suffered a mortal wound, and more than 2,500 British lay dead or wounded. Congress passed a resolution of thanks "for the valor and good conduct of Major Daniel Carmick, of the officers, noncommissioned officers, and Marines under his command." Had Carmick not died in November 1815 from wounds received at New Orleans, he may have survived to become one of the Marine Corps' great commandants.

As for Marine Commandant Franklin Wharton, the same cannot be said. After the Battle of Bladensburg, Wharton saved the Marine paychest but fled from Washington. The Marines

Top: *After the Battle of Bladensburg, a stubborn force of Marines temporarily stopped the British force under General Robert Ross on the road to Washington, D.C.*

Above: *Captain Samuel Miller, commanding 114 Marines and a handful of bluejackets, hold off the British on the Bladensburg Road.*

Right: *On any day at sea, Marines perform exercises such as scampering up the rigging to reach firing platforms in the tops.*

marched on Washington, and along the way scattered 6,000 local militiamen at Bladensburg, a few miles outside the capital. The militia fled at the first sound of musket fire, but 114 Marines under Captain Samuel Miller and a handful of sailors under the command of Commodore Joshua Barney stood their ground. Having nothing more than muskets and a single 18-pounder cannon, Miller and Barney delayed the British advance for two hours and inflicted 250 casualties. The British pressed into Washington, burned the White House, but left the Marine barracks untouched. Ross's veterans mounted an unsuccessful attack on Baltimore and withdrew the same way they came.

On 11 September 1814 the second British prong – an army of 11,000 under Major General George Prevost – moved across Lake Champlain for a thrust down the Hudson Valley to New York. To oppose this threat Captain Thomas Macdonough could muster only 1,500 regulars and Marines and 3,000 militiamen. In an action on the

ARCHIBALD HENDERSON – MARINE OF VISION

Thirty-eight-year-old Archibald Henderson, a fiery and forceful redhead, grew up near the present-day Marine base at Quantico, Virginia, and in 1806 received a commission in the Corps. As a captain of Marines on the *Constellation*, he led his detachment in the capture of the frigate HMS *Cyane* in 1813 and the sloop-of-war *Levant* in 1815 – two months after the War of 1812 ended. For his bravery Henderson received the brevet of major.

The Peace Establishment Act of 1817 authorized a paltry 50 officers and 942 enlisted men for the Corps, but funding never provided for more than half that number. After Henderson became commandant on 17 October 1820, he compelled all new officers to come to the Marine Barracks for instruction. This program evolved into the Basic School of the future.

President Andrew Jackson, a parsimonious Democrat, attempted to merge the Marine Corps into the organization of the Army "as the best mode of curing the many defects of its organization." The so-called "defects" had more to do with the last two commandants – Wharton and Gale – than with the men in the Corps. Henderson had friends in Congress, however, and played an astute game of politics. He preserved the Corps, although the 1834 "Act for the Better Organization of the Marine Corps" provided that the president could assign duties to the Marines however he wished. The act also specified that the Corps, ashore or afloat, would be part of the Navy Department but not part of the Navy itself.

In May 1836 President Jackson exercised his option and sent a two-battalion regiment of Marines against the Seminoles and Creeks in Florida and Georgia. Henderson took command of the regiment, pinning a note to his door that read: "Gone to fight the Indians. Will be back when the war is over. A. Henderson. Col. Comdt."

Henderson brigaded his Marines with the Army's 4th Infantry Regiment. Using assorted Creek and Georgian volunteers, he forced a band of Seminoles to the banks of the Hatchee-Lustee River. In an action filled with more noise than killing, Henderson persuaded Seminole chiefs to move to a reservation. In recognition for his services, Henderson received promotion by brevet to brigadier general.

Commandants do not normally fight wars, but Henderson would have taken to the field during the Mexican War if his sixty-three years of age had let him. Though confined to Washington, he did much to enhance the reputation of the Corps by demonstrating its usefulness in sea-land expeditions. After thirty-eight years as commandant, Henderson died in office on 6 January 1859, two years before the outbreak of the Civil War. For the United States, his annual pay and emoluments of $2,636.16 were a bargain. The volatile years of the Civil War fell to the next commandant, Colonel John Harris, whose uninspired leadership would exasperate Gideon Welles, the new secretary of the Navy.

▶ **1815**

8 JANUARY: Andrew Jackson, together with Marines under Major Daniel Carmick, defeat the British at New Orleans.

20 FEBRUARY: Captain Archibald Henderson leads Marines in the victory of the USS *Constitution* over *Cyane* and *Levant*.

1820

17 OCTOBER: Major Archibald Henderson becomes the 5thcommandant and holds the position until his death in 1859.

Left: *Brevet Brigadier General Archibald Henderson served the Marine Corps as its commandant for thirty-eight years, the longest in the history of the Corps.*

Below: *On 8 January 1815 Marines fought the final battle of the War of 1812 near New Orleans and distinguished themselves under the command of General Andrew Jackson.*

accused Wharton of cowardice, and incoming President James Monroe urged him to resign. Marine Captain Archibald Henderson brought charges against Wharton for neglect of duty and conduct unbecoming an officer and a gentleman. During the war Henderson had distinguished himself as an exemplary fighter while commanding a Marine detachment on *Constitution*. Tried in September 1817, Wharton won acquittal but not exoneration, and he died soon after.

Major Anthony Gale replaced Wharton as commandant and proved to be a drunken dunderhead who soon fell afoul of the secretary of the navy. Two years later another court-martial ensued. Gale, accused of "being intoxicated in common dram shops and other places of ill-repute," pleaded not guilty by reason of insanity and was dismissed from the service.

On 17 October 1820, the Marines finally received as their fifth commandant perhaps the only man in the Corps who could preserve and elevate this unique arm of the service to the mis-

1824

12 MARCH: Brevet Major Robert D. Wainwright and Marines from Boston quash riots in Massachusetts state prison.

1832

8 FEBRUARY: Brevet Captain Alvin Edson leads attack against Malay pirates in Sumatra.

1836

23 JUNE: Colonel Henderson leads 462 Marines into the Second Seminole War.

1837

27 JANUARY: Colonel Henderson wins Battle of Hatchee-Lustee River against the Seminoles.

1845

30 OCTOBER: President Polk sends 1st Lieutenant Archibald Gillespie to California with secret orders.

Right: *In 1843 Commodore Matthew C. Perry landed a detachment of Marines on Liberia in an effort to stop the slave trade. A Marine sergeant saved the commodore's life by shooting Ben Crack-O, the chief of the Berribees, thus paving the way for a settlement.*

sions that lay far into the future. Lieutenant Colonel Archibald Henderson would dominate and serve in that post through thirty-nine years and ten presidential administrations.

Henderson put every man in the Corps to work. Having inherited Haitian problems from his predecessor, he landed Marines at Port-au-Prince and Cape Haitien. On Commodore David Porter's Caribbean Squadron, he supplied Marines to help suppress piracy. In 1832 Marines on the USS *Lexington* landed on the Falkland Islands and freed American whalers captured by Argentinians. On the other side of the world Marines participated in a punitive expedition to western Sumatra after Malay pirates murdered the crew of the American merchantman *Friendship*.

Domestic problems also required help from the Marines. In 1824 Boston called upon the Marines twice – once when fires threatened the city, and again when inmates at the Massachusetts state prison mutinied. Major Robert D. Wainwright and 30 men from the Marine Barracks broke into the prison, faced off against 283 inmates, and ordered the prisoners to disperse. When they refused, Wainwright pulled out his watch and said, "You must leave this hall. I give you three minutes to decide. If at the end of that time a man remains, he will be shot dead. I speak no more." For two minutes not a person moved. Then two or three inmates standing in the rear departed, followed gradually by others. Before the last thirty seconds expired, "the hall cleared as if by magic."

In 1833, when arsonists set fire to the U.S. Treasury, men from the Marine Barracks at "Eighth and Eye" helped quench the flames and guard the funds. Two years later Lieutenant Colonel Gamble's Marines from the Brooklyn Navy Yard fought another fire, this time blowing firebreaks and saving Manhattan.

After bringing the Creek war to an end during the summer of 1836, the Seminoles proved far less compliant. For the next six years they held out in the swamps of the South, forcing the Navy in 1838 to form a combination of patrol craft, revenue cutters, barges, and canoes capable of penetrating the upper reaches of the swamplands. This so-called "Mosquito Fleet" contained at times as many as 190 Marines, one-fifth of the flotilla's strength. Many men lost their lives. The war subsided in 1842 on Seminole terms and without a treaty.

MARINES WITH WILKES

Wherever the Navy went, so went Marines, even to the shores of the frozen Antarctic wasteland. The voyage of exploration by Navy Lieutenant Charles Wilkes began in June 1838 and lasted exactly four years. After exploring the coast of Antarctica, Wilkes charted the Fiji Islands, Samoa, parts of the Philippines, and the Pacific Northwest. Each of the five ships in the squadron sailed with a complement of Marines. The men came in handy wherever Wilkes chose to stop, driving off attacks in the Fiji Islands, fighting spear-throwing natives on Drummond Island, and dispersing angry Chinese when a mob laid siege to the American compound at Canton. By 1845 Marines had been many times around the world. They learned to fight at sea and in the deserts,

cities, swamps, and jungles of the world. But they were still a small military force of specialized skills trying to find a niche in the growing nation.

Henderson knew that the expansion of the United States would bring new challenges for the Marine Corps. He watched with interest when in 1836 Texas won its war of independence from Mexico. He saw it as a harbinger of things yet to come and grew more certain when in 1845 the United States annexed Texas.

Trouble continued to brew. In 1845 President James K. Polk's special emissary, 1st Lieutenant Archibald H. Gillespie, USMC, disguised himself as a whiskey agent and carried secret orders through Mexican territory to Commodore John D. Sloat, commanding the Pacific Squadron on the West Coast. Polk wanted to grab New Mexico and California, and the message carried by Gillespie contained instructions for Sloat to counter British

intrigues on the Pacific coast and to cooperate with Captain John C. Frémont's armed "scientific expedition" should war break out with Mexico. Gillespie did not find Frémont until 9 May 1846. Nine days later the invasion of Mexico commenced.

On 18 May 1846, fifteen miles upriver from the mouth of the Rio Grande, the first American force set foot on Mexico — Marine skirmishers from a naval force commanded by Captain John H. Aulick. Aulick's attack on the town of Burrita preceded by two hours General Zachary Taylor's invasion of Mexico. The Marines returned to their ship as the Navy began to establish its blockade of Mexican ports.

To keep General Taylor supplied required bases along the Mexican coast. Captain Alvin Edson, senior Marine officer attached to Commodore David Conner's Gulf Squadron, organized a 200-man battalion of Marines by combining all the detachments in the squadron. Supported by Conner's guns and augmented by bluejackets, Edson's force landed at Frontera and San Juan Bautista and on 14 November 1846 captured Tampico. Two days later Taylor occupied Saltillo, where he maintained a defensive posture while waiting for General Winfield Scott to land. Scott's army, however, did not land. After Taylor defeated Santa Anna at Buena Vista on 22-23 February 1847, Scott decided to put his forces ashore at Veracruz.

The Navy thought the campaign afloat needed a more energetic commander and sent Commodore Matthew C. Perry (Oliver Hazard Perry's younger brother) to replace Conner. On 9 March 1847, supported by the Gulf Squadron under Perry, Scott's army landed at Veracruz and began

Left: *Marines and sailors used small boats and dugouts to search for well-concealed Indians during the Seminole Wars of 1835-1842. Search parties could pass within a few yards of the camouflaged Seminoles and never see them.*

Below: *In 1847, during the Mexican War, Marines under the command of Commodore Matthew Perry storm ashore on the Tabasco River to capture the town of San Juan Bautista. The Marines staged many raids, and were among the first to set foot on Mexico proper.*

Below: *When General Scott landed his army at Vera Cruz, he also brought detachments of Marines serving on board the ships to help clear certain sections of the city, which the leathernecks promptly did.*

an 18-day siege. General Scott wanted Alvarado secured to protect his flank, so Perry organized a landing force of 1,500 men. Captain Edson took a battalion of Marines and a battery of field artillery ashore and on 1 April 1847 captured Alvarado. Seventeen days later, in another hotly contested landing, Marines and bluejackets captured the town of Tuxpan.

Scott pushed westward, making good progress. On 18 April 1847 he routed Santa Anna's army at Cerro Gordo, but he began running out of men when he reached Puebla. Four thousand American soldiers stopped fighting because their agreed term of service had expired. Aware of Scott's plight, Archibald Henderson began stripping every navy yard of Marines. He dipped into the increase of 1,000 men approved by Congress on 3 March 1847, formed a full Marine regiment, and a few days later shipped the first battalion off to reinforce Scott. With the approval of the secretary of the navy, Henderson formed a second battalion, drawing from the Gulf Squadron the Marines under Captain Edson. He put the full regiment under Brevet Lieutenant Colonel Samuel E. Watson, a veteran Marine who had served under Scott in 1813. Henderson's rapid mobilization of troops in reaction to Scott's plight became one of the stellar traditions of the future Marine Corps.

Scott never received all the Marines that Henderson so rapidly folded into a single regiment. Perry wanted Marines as badly as Scott did. When they arrived off Vera Cruz, Perry ignored orders from the secretary of the navy and kept all but 357 Marines for his Gulf Coast naval brigade.

MARINES WANT MORE ACTION

Scott took his portion of the Marine regiment and folded it into an Army division under Franklin Pierce, who later became the 14th president of the United States. On 16 July the column started on a three-week march to Puebla, Scott's forward base. Three weeks later, after being attacked six times by guerrillas, the battalion arrived in good order and reported to Watson. Brigadier General John A. Quitman incorporated the battalion into the 4th Army Division and gave Watson command of an Army brigade. Watson put the Marine battalion under Major Levi Twiggs, a veteran hardened in the Florida wars, and two days later Scott began the march to Mexico City with 11,000 men.

During the battles at Cherubusco, Contreras, and Molino del Rey the Marines grumbled because General Quitman saddled them with the

chore of protecting Scott's siege and supply trains. It soon became clear to Scott that the key to Mexico City led through Chapultepec Castle, where 800 defenders looked down upon the approaching Americans. The general planned to attack the southern face with Quitman's division, and Quitman chose Major Twiggs to lead the storming party.

Twiggs knew about Marines. He had fought beside them before. He formed the battalion for the assault and put Captain John G. Reynolds, a Marine company commander and one of ablest men in the Corps, to head the first wave. Into the storming party went forty Army and Marine volunteers, selected with care from the entire division. Quitman then chose Colonel Watson to support the storming party and lead the division in the attack. On 12 September, while Scott's batteries pounded the fortress, Quitman lost seven Marines who had been reconnoitering the ground over which Reynolds's storming party would advance in the morning.

At daylight on 13 September, Scott's artillery opened on Chapultepec and pounded the fortress for two hours. At eight o'clock the guns fell silent. Twiggs pressed forward, Reynolds's men in the lead with pickaxes, crowbars, and scaling ladders. Behind the storming party moved Watson's battalion and the rest of Quitman's division. Mexican guns pinned down Reynolds's pioneers, but the Marines got tired of waiting and wanted to move off the causeway and attack. Watson restrained them, waiting for buglers to sound the general charge. A few minutes later Reynolds's

storming party swept over the castle walls, bayoneting the enemy as they advanced. With those that followed, the Marines collected 550 prisoners – including a general and ten colonels – and captured seven guns and a thousand muskets at a cost of twenty-four casualties. Second Lieutenant Charles A. Henderson, the commandant's son, lay among the wounded. Thirteen of the twenty-three Marine officers at Chapultepec received brevets for bravery.

Marine Captain George H. Terrett of Company C ignored the action at Chapultepec. With sixty-seven Marines he outflanked the Mexican artillery on the causeway, and instead of wheel-

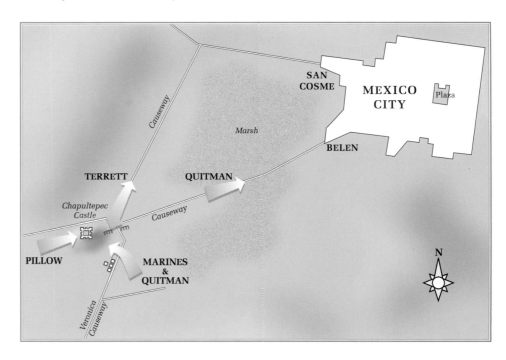

▶ **13 SEPTEMBER:**
Marines seize fortress
of Chapultepec and
the next day occupy
the National Palace
and the Halls of
Montezuma.

1853

14 JULY: Major Jacob
Zelin lands the first
Marines on Japan with
Commodore Perry's
mission.

ing toward the fort, he pursued the enemy fleeing toward Mexico City. Along the way he annexed two light artillery sections from Magruder's Battery and broke up a counterattack by Mexican lancers. Near the San Cosme gate leading into the city, the Marines incorporated twenty-six men from Lieutenant Ulysses S. Grant's command, gained the gateway, and became the first Americans to enter the city.

On the causeway leading to the Belen Gate, General Quitman's force pressed forward with Reynolds's Marines still in the van. Night intervened and Quitman stopped outside the city. During the night Mexican forces quietly evacuated the city. Early in the morning Quitman entered through the gate and formed his men under the shadow of the cathedral in the Grand Plaza. The general gave Reynolds's battalion, which had already tallied thirty-nine casualties, the task of mopping up the city and clearing thieves from the Placido Nacional. Second Lieutenant A. S. Nicholson, later adjutant and inspector of the Corps, climbed to the top of the Palace of the Montezumas, cut down the Mexican flag, and raised the Stars and Stripes. As General Scott rode into the Placido Nacional, he found the surrounding streets already guarded by U.S. Marines.

The Marines now had another stanza for what would one day become The Marines' Hymn. For forty years their standard carried only the traditional motto, *To the Shores of Tripoli.* During the Henderson era the Corps also used two unofficial mottoes. One was *By Sea and By Land,* an obvious translation from the British Royal Marines' *Per mare per Terram;* the other, *Fortitudine,*

which richly sprouted from Marine tradition. When the Marines returned to Washington in 1848, the city presented General Henderson with a new blue and gold standard, emblazoned with the words: "From Tripoli to the Halls of the Montezumas." A future lyricist discovered that no appropriate word rhymed with Montezumas, so he reversed Marine chronology and put Tripoli at the end of the stanza. When The Marines' Hymn was adopted remains a mystery, but its melody dates back to 1859 and Jacques Offenbach's opera, *Genevi ve de Brabant.*

During the Mexican War, Marines also engaged in action on the West Coast. On 9 July 1846 Commodore Sloat learned of General Taylor's invasion of Mexico and put a detachment of Marines and sailors ashore at Yerba Buena. The party landed without opposition and raised the colors over the future city of San Francisco. Two days earlier, without Sloat's knowledge, the USS *Savannah* landed eighty-five Marines under the command of Captain Ward Marston and captured Monterey. Commodore Robert F. Stockton replaced Sloat and immediately sent Fr mont's California Battalion south to capture San Diego.

On 6 August Stockton sent 350 Marines and bluejackets ashore under Lieutenant Jacob Zeilin, a future commandant of the Corps, to attack Ciudad de los Angeles. After Zeilin captured the city, Stockton named the ubiquitous Captain Archibald Gillespie, USMC, as Military Commandant of the Department of Southern California, and gave him a garrison of volunteers who were, as Gillespie reported, "perfect drunkards."

Observing the numerical weakness of the American force, 600 Southern Californians of

Right: *Captain William
A. T. Maddox
responded to the call
in the nation's capital
when the Plug-Uglies
came onto the streets
with a brass cannon
and put the
Washington police to
flight. He placed his
company at the
Northern Liberties
Market, the polling
place under assault,
and helped to drive
the Plug-Uglies away.*

THE MARINES' HYMN

*From the halls of Montezuma
To the shores of Tripoli
We fight our country's battles
In the air, on land, and sea.
First to fight for right and freedom,
And to keep our honor clean,
We are proud to claim the title
Of United States Marines.*

*Our flag's unfurl'd to every breeze
From dawn to setting sun;
We have fought in every clime and place
Where we could take a gun.
In the snow of far-off northern lands
And in sunny tropic scenes,
You will find us always on the job –*

*The United States Marines.
Here's health to you and to our Corps
Which we are proud to serve;
In many a strife we've fought for life
And never lost our nerve.
If the Army and the Navy
Ever gaze on Heaven's scenes,
They will find the streets are guarded
By United States Marines*

Left: *"Horse Marines 1846, San Diego,"* from a painting by Waterhouse, one of the Marines' most prolific artists. Marines, unused to horses, were formed into cavalry units of sorts, abandoned after this incident."

Spanish extraction revolted against Gillespie's fifty-nine "perfect drunkards." The attack proved to be sobering. Gillespie spied four spiked and rusty gun barrels, set his gunner's mate to work melting down lead pipes for grapeshot, and for seven days held off the attackers. Overwhelmed by numbers, Gillespie finally surrendered on 30 September and marched out of Los Angeles with his troops, guns, and unfurled flag to the waiting USS *Vandalia* at San Pedro.

Not until 8 January 1847, after Brigadier General Stephen W. Kearny, USA, arrived from an overland march was Stockton able to combine the forces of the Army, Navy, and Marines – including Gillespie's volunteers – into a force large enough to retake Los Angeles and settle the issue of California. Though wounded for a second time, Gillespie raised the same flag over the city that he had lowered the previous September. He and Zeilin received brevets to major for their services in California.

UNIFORM CHANGES

After the Mexican War, Marine privates still drew only six dollars a month in pay, but Commandant Henderson began to initiate a number of changes. He made several revisions to the Marine uniform, finally settling on the blue, white, and scarlet colors like those used during the War of 1812. Enlisted men wore white cross-belts, white trousers for summer, and light blue trousers for winter. Officers and NCOs wore similar trousers distinguished by dark blue stripes edged with scarlet. Then, as now, the Marine Band wore scarlet coats. To supplement a private's wretched pay,

every enlisted man now received an annual clothing allowance of thirty dollars. He could not spend it frivolously because Uniform Regulations of 1859 prescribed that he carry and maintain at all times, the following:

1 uniform cap	1 blanket
2 uniform coats	8 pairs of socks
2 sets of epaulettes	8 pairs of drawers
7 pairs linen trousers	4 fatigue caps
8 pairs woolen trousers	4 fatigue coats
	8 blue flannel shirts
12 shirts	2 stocks, leather
6 pairs of shoes	1 greatcoat

Below: *In 1825, to celebrate the opening of the Chesapeake and Ohio Canal, the Marine Band provided music for the ceremony. The band had always been a favorite of the presidents, and Marine bandsmen answered the call whenever a special occasion called for music.*

▶ **1856**

20 NOVEMBER:
Marines land at
Canton and capture
four barrier forts
protecting the city.

Right: *In 1859 a first
sergeant's dress
uniform consisted of a
double-breasted frock
coat with sleeve
chevrons, introduced
that year into the
Corps. The shako cap
resembled the one
worn by the Army, and
the trousers, sky blue
in color, contained a
red welt down the
seam. The red sash
identified staff
noncommissioned
officers.*

A Marine private owned a greater wardrobe than the ordinary civilian of 1859 or the typical G.I. of World War II. For those Marines who served at sea, it is a wonder they squeezed so much apparel into a single ditty bag. If clothing did not overwhelm the typical enlisted man, his next stop at the Marine Corps Depot of Supplies would, for there, depending upon his particular specialty, he would receive from Major D. J. Sutherland's four-story quartermaster house at 226 South 4th Street in Philadelphia an assortment of the following:

Musket	Drum
Bayonet belt	Fife
Scabbard	Knapsack
Cartridge box	Haversack
Cartridge box belt	Canteen
Sword, NCO only	Slings, musket
Sword, musician only	Sling, drum
Sword belt	

Right: *In 1852 the
Marine Corps
established a basic
"fatigue" uniform. The
fatigue coat (left)
resembled the Army
coat but carried hash
marks that would later
evolve in service
strips. The leather
stock (below) dated
back to early 1800s.
The "sky blue" wool
trousers matched the
coat. The "wheel hat"
became standard issue
in 1852, as did the
"brogans."*

After the Mexican War, Commandant Henderson cut the force of the Corps back to its authorized peacetime enlisted strength of 1,224 Marines. For the next fifteen years the Corps would be stretched thin with duty around the world. Between 1846 and 1860 the threefold expansion of foreign trade doubled America's maritime commerce. The California gold rush added to the number of merchant vessels rounding Cape Horn for San Francisco. The nation continued to expand at a dizzying pace, and with it the demand for Marines to serve from China to South America.

During a mid-nineteenth century religious uprising in Teiping, the fifteen-year Chinese conflict claimed twenty million lives. From Shanghai to Canton, Marines stationed on naval vessels frequently landed to protect American citizens and their property from attacks by frenzied mobs. In September 1856 the situation below Canton on the Pearl River developed into the hottest fighting since 1847 when four "Barrier Forts" – garrisoned with 4,000 Chinese and armed with 176 cannon – opened without warning on U.S. merchantmen. On 16 November Commodore James Armstrong brought the *San Jacinto* up the Pearl River with the sloops-of-war *Portsmouth* and *Levant* and anchored them off the forts. On 20 November Captain John D. Sims, USMC, took 287 Marines and sailors ashore and in three days of hard fighting captured all four forts, killing an estimated 500 Chinese and routing an army of thousands. Sims lost seven men killed and twenty wounded.

During the 1850s a more sinister chord of dissent began dividing the nation, an outburst of factional friction between the North and the South. Waiting in the center of the controversy were the nation's armed services, and waiting in particular was the aging Archibald Henderson and the U.S. Marine Corps.

Above: The 1859 officer's fatigue dress consisted of a frock coat with Russian-style shoulder knots and somewhat resembled the Army cavalry coat for enlisted men. The officer's kepi contained a "French Braid." The white buff leather sword belt, except for the color, and the officer's sword followed the Army pattern.

Left: In 1859, the Marine Corps introduced new enlisted fatigue dress: a single breasted frock coat with only a red welt at the base of the collar, a fatigue cap patterned after the French kepi, and a fatigue pullover used as a work garment mainly during sea duty.

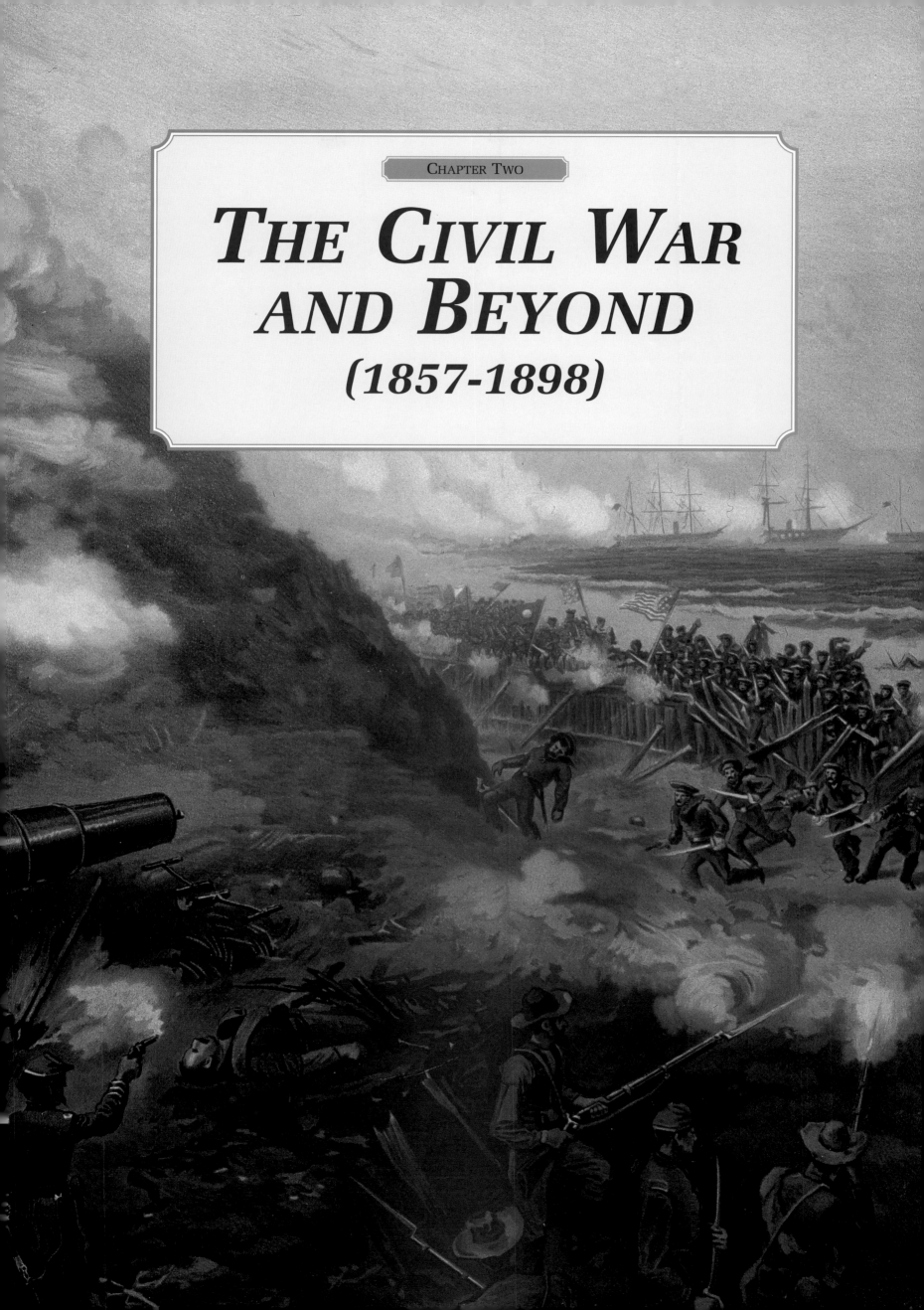

Chapter Two

THE CIVIL WAR AND BEYOND

(1857-1898)

Previous page: *U.S. Marines and bluejackets are cut down by Confederates on the approach to Fort Fisher, January 1865.*

Above right: *In 1859 Colonel John Harris became the sixth commandant of the Marine Corps. Though marvelous opportunities existed during the Civil War, his lackluster administration did nothing to advance the reputation of the Corps.*

Right: *On 18 October 1859, a detachment of Marines under the command of Brevet Colonel Robert E. Lee rushed the engine house at the Harpers Ferry Federal Armory and captured the abolitionist John Brown and his men, freeing a dozen townsfolk who had been taken as hostages.*

By 1857 seventy-four-year-old Commandant Archibald Henderson had nurtured the Marine Corps through thirty-seven years of its brief and often tangled history. He observed the conflict brewing between the North and South and the growing dissention within the nation, but when the self-styled "Plug-Uglies" of Baltimore thought they could disrupt the 1 June 1857 elections in Washington, D.C., Henderson stepped into the fight.

After the armed gang from Baltimore overwhelmed the Washington police, the mayor called Marine headquarters for help. On Fifth and K streets the "Plug-Uglies," carrying an assortment of arms and a shotted brass cannon, came face to face with the old commandant – a gray-haired gentleman dressed in civilian clothes carrying a gold-headed cane. They did not know who he was or that he was made from the same fiber as "Old Ironsides." They paused when the elderly figure, backed by a company of Marines led by Captain Jacob Zeilin, stood before the muzzle of their brass cannon and sternly said, "Men, you had better think twice before you fire this piece at the Marines."

A drunken "Plug-Ugly" came within two feet of the general and raised a pistol. A private standing nearby knocked the pistol to the ground. Hender-son grabbed the thug by the arm and marched him off to the town jail, leaving Zeilin to deal with the mob. When the "Plug-Uglies" opened fire, the Marines returned an answering fire, and as they reloaded, the rioters "took to their heels and fled."

Eighteen months later, on 6 January 1859, Henderson died in office. Whether he could have changed the course of the onrushing Civil War is doubtful, but he brought the Marine Corps through thirty-nine years of its most troubling times. He became indeed, "The Grand Old Man of the Corps," and his name will never be forgotten. Had Henderson lived another ten months, he would have seen the beginning of the strife that began to tear the nation asunder, and with it the men of his Corps.

On 7 January 1859 John Harris of Pennsylvania became the sixth commandant of the Marine Corps. He had entered the Corps during the War of 1812 and served with distinction in the Seminole Wars and the Mexican War. Like fellow Pennsylvanian, President Franklin Buchanan, his sympathies tended toward the South. Five years later Secretary of the Navy Gideon Welles would write: "His death gives embarrassment as to a successor." But on 16 October 1859 the country was still united and at peace, except in the mind of John Brown, a

fanatic abolitionist who late that night seized the federal armory at Harpers Ferry, Virginia, in an effort to propagate a slave revolt.

On the morning of 17 October the governor of Virginia wired President Buchanan for help. The only force available in Washington was Harris's Marines, and the only distinguished officer available to lead them was Brevet Colonel Robert E. Lee of the U.S. Army. Harris dispatched eighty-six Marines under Lieutenant Israel Greene by rail to Harpers Ferry with instruction to wait until Lee arrived by another train. In the meantime John Brown and his men holed up in the armory's engine house with several hostages and skirmished with townsfolk, railroaders, and militia.

ONE-MINUTE ACTION

At daylight on 18 October, Lee ordered Greene to organize a detail to break down the doors of the engine house and seize Brown's raiders. Greene, a veteran of the Mexican War, picked his volunteers and waited while Lieutenant James E. B. "Jeb" Stuart, USA, delivered an ultimatum to Brown. When the grizzled abolitionist refused to surrender, Greene and his men battered down the swinging doors of the engine house with a ladder

and rushed inside. In the turmoil, one of the raiders killed Marine Private Luke Quinn. When a hostage pointed to Brown, who was reloading his Sharps rifle, Greene cut down the trouble-maker with his sword.

In barely more than a minute, the insurrection came to an end. Days later, after Brown and several of his men recovered from their wounds, Greene escorted them to Charles Town, Virginia, where the raiders were tried for treason and hanged by the State of Virginia.

The seeds for the American Civil War, which were sown during the debates over slavery during the formation of the Constitution, began to sprout with the election of Abraham Lincoln on 6

> While some historians marked the affair at Harpers Ferry as among the first actions leading to the Civil War, Lieutenant Greene put it in perspective when he wrote:
>
> '[Colonel Lee] treated the affair as one of no great consequence, which would be speedily settled by the Marines. It was. '
>
> ISRAEL GREENE, "THE CAPTURE OF JOHN BROWN," NORTH AMERICAN REVIEW, DECEMBER, 1885.

Above: *In 1842 the Federal Armory at Harpers Ferry began producing percussion musket and bayonets, such as the model pictured above. By coincidence, the Marines assaulting John Brown's engine house in October 1859 carried the very rifle-muskets and bayonets produced by the armory.*

Left: *After freeing the hostages from the Harpers Ferry engine house, Lieutenant Israel Green's Marine detachment rounded up John Brown's raiders and hauled them off to jail. During the scuffle, Green wounded Brown and laid him on the ground.*

► **1861**

7 MARCH: Gideon Welles becomes secretary of the navy.

12 APRIL: The Civil War begins when Confederate shore batteries fire on Fort Sumter.

21 JULY: Major John G. Reynolds leads 365 Marines into the First Battle of Bull Run and reports 44 men killed, wounded or missing.

28 AUGUST: Marines participate in a successful amphibious attack on Hatteras Inlet.

Above right: Marines who fought in the Civil War wore pretty natty uniforms. An officer stands at the left of five enlisted men under his command.

Below: Marines at the Harpers Ferry carried a black leather cartridge box with sling, a baldric with bayonet and scabbard, a pack marked "USM," and a white buff waist belt for carrying percussion caps.

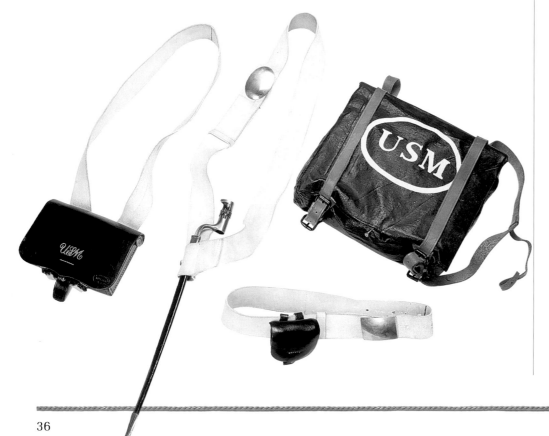

November 1860. Seven states of the South, beginning with South Carolina, seceded before the new president took office. By then, former Senator Jefferson Davis had already been seated as president of the new Confederate States of America. Lincoln had barely settled into his new responsibilities when on 12 April 1861 shore batteries in the harbor of Charleston, South Carolina, opened on the federal garrison at Fort Sumter and the Civil War began in earnest.

Like the politicians who fueled the war, men in all branches of the military saw the "irrepressible conflict" coming. Loyalty to their native state dominated the emotions of men in the armed services and ripped the Marine Corps apart. While the Army lost one-third of its officers – among them Robert E. Lee – and the Navy one-sixth, the Marine Corps lost half of its officers.

Two majors, Adjutant and Inspector Henry B. Tyler and veteran of the Mexican War George H. Terrett, joined the South. Other veterans like Captain John D. Simms (Barrier Forts), and Israel Greene (Harpers Ferry) went with them. To make up the losses, Congress increased the strength of the Corps to 93 officers and 3,074 enlisted men. Lincoln used his discretionary war powers and added a thousand more. Neither augmentation met the demands of war. At no time did the Corps exceed 3,900 men. Most of the newly appointed officers had no previous military training and received little on their way to war. Commandant Harris assigned them to Union warships on blockade duty and never as a united fighting force. On the other end of the spectrum the Confederate Marine Corps never attracted many volunteers, reaching peak strength of about 600 men.

FIRST BULL RUN

Many of the raw recruits joining the U.S. Marines in the early days of the war added a sad chapter to the history of the Corps. Major John G. Reynolds created a 353-man battalion from new officers and enlisted men and tried to whip them into fighting shape. Only seventeen officers and NCOs had previous experience, among them Major Jacob Zeilin, commanding a company. On 21 July 1861 Reynolds rushed the battalion into the First Battle of Bull Run. After three assaults on Henry House Hill and suffering forty-four Marine casualties, among them Zeilin, the Union Army broke and ran. The Marines soon followed, chased by the Confederate cavalry of Colonel "Jeb" Stuart. Neither side had a battle plan. The clash of arms demonstrated incompetence on both sides as well as a lack of tactical leadership.

Above: *During the
Civil War, officers wore
the brass emblem
shown here on their
fatigue caps.*

Commandant Harris had the unpleasant task of reporting to Secretary of the Navy Welles "the first instance in [Marine Corps] history where any portion of its members turned their backs to the enemy" – a truly bitter pill for such a proud force to swallow.

Colonel Harris did a poor job managing the Corps or finding worthy assignments for his men. On 20 August 1862 Secretary Welles grumbled, "Almost all the elder officers [of the Marine Corps] are at loggerheads and ought to be retired." Frustration within the Corps reached a peak when old line officers like Reynolds lobbied for Harris's ousting. Harris responded by court-martialing Reynolds. Nobody liked Harris. Reynolds won acquittal but lost most of his leverage. Not satisfied with the outcome, he preferred charges against Harris. Gideon Welles called it the last

straw. He foresaw interminable quibbling within the Corps and "a series of courts-martial for a year to come." He closed the squabble by sending both men a letter of reproof. Lieutenant Robert W. Huntington, a Reynolds advocate, wrote: "I know [Reynolds] is not perfect, but since I left his command, I have arrived at the opinion that I shall not again serve under any officer in the Navy or the Marine Corps where discipline is better observed."

Despite internal strife, the Marines worked their way into the Civil War. They served at sea – from Chesapeake Bay to the Rio Grande – in the Navy's amphibious strangulation of the southern seaboard. On 28 August 1861, six weeks after the disastrous Bull Run debacle, a 250-man assault force composed of Marines and Army regulars landed from surfboats to storm Fort Clark at Hatteras Inlet, North Carolina. A bombardment from

Above: *Prior to the
Civil War the officer's
fatigue emblem,
discontinued in 1859,
was embroidered gold
thread.*

Left: *Marines spent
much of their time
during the Civil War
serving as guards.
Here they are
conveying the crew of
the captured CSS*
Falmouth *from the
Brooklyn Navy Yard to
prison.*

Right: *On 27 August 1861, Marines and army regulars disembark from the USS Minnesota and in the first amphibious assault of the war storm Hatteras Inlet.*

Below: *The popular 1863 Sharps rifle went through many modifications. It was breechloaded and far more accurate than a musket.*

Bottom: *In the 1850s, the Marine Corps adopted an enlisted man's overcoat with a wrist length detachable cape.*

the *Minnesota, Wabash, Susquehanna,* and *Cumberland* softened the resolve of the fort's garrison and at 2:00 p.m. the Marines entered the works and raised the Stars and Stripes. The next morning, on the opposite side of the inlet, Fort Hatteras surrendered after a shell touched off the garrison's magazine. The first joint amphibious operation of the war went without a hitch, closing Hatteras Inlet to British blockade-runners and Confederate privateers.

The next Union objective – the capture of Port Royal, South Carolina – involved Flag Officer Samuel F. Dupont, 50 ships, 13,000 infantry, and a 300-man Marine battalion under Major Reynolds. This time the Marines were not so lucky. DuPont piled them into an old unseaworthy transport that foundered on the way to Port Royal. Reynolds found near-miraculous ways to save all but seven of his 300 men and half of his equipment. Soon after the near catastrophe, Commandant Harris disbanded the amphibious battalion, detached the men, and assigned them to various war ships.

In early 1862 a number of Marines were lucky enough to draw duty under Flag Officer David G. Farragut, who took them into the Mississippi River and put them to work in their preferred profession. On the night of 24 April 1862 Farragut fought thirteen of his warships through a Confederate cordon of fire laid down by Forts Jackson and St. Philip. The next day, after destroying the Confederate river flotilla, Farragut lay off New Orleans and demanded the surrender of the city from a group of obstinate politicians. Having at hand no Army troops to support his demand or to occupy the city, Farragut turned to his Marines.

Second Lieutenant John C. Harris of the screw-sloop USS *Pensacola* took the first Marines ashore. Armed with rifled muskets and two boat howitzers, Harris's detachment rowed to shore. A snarling crowd of civilians brandishing pistols, knives, and clubs met them near the levee. Harris set up the howitzers to bear on the mob, formed his men, marched them to the nearby by U.S. Mint, hauled down the Confederate banner, and broke out the Stars and Stripes.

Captain James L. Broome, Farragut's senior Marine officer, formed a 300-man battalion from the remainder of the squadron. Following the tactics of Harris, Broome ignored the mob, led his battalion through the narrow streets, stopped at the customhouse to raise the American flag, and placed a guard before proceeding to city hall. For three days Broome held New Orleans, waiting for Major General Benjamin F. Butler to bring his Army occupation force of 12,000 men upriver to the Crescent City.

CAPTURE OF VICKSBURG

For the next year Farragut kept much of his Western Gulf Squadron in the Mississippi, on occasion running up the river to confer with General Grant. During one excursion Captain Broome made an interesting observation he shared with Grant, who had been unable to flank Vicksburg from the north. Broome had studied the terrain below Vicksburg while Grant had never seen it. On 23 March 1863 Broome suggested that Grant attack the city from the south by moving the Army down the western shore and crossing the Mississippi below Grand Gulf. He also suggested that every soldier carry a week's rations and live off the country as the Union Army circled to the rear of Vicksburg. A month later Grant put Broome's plan into operation, and on 4 July 1863 Vicksburg surrendered after a month-long siege.

Union efforts to stop blockade-running had been as frustrating as the capture of Vicksburg, but for different reasons. By 1863 the two ports most frequently used by British blockade-runners laden with munitions for the Confederacy were Charleston, South Carolina, and Wilmington, North Carolina. The Navy wanted to put both ports out of business. Efforts by the South Atlantic Blockading Squadron to get inside Charleston harbor had been repulsed by the guns of heavy shore batteries; in particular, those of Forts Wagner and Sumter. Fort Fisher, at the mouth of the Cape Fear River, protected Wilmington and successfully kept the North Atlantic Blockading Squadron out of the river and at sea. Welles chose to attack the Charleston forts first and in August 1863 sent the backbone of the

Navy's new ironclad fleet – nine monitors and the powerful USS *New Ironsides* – along with more than 3,000 soldiers to invest Charleston harbor and capture Fort Wagner on Morris Island.

To reinforce the Army in the attack on Fort Wagner, the Marines provided a 300-man battalion under Major Zeilin. Zeilin envisioned an opportunity to bring a glorious new chapter to the history of the Marine Corps. He attempted, though unsuccessfully, to increase the size of the battalion to a full regiment and instill in his men the fundamentals of amphibious warfare. Zeilin

▶ **1862**

15 MAY: Corporal John F. Mackie becomes the first Marine in the Civil War to receive the Medal of Honor.

26 APRIL: Marines under Captain John L. Broome seize the former federal buildings at New Orleans.

Left: *A officer from the Mississippi Marine Brigade (which was actually a creation of the Army and no part of the Marine Corps) runs into a group of Confederate guerrillas while on patrol in Arkansas.*

Below: *During the Civil War, Sergeant Will Potts wore the enlisted man's kepi shown at the far left. The Marine Corps dress shako shown below was worn from the 1850s through most of the 1880s.*

Left: *This style of Civil War epaulettes were worn from 1859 to the 1870s by noncommissioned officers. The pair shown were also worn by Sergeant Will Potts.*

▶ 1864

10 JUNE: Jacob Zeilin becomes the seventh commandant of the Marine Corps.

1865

15 JANUARY: Marine amphibious operations at Fort Fisher, North Carolina, end in disaster.

Above right: The Marine guard on board the USS Kearsarge *standing at attention during inspection. The* Kearsarge *fought the famous naval battle in the English Channel and sank the Confederate commerce raider* Alabama.

Right: Boats filled with Marines and bluejackets from Admiral David D. Porter's North Atlantic Blockading Squadron disembark from their ships and row ashore in the largest and most disorganized amphibious attack of the Civil War, the 15 January 1865 assault on Fort Fisher.

never landed, nor did his Marines. In August he became ill and had to be invalided north, but his ideas of amphibious warfare continued to burn as hotly as his fever.

On 7 September, after Fort Wagner fell, the Navy formed five 100-man detachments – one of Marines and four of bluejackets – to storm Fort Sumter. Captain Charles G. McCauley led the 106-man Marine detachment, but the men were mostly new recruits and not yet full-blown Marines. The 8 September night attack failed miserably. The five-unit force got confused in the dark, Confederate sentinels opened fire, and Confederates manning the ramparts at Fort Sumter sent the five units fleeing for safety. Among the Marines who landed on Fort Sumter, forty-four were killed, wounded, or captured. Not until February 1865 did Charleston, the so-called "hotbed of secession," surrender.

As the war wound down, the Marines continued to look for one last opportunity to prove their worth. Most of the force watched the war from ships at sea, their boredom on occasion inter-rupted to chase blockade-runners. In mid-December 1864 Marines attached to the North Atlantic Blockading Squadron finally got their chance. When Rear Admiral David D. Porter took command of the squadron, he had his eye on the destruction of Fort Fisher – the gateway to Wilmington, North Carolina. Success could only be achieved with an amphibious assault, but the attempt ended in failure.

MARINE MEDAL-WINNERS

Marines were not a wholly unrecognized factor during the Civil War. Eighteen men received the Medal of Honor, among them Corporal John Mackie. On 11 May 1862 the Confederates evacuated Norfolk, Virginia, and scuttled the CSS *Virginia* (*Merrimac*). Mackie traveled up the James River on the ironclad USS *Galena* as she pursued the enemy. At Drewry's Bluff, eight miles short of Richmond, Confederate shore batteries opened

TO THE SHORES OF FORT FISHER

Marines attached to the North Atlantic Blockading Squadron sat through the first attack on Fort Fisher and watched as General Butler bungled another military operation. Butler put half of his 6,500-man force ashore and then deserted them, leaving Admiral Porter with the chore of rescuing the Army from under the guns of Fort Fisher.

General Grant, who never liked Butler, replaced him with Major General Alfred H. Terry and told Admiral Porter to try again. Terry intended to make the assault with 8,500 men, but Porter, not content to pummel the fort with his guns, wanted a larger piece of the action. So on 15 January 1865, after softening-up Fort Fisher for two days, Porter formed a diversionary landing force of 400 Marines and 1,600 bluejackets. Marines, armed with rifled muskets, were to go ashore and after landing reform into companies with bluejackets. The plan contained a major flaw because it compelled Marines to come from a number of different ships, land under fire, and form into loose combat groups. Once ashore, Porter expected the Marines to advance on the fort, dig rifle pits in the sand, and support the bluejackets in one grand final assault. The plan, according to future Admiral George Dewey, was "sheer, murderous madness" because the naval officers entrusted with the operation had no experience with amphibious operations or assault tactics.

Nonetheless, Marines and bluejackets tumbled into boats and landed on the neck of the peninsula east of Fort Fisher. When every steam whistle in the squadron screeched in unison, Porter's ships ceased fire. Marines and bluejackets leapt to their feet and dashed forward with a whoop, screaming and yelling so loud that no order from any of the officers could be heard. A hail of fire from the fort cut down the men and sent them reeling back in an "every man for themselves" retreat. Captain Lucien L. Dawson, commanding the Marines, tried to carry out his part in the assault, but Fleet Captain K. Randolph Breese, in charge of the amphibious assault, could not issue a clear order or one that made sense. As the bluejackets fell back, Dawson's force followed,

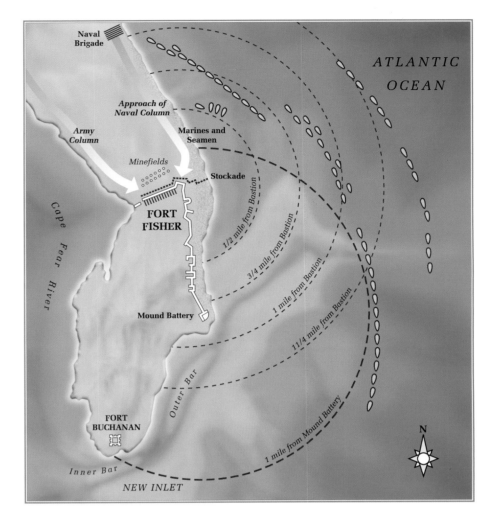

Above: The disposition of the North Atlantic Blockading Squadron during the 15 January 1865 bombardment and amphibious assault on Fort Fisher.

Below left: Marines and bluejackets sweep along shore as they race toward heavily fortified Confederate positions at Fort Fisher.

Below right: During the closing days of the war, Confederates at Fort Fisher repulse the charge of Union Marines and bluejackets.

leaving behind 309 dead sailors and Marines.

Breese attempted to blame the failure of his attack on Marines. Porter would later become a warm friend of the Corps, but with regard to the assault on Fort Fisher, he accepted Breese's cock and bull story. General Terry, thanks in part to the diversionary attack by Marines and bluejackets, flanked the fort and captured it a few hours later.

But, for the Marine Corps, there would be unfortunate consequences. Blame for Breese's failure resonated for thirty years, encouraging some Navy officers to question the continued usefulness of the Corps as an independent force. The failure at Fort Fisher set back progress on amphibious operations until the Spanish-American War.

Right: Marine Medal of Honor winner John Mackie sharp-shoots through an open gun port on the USS Galena, rallying survivors after a direct hit from a Confederate shell knocked the ironclad out of commission.

Far right: Brigadier General Jacob Zeilin, the seventh commandant of the Marine Corps, served twelve years and brought the Corps out of the doldrums after the Civil War and prevented it from being transferred to the U. S. Army.

from the heights. A direct hit caused an explosion on *Galena*, killing and wounding a number of men and putting the ironclad out of commission. Mackie rallied the survivors, carried off the dead and wounded, and put three of the ironclad's guns back in action. For heroism under fire, Mackie received the first Medal of Honor awarded a Marine.

The war all but ended on 9 April 1865 without the Corps having established a meaningful presence. Aside from a rare flash of individual heroism, the Corps' minor influence on the outcome of the war left no sound foundation for the future. Judging from the Corps' casualty figures of 148 killed in action and 312 dead from other causes, the losses represented a pittance compared with the 600,000 men who were killed, wounded, or died of disease. Such unspectacular service did nothing to improve the waning morale of a once-proud and elite branch of the services.

The salvation of the Corps began on 12 May 1864 when Commandant Harris died in office. A month passed while Lincoln and Welles pondered the viability of the Corps. On 9 June the secretary of the navy made the decision, writing in his diary: "Concluded to retire the Marine officers who are past the legal age, and to bring in Zeilin as commandant of the Corps. There seems no alternative." On 10 June Lincoln retired every Marine officer senior to Zeilin and appointed him seventh Commandant of the Marine Corps – the first commandant to take office since Burrows by selection rather than by seniority.

Fifty-eight-year-old Colonel Jacob Zeilin, commissioned in the Marine Corps in 1831, became a seasoned seagoing officer by the time of the Mexican War. He distinguished himself on the West Coast, and by the end of the war had become the fleet Marine officer of the Pacific Squadron. Long

recognized as a determined fighter, Zeilin fought hard to preserve the Corps, using men like Farragut and Porter to espouse his cause. He brought other qualified witnesses before the Committee on Naval Affairs, which in February 1867 finally concluded: "No good reason appears either for abolishing…the Marine Corps, or transferring it to the Army; on the contrary, the Committee recommends that its organization as a separate Corps be preserved and strengthened…and its com-

---

Colonel Zeilin found himself soon beset by problems when Congress passed the following:

'*Resolved, That the Committee on Naval affairs be directed to consider the expediency of abolishing the Marine Corps, and transferring it to the Army…*'

HOUSE REPORT NO. 22, 39TH CONGRESS, 2ND SESSION, 21 FEBRUARY 1867.

Admiral Farragut, the first full admiral of the Navy, set the matter straight when he wrote:

'*I beg leave to say that I would consider it a great calamity if the Marine Corps should be abolished or turned over to the Army. In its organization it should be naval altogether. A ship without Marines is no ship of war at all.*'

Congress might not have appreciated Farragut's opinion when he added:

'*The past efficiency of our Marine Corps fills one of the brightest pages in the history of our country, and the man who proposes such a measure cannot know the Service, or is demented.*'

FARRAGUT'S LETTER IN *LETTERS FROM NAVAL OFFICERS IN REFERENCE TO THE UNITED STATES MARINE CORPS*, JOHN HARRIS, WASHINGTON: 1864.

19 NOVEMBER:
Secretary Gideon
Welles approves the
globe and anchor as
the Marine Corps
emblem.

1871

10 JUNE: Captain
McLane Tilton leads a
Marine battalion
against forts along
Korea's Han River. Six
Marines win the
Medal of Honor.

Marine Landings Between the Wars

Formosa (1867)
Japan (1867)
Japan (1868)
Uruguay (1868)
West coast of Mexico (1870)
Korea (1871)
Colombia (1873)
Hawaiian Islands (1874)
Egypt (1882)
Isthmus of Panama (1885)
Korea (1888)
Egypt (1888)
Samoa (1888)
Hawaiian Islands (1889)
Argentina (1890)
Chile (1891)
Bering Sea area (1891)
Navassa Island (1891)
Korea (1894)
Nicaragua (1894)
North China (1894)
North China (1895)
Isthmus of Panama (1895)
Nicaragua (1896)

manding officer shall hold the rank of brigadier
general." Welles accordingly promoted Zeilin to
brigadier general, and the Corps' existence
remained unchallenged for another seven years.

For the next three decades service at sea continued to be the primary role of the Marines, but
the gradual demise of sailing ships meant that the
Corps would no longer be needed as sharpshooters in the tops. To justify their existence, the
Marines needed to develop a different tactical
approach to warfare, but for the next thirty years
they served mainly as peacekeepers and protec-
tors of American interests in foreign countries.
Their landings ranged all over the globe.

The presence of Marines in foreign lands usually stemmed any threats towards Americans, but
in 1871 Korea – "The Hermit Kingdom" – asked
for trouble when a shipwrecked American crew
from the *General Sherman* sought refuge on the
Han River and were murdered. To eliminate such
atrocities in the future, the State Department
asked the American Minister to China to visit
Korea and negotiate a treaty of amity and commerce. In May 1871 minister Frederick Low
embarked aboard the USS *Colorado*, and in the
company of four other warships sailed for the
Salee River on the west coast of Korea. The recep-
tion was not quite what Low expected as the

Above left: *In June
1871, Marines and
bluejackets disembark
from the vessels of the
Asiatic Fleet to storm
the forts situated along
Korea's Salee River,
acting in reprisal to
attacks on merchant
vessels seeking shelter
from typhoons.*

Battle of the Salee River

On 30 May 1871 Rear Admiral John Rodgers brought his squadron to anchor above the Korean city of Inchon, which in 1950 would become the site of an amphibious landing of historical significance. Rodgers's mission was one of peace, but nobody notified the Koreans.

On 1 June a Navy surveying team began working up the Salee River channel to mark the way to Seoul. One of five forts covering the approaches to the Han River fired on the party. Rodgers stopped and demanded an apology. After waiting ten days for a response, the admiral organized a punitive expedition of bluejackets and Marines. Captain McLane Tilton, commanding a two-company Marine battalion, expressed reservations about going into battle with obsolete muzzle-loading muskets. He did not know that the cannon in Korean forts dated as far back as 1313 A.D.

On 10 June the mixed brigade landed on the mud flats of Kanghwa-Do. Men sank to their knees in the mud. The assault could have been disastrous had not *Monocacy* and *Palos* worked inshore and blasted the first Korean fort. The Marines thrashed through the muck and began working their way toward the fort. Tilton found the bastion deserted, so he spiked the guns and advanced upriver to the next fort while bluejackets remained behind to create a redoubt.

On the following morning Tilton's Marines overran the second fort, dismantled the battlements, and directed the main assault against "The Citadel," the fort that had fired upon the survey party. To reach the citadel required an advance across ridges teeming with white-robed Koreans firing old matchlocks.

The citadel stood atop a 150-foot conical hill that could only be reached by going straight up. Tilton steeled his Marines for the assault. The enemy met them with a fusillade of bullets that hit no one, but Marine muzzle-loaders toppled forty Koreans on the ramparts. As bluejackets and Marines trudged upwards, they dodged rocks hurled down the hill by the fort's defenders. The Koreans began singing "melancholy" chants, which intensified as the brigade drew closer. The first Americans over the wall encountered a shower of spears. Korean marksmanship remained deplorable. Only twenty Koreans surrendered – 243 of them died in combat.

In the closing minutes of the battle Corporal Charles Brown and Private Hugh Purvis hauled down the Korean flag, a yellow banner twelve feet square. Six Marines received the Medal of Honor, among them Brown and Purvis. Since only two Marines lost their lives in the scuffle, it marked the only time in modern warfare where the number of Medals of Honor exceeded by three times the number of American casualties.

Right: In June 1871, Marines land from ships and drag artillery through the mud; the guns would be needed to storm a series of Korean forts along the Salee River.

Below: Marines and bluejackets come ashore along mud flats, build a redoubt, and advance up the shore until reaching the citadel, which they quickly capture.

Below right: The Koreans, using antiquated weapons, were no match for the Marines, which quickly overran their fortified earthworks, killing hundreds as they advanced.

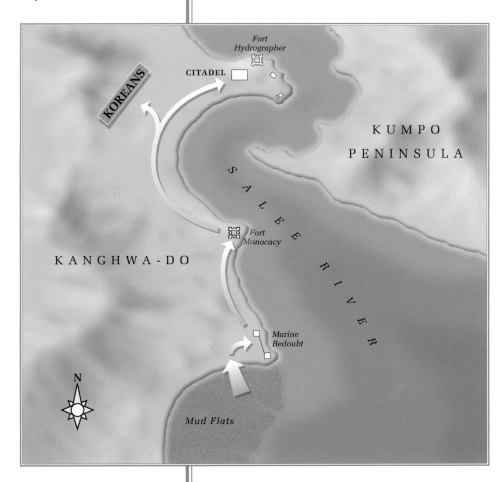

poorly armed Koreans attacked members of his party, leading to one-sided actions in which American forces overwhelmed the Koreans.

In 1874 Commandant Zeilin warded off another challenge by some members of Congress to disband the Marine Corps and give shipboard duties to soldiers or sailors. The proposals were "defeated by the efforts of better informed legislators," but this time the Corps escaped dissolution by the narrowest of margins. As a part of the compromise, Congress cut back the already skimpy Corps' budget, reduced the officer corps to seventy-eight, and ordered that the commandant's rank be reduced from brigadier general to colonel whenever Zeilin retired. A floor fight in the House of Representatives barely succeeded in preserving the Marine Band. Zeilin, though disgusted with Congress's bickering, stayed in command until the nation's Centenniel celebration on 4 July 1876. Unlike his predecessor, he did not want to remain in office until he died, and on 31 October he retired.

IMPROVEMENTS UNDER MCCAWLEY

On 1 November 1876 forty-nine-year-old Charles G. McCawley, a notable officer and veteran of the Mexican and Civil Wars, took over the reins of office and became the Corps' eighth commandant. With a smaller budget to run the Corps, he methodically established higher enlistment standards, provided better training for recruits, and, beginning with the Annapolis class of 1881, recruited all his officers, fifty in number, from the Naval Academy. Five of his selections would become commandants; thirteen others would become generals.

As an administrator McCawley drew up the first standardized table of organization for the Corps. As an entrepreneur he started a clothing factory in Philadelphia and produced the first mass-produced uniforms, which continued in production through World War II and the Korean War. Having an appreciation for all forms of advanced technology, he soon had clerks using typewriters and the telephone. He used Marines stationed stateside to support the Treasury Department in the destruction of illegal distilleries, the enforcement of revenue laws, and when labor riots erupted in Philadelphia and Baltimore he sent Marines to quell the disturbances. Problems at home and abroad kept McCawley busy for fifteen years.

During the summer of 1882 *fellah* mobs in Alexandria, Egypt, rioted against the intrusion of foreigners. Britain's Royal Navy responded and bombarded portions of the city. On 14 July, as fires spread through Alexandria, Captain Henry C. Cochrane, commanding the European Squadron's Marines, sent 73 of his men and 60 bluejackets into the center of the city to guard the

American Consulate. Cochrane, a brilliant officer and notorious disciplinarian, marched his men through mobbed streets, formed a cordon around the consulate, and established a riot-free zone, a courageous action that drew praise from Lord Charles Beresford, who wrote, after arriving with a force of 4,000 men: "To your smart, faithful force, great credit is due...I have represented these facts to my government."

In 1885 the Marine Corps operated for the first time as a brigade when called to duty at Aspinwall (now Colon, Panama). Revolution between Panamanians and the Colombian government threatened American transit across the isthmus and broke an agreement guaranteed by treaty. Brevet Lieutenant Colonel Charles Heywood collected a battalion of Marines from four navy yards and rushed them to Aspinwall. When later joined by a second battalion from Pensacola and Boston, Heywood fought his way across the 47-mile isthmus and encamped outside Panama City. When a third battalion arrived from the West Coast, he formed the Marines into the Corps' first brigade.

▶ **1876**

1 NOVEMBER: Charles G. McCawley becomes the eighth commandant of the Marine Corps.

1880

1 OCTOBER: John Philip Sousa becomes the 17th leader of the Marine Band.

Above left: *The typical enlisted Marine in 1884 wore a comfortable wool or cotton uniform, well fitted, with stripes showing his rank stitched to his sleeves.*

Below: *During the summer of 1882, after quelling* fellah *mobs in Alexandria, Egypt, American and British Marines stand together in review as officers pass by near the British and American consulate buildings.*

▶ **1882**

14 JULY: Marines assume a new role and become a peacekeeping force in Alexandria, Egypt.

1883

3 MARCH: Congress authorizes the construction of four steel warships, which later threatens the assignmentof Marines to ships of war.

1885

18 JUNE: Marines land in Panama to safeguard passage of Americans across the isthmus.

Right: John Philip Sousa emerged from relative obscurity to become the seventeenth director of the Marine Band, and under his leadership made it the finest band in the nation.

Below right: Marine band members became the most nattily dressed ensemble in the nation, right down to their white, spiked Prussian-style helmets.

Below: The fancy dress band shoulder knots of the 1880s contained a lyre in the center to designate that the wearer was a band member.

By the time Commander Bowman H. McCalla arrived to assume overall command, Heywood had matters under control. During the height of the disturbance, the captain of a British man-of-war lying in Panama City's harbor learned that the Marines had arrived. To the good news he laconically replied, "Tranquility is then assured."

Under the leadership of Zeilin and McCawley the Marine Corps survived the congressional cost-cutters for twenty-seven years, but on the eve of McCawley's retirement in 1891, a cabal of young naval officers, led by Lieutenant William F. Fullam, launched a campaign to force Marines off ships of the Navy. Fullam's argument stemmed from the creation of the "New Navy" of the 1890s, which no longer carried sail. Even Admiral Porter, a supporter of the Marine Corps, admitted that the change transformed "Our seamen…into coal heavers, our officers had little to do but walk the deck."

THE PRESIDENT'S OWN

In 1880 Commandant Colonel McCawley stared glumly at his pathetic collection of Marine musicians and lamented, "The Band gives me more trouble than all the rest of the Corps put together." On 1 October he solved the problem for $94 a month when he appointed John Philip Sousa as its seventeenth director. He had no idea what a marvelous change the portly, bewhiskered young man would make on the floundering band.

On 9 June 1868 Antonio Sousa, himself a member of the band, decided that his obstreperous thirteen-year-old son needed discipline and signed him up as a "music boy," an apprenticeship with the Corps for a period of "seven years, five months, and twenty-seven days." Twelve years later Antonia found himself playing trombone under the direction of his son. During those years the younger Sousa wrote music and became popularly known as "The March King," a fitting sobriquet for the man who composed 136 marches.

Sousa led the Marine Band for twelve years, and during that time he elevated it from the doldrums to the finest military band in the country. For the dedication of the Statue of Liberty on 4 July 1886, the nation would have none other than Sousa and the Marine Band for the ceremony.

After his long service with the Marine Corps, Sousa formed his own band and toured throughout the world. When the United States entered World War I, sixty-two-year-old John Philip Sousa joined the Naval Reserve with the rank of lieutenant and became the first musician ever to become a naval officer. He loved life and he loved music. On George Washington's two-hundredth birthday in 1932, he conducted the combined bands of the Army, Navy, and Marine Corps. Fourteen days later he died. The last composition ever played under his baton was the immortal *Stars and Stripes Forever*. For four days his body lay at rest in the Marine Band Auditorium.

On 10 March 1932 eight white horses drew his caisson to his final resting place in Congressional Cemetery. As the procession began, the Marine Band played *Semper Fidelis* in dirge time. The great band that Sousa organized in the late 19th Century is today a living legacy of the U.S. Marine Corps. From the original thirty-two drums and fifes, the Marine Band has become a national treasure and is still, as Thomas Jefferson once said, The President's Own.

> *'I have had the Marines under my observation since the year 1824, when I first joined an American man-of-war, a period of 66 years, and all during that time I have never known a case where the Marines could not be depended upon for any service.'*
>
> ADMIRAL OF THE NAVY DAVID D. PORTER.

Fullam's arguments were not new, but they were articulately and persuasively presented. Over the objection of the Navy Department, Fullam's proposal caught the eye of the Senate. As this new attack on the Marine Corps gathered momentum, McCawley resigned at the age of sixty-four, and on 30 June 1891 Colonel Charles Heywood became the ninth commandant of the Marine Corps.

During the debate over the future of the Marine Corps, Heywood kept out of the political arena but did battle through his friends in the Navy Department. In August 1894 a Senate bill proposed that a Corps of Marine Artillery be formed and transferred into the Army. The bill mimicked a concept practiced by Germany and Britain for fortress and coast defense and exasperated Secretary of the Navy Hilary A. Herbert. The secretary convinced the Senate Navy Affairs Committee to pigeonhole the legislation, and for all practical purposes he also pigeonholed Fullam and the lieutenant's petitioners. The most influential voice in the decision came from Captain Henry C. Taylor, President of the Naval War College, who said that if the Corps was integrated into the Army, "...I do not doubt that those seamen, and the officers [who] command them, would evolve...into a new corps, identical to the present Marines."

Though Secretary Herbert shut down the Fullam machine, Captain Robley D. Evans, USN, spurted into the debate and asked the Navy Department to omit Marines from the new battleship *Indiana* (BB-1), which he had been assigned to command. "Fighting Bob" was not the type of man to take lightly. Evans still blamed the errant 1865 amphibious landing at Fort Fisher on the Marines. He had a reason for his ire: he had nearly lost his leg in the furtive assault.

On 1 November 1895 Secretary Herbert took Evans aside and made it clear that a Marine detachment consisting of "one captain, one subaltern, and 60 noncommissioned officers, privates, and musics" would be on the USS *Indiana* when she sailed. The Marines were "to be part of the working force of the ship; would man certain guns under their own officers and would assist in such all hands evolutions as provisioning, coaling, and ammunitioning." Herbert's proclamation set the pattern for the duties of Marines aboard a ship for the next century. Colonel Heywood promptly detailed 1st Lieutenant Lincoln Karmany as Evans's Marine officer. The relationship chilled after word got back to Captain Evans that Karmany surreptitiously referred to him as "Frightened Bob."

While the scuffle between the Senate and the Navy Department waxed and waned, Heywood went about the business of professionalizing the Marine Corps. He created the School of Application in Washington for new lieutenants and select enlisted men. Besides infantry drill and tactics, the school stressed training in naval gunnery, mine warfare, electricity, and high explosives. When the Bureau of Ordnance refused to transfer eighteen rapid-fire guns for training Marines, Heywood went to Secretary Herbert and got them.

MARKSMANSHIP PROGRAM

The commandant's new school would later evolve into the Marine Basic Schools system. He increased the number of bases from twelve to twenty-one. One would become Parris Island at Port Royal, South Carolina, the most important training area for Marines on the eastern seaboard. Heywood de-emphasized drill and placed great emphasis on target practice, and the Marine Corps soon bragged of having the best marksmen in uniform. When the Navy tried to induce the Marine Corps to accept a few new bolt-action 6mm Lee magazine rifles, Heywood held onto his old single-shot Springfields until Congress

> *'The Corps has always been so distinguished in its discipline and efficiency that I should regard the withdrawal of the guards from our ships and Navy Yards as a positive misfortune for the Navy. The proposition to supply these places with bluejackets is not worthy of serious consideration.'*
>
> REAR ADMIRAL STEPHEN B. LUCE
> (FOUNDER OF THE NAVAL WAR COLLEGE)
> TO COLONEL HEYWOOD, 15 FEBRUARY 1894.

Left: The Marine bugler of 1887 wore epaulets similar to those of a band member, service stripes lower down the sleeve, a white or buff belt with a polished brass buckle, and a kepi. The uniform fitted well and was comfortable.

Above: *The blue dress bell crown cap with the globe and anchor became popular in the early 1900s. The fancy spiked black dress helmet to the right was worn from 1892 to 1906 and copied headgear being worn in Germany and Austria.*

Below: *At Marine Headquarters in Washington, three Marine officers in dress uniforms pose for a photographer while Assistant Surgeon Thomas Rhodes, USN, kneels behind them.*

‘*There were many kinds of uniforms to be seen in Washington in those war days, but they were so shabby in comparison to those worn by the Marines. While out on liberty in the city, we were frequently taken for brigadier generals by volunteer soldiers and they would sometimes present arms to us. We returned the salute…as we considered they were saluting the uniform and not the man.*’

A CIVIL WAR VETERAN IN RECRUITER'S BULLETIN, JANUARY, 1918.

granted him enough money for 3,000 Lees, better target ranges, and sufficient ammunition for the Marines to continue his marksmanship program. The training included artillery practice because Heywood believed "It is as Artillerymen aboard our new floating batteries that their importance must be felt and acknowledged in the future."

At the height of Senate debate to fold the Marine Corps into the Army, Heywood probably did his cause some damage by demanding $31,000 to feed his men the prescribed Navy ration and another $50,000 for new bunks with mattresses to improve barracks life. He asked no more for his Marines than what Congress granted the Army. In the end he got most of what he wanted, including enough money to provide better-quality material for dress and undress uniforms, a comfortable dark blue billed cap, better shoes, and red trouser stripes for corporals.

Throughout the early 1890s the Marine Corps remained what it had always been: ship's guards for security duty, marksmen, and the core of the landing party. Heywood began expanding the role to include gunnery. He knew that the Corps must evolve with the New Navy and the emergence of American imperialism. The Spanish–American War, hovering on the horizon, would give him that chance.

USS *MAINE* EXPLODES

The opportunity for war came with an unexpected event. On 15 February 1898 the battleship USS *Maine* mysteriously exploded and sank in Havana's harbor with the loss of 238 sailors and 28 Marines. A naval court of inquiry headed by Captain William T. Sampson looked into the disaster and conjectured that the effects of the blast "could have been produced only by…a mine situated under the bottom of the ship." Angry Americans concluded that the Spaniards were to blame, though more recent research attributed the explosion to a fire in the coalbunker that ignited an adjacent magazine.

Newspaper mogul William Randolph Hearst fanned the flames of public opinion, reminding the country of the brutal methods used by Spain in crushing the recent Cuban insurrection. "Remember the Maine" became the hue and cry of Americans. Assistant Secretary of the Navy Theodore Roosevelt sensed the mood of the country. On 25 February he coaxed the secretary of the navy to take a day off and secretly cabled Commodore George Dewey, commanding the Asiatic fleet, to prepare for operations in the Philippines. Dewey paced the deck of the cruiser *Olympia* (C-6), waiting for the order that would cut his squadron loose on the Spaniards.

Rarely had Congress moved so fast, acting unanimously on 8 March to appropriate $50 million for national defense. Two weeks later the

1 MAY: The first Marine school – The School of Application – is established for newly commissioned officers.

30 JUNE: Charles Heywood becomes the ninth commandant of the Marine Corps.

1894

6 JULY: Marines land on Nicaragua to safeguard American citizens.

1896

20 July: Congress establishes the Marine Good Conduct Medal to reward enlisted men for blameless service.

Navy Department formed the Flying Squadron for the defense of the eastern seaboard with Acting Commodore Winfield Scott Schley in command. On 26 March, urged by Congress to take action, President William McKinley sent an ultimatum to the Spanish government demanding, among other things, independence for Cuba. On 9 April Spain agreed to an armistice with Cuban rebels, but the concession came too late. Two days later McKinley asked Congress for authority to intervene in Cuba. On 19 April Congress approved American intervention in the island. When Secretary of the Navy John D. Long cabled the Asiatic Squadron, he was somewhat surprised to find Commodore Dewey already primed and ready to leave for the Philippines.

Commandant Heywood now had his war, a promotion to brigadier general, and an authorization to recruit more men. The increase brought the Corps to 119 officers and 4,713 enlisted men, and he expected the Marines to make the most of it. He also had a radically new weapon. In 1896 he finally adopted the Lee Navy rifle, a high-velocity, clip-fed, bolt-action .236 caliber rifle using smokeless powder – the first of its kind in the U.S. armed forces – and in 1898 the Corps took their Lees to war.

Above left: The Marine detachment on board the USS Olympia *pose with their weapons for a group photograph. A few weeks later they entered Manila Bay with Commodore George Dewey's Asiatic Fleet.*

Above: The globe and anchor became the standard insignia for the spiked helmet from the 1880s to 1904.

Far left: The Good Conduct Medal is pinned to the chest of the Spanish American War era full dress quartermaster's uniform.

Left: An 1890s collage includes a Krag leather pouch, full dress shoulderboards, shako insignia, 1st sergeant chevron, and pith helmet insignia.

▶ 1898

7 FEBRUARY: The gunboat *Alert* lands Marines and bluejackets on Nicaragua to protect the U.S. Consulate.

15 FEBRUARY: Twenty-eight Marines lose their lives when an explosion rocks the USS *Maine* at Havana.

21 APRIL: Congress approves war against Spain.

1-3 MAY: Marines occupy Cavite Naval Station in the Philippines after Commodore Dewey destroys the Spanish fleet.

Above right: Lieutenant Dion Williams and his detachment of Marines from the USS Baltimore *salute Admiral Dewey during his first visit to the Cavite navy yard.*

> *'Take the best position for holding the rifle. Aim it correctly, hold it steadily, and pull the trigger without deranging the aim.'*
>
> MARINES' MANUAL, THE CORPS' FIRST HANDBOOK.

On the morning of 1 May 1898, nine days after the outbreak of war, Dewey steamed into Manila Bay with seven ships, and before lunchtime wiped out Spanish Admiral Montojo's squadron. Forty-eight hours later Marines under the command of 1st Lieutenant Dion Williams landed from the

USS *Baltimore* (C-3) and secured the Cavite Navy Yard. Being the first U.S. troops to land on Spanish territory, the Marines were also the first to hoist the American colors on Spain's domain. Then they waited until July, rotating guard duty ashore, for an occupying force from the Army to arrive. "If there had been 5,000 Marines under my command at Manila Bay," Dewey grumbled, "the city would have surrendered to me on 1 May 1898," implying that an insurrection that followed could have been avoided.

While Dewey waited for the Army to arrive, Captain Henry Glass stole over to Guam in the USS *Charleston* (C-2) and bombarded the island. The local Spanish authorities had not yet learned

Right: Marine equipment in the 1890s consisted of leggings, which can also be seen in the above photograph. In 1884 Marines wore a white cork "pith" helmet or, when in the field, a soft campaign hat with the globe and anchor ornament. The dark blue wool flannel fatigue shirt gave way to cotton in the tropics. The 1899 "Mills" cartridge belt with bayonet was for the 30/40 Krag rifle. The Navy/Marine cartridge belt below was for the Lee 6mm rifle.

Left: *Lieutenant Colonel Robert W. Huntington's Marine Battalion form at Portsmouth, New Hampshire, before completing the successful landing and occupation of Guantanamo Bay, Cuba, during the Spanish-American War.*

of the war and thought it was a salute. Marines under 1st Lieutenant John Twiggs Myers went ashore and raised the American flag, confounding all 56 Spanish marines garrisoning the island as to the reason.

SERVICE IN CUBA

On the other side of the globe Marines planned to land on some undetermined site on Cuba. On 17 April, four days before the war declaration, Heywood ordered Lieutenant Colonel Robert W. Huntington to prepare a Marine battalion for service in Cuba. Huntington mixed the new recruits in among the veterans, formed them into five companies of infantry and one of artillery, requisitioned four 3-inch landing guns from the Brooklyn Navy Yard, and on 22 April marched 647 Marines through the streets of Brooklyn to an old merchantman re-christened USS *Panther*. That afternoon, accompanied by cheers and steam whistles, Heywood watched as the battalion sailed for Key West. He had seen to their needs personally, ensuring that the battalion had "all the equipment and necessities for field service prevailing in Cuba, including mosquito netting, woolen and linen clothing, heavy and lightweight underwear, three months' supply of provisions, wheelbarrows, pushcarts, pick-axes, shovels, barbed-wire cutters, wall and shelter tents, and a full supply of medical stores."

Huntington and the *Panther*'s cantankerous skipper, Commander G. C. Reiter, had both been in the service since 1861. Reiter harbored an old grudge against the Corps, and when relations began to sour during the voyage south, he decided "to put the Marines on their mettle" by dumping the battalion ashore at night near a swamp swarming with bloodthirsty insects.

Huntington's junior officers fretted over being marooned on a Florida key while the war passed them by. Huntington ignored the complaints and put the men through tactical exercises while waiting for orders.

On 28 May Schley's Flying Squadron cornered the Spanish Fleet at Santiago and set up a blockade. To support the blockade, Navy Secretary Long recognized the need for a supply base somewhere along the Cuban coast. He cabled Rear Admiral William T. Sampson, Atlantic Fleet commander, and asked, "Can you not take possession of Guantanamo, [and] occupy as a coaling station?" Sampson replied: "Send Colonel Huntington's Marines."

On 7 June Reiter loaded the Marines back on *Panther* and headed for Guantanamo Bay, located

Above: *From left to right, First Lieutenant Herbert L. Draper, Colonel Robert W. Huntington, battalion commander, and Captain Charles L. McCawley, assistant quartermaster, await orders that will eventually take the battalion to Guantanamo Bay.*

▶ **10 JUNE:** The 1st Marine Battalion lands at Guantanamo Bay, Cuba. Sergeant John Quick earns the Medal of Honor.

21 JUNE: Marines capture Guam.

10 DECEMBER: The United States and Spain sign a treaty of peace.

Right: After making an amphibious landing Marines under the command of Colonel Huntington take positions at Guantanamo Bay and repel a heavy attack by the enemy.

THE SPEARHEAD AT GUANTANAMO BAY

On 10 June 1898, supported by the guns of the battleship *Oregon* (BB-3), the band played as Huntington landed his battalion near Fisherman's Point inside Guantanamo Bay – the first American troops on Cuban soil. Commander G. C. Reiter refused to unload the small arms ammunition because he wanted it for ballast. Commander McCalla of the USS *Marblehead*, the senior officer present, exploded. Using a few unprintable expletives, he told Reiter in no uncertain terms to use his own officers and men to "break out or land" whatever ammunition and supplies Huntington "may desire." In appreciation for the support, the Marines named their beachhead Camp McCalla.

For four days enemy snipers kept up a desultory fire on Camp McCalla while Huntington's scouts probed the countryside in search of the enemy's weakness. Near the village of Cuzco, a few miles from the Marine camp, scouts discovered a fortified well that provided the Spanish with fresh water. Huntington organized two rifle companies and seventy-five Cuban guerrillas under fifty-two-year-old Captain George F. Elliott (later tenth

commandant of the Marine Corps) to take out the well. With fire support from the dispatch boat *Dolphin*, Elliott's force defeated a 500-man Spanish detachment and wrecked the windmill and well at a cost of six killed and sixteen wounded. The booming voice of another future commandant, 1st Lieutenant Wendell C. Neville, could be heard throughout the action as he led his men into the fight.

Marine Sergeant John H. Quick distinguished himself in the heat of battle by performing a role that would increase in importance during future wars –spotting for artillery. As the Marines advanced into the Cuzco Valley, supporting fire from the *Dolphin* came dangerously close to falling among the advancing Marines. Quick, who improvised a semaphore flag, stood calmly on a rise wigwagging his flag to direct the gunship's fire while bullets whistled around his ears.

Stephen Crane, a war correspondent with the Marines, wrote of Quick: "I watched his face, and it was as grave and serene…betraying only one sign of emotion. As he swung the clumsy flag to and fro, an end of it caught on a cactus pillar. He looked annoyed." After the fight, the sniping ended. For his courage and heroism at Guantanamo Bay, Sergeant Quick received the Medal of Honor.

Above: As the Marines push inland, they beat off repeated attacks by Cuban guerrillas and destroy a 500-man Spanish detachment protecting the enemy's water supply.

about forty miles east of Santiago. During the day three U.S. naval vessels shelled enemy positions in the bay, tipping off General Felix Pareja and 7,000 Spanish troops that trouble was on the way.

The operations of Huntington's battalion at Guantanamo Bay heralded an important development in Marine warfare that eventually defined the future of the Corps. In 1898, nobody envisioned the term Fleet Marine Force. But Huntington's Marines, combined with the irascible and uncooperative Commander Reiter, proved the value of unifying a strong assault force with an armed attack transport for amphibious operations. The mission of Huntington's battalion involved a landing on enemy shores to secure an advanced base for the fleet. As part of the fleet, and drawing upon the firepower and logistics of the Navy, Huntington moved quickly upon the

objective and secured a beachhead. It worked so well that Huntington's fleet landing force set a pattern for the employment of Marines that was followed through every war of the 20th Century in which they were involved.

In contrast to the Marines, the U.S. Army landed 17,000 troops near Santiago where, after an extended and drawn battle, forces under Major General William T. Shafter finally whipped General Linares's 35,000-man army at San Juan Hill. The battle demonstrated unpreparedness on both sides. Unlike Huntington's fast attack at Guantanamo Bay, Shafter's casualties told the story. The Army lost four men to disease for every man killed: fifty percent of the soldiers setting foot on Cuba suffered from yellow fever, malaria or enteric disease. Huntington's Marines sustained only two percent casualties, no deaths from sick-

Far left: *Marines post guards around Camp McCalla while volunteers from the ships come ashore to dig trenches and perform picket duty to give the fighters a rest.*

Far left: *Marines post guards around Camp McCalla while volunteers from the ships come ashore to dig trenches and perform picket duty to give the fighters a rest.*

Left: *The first Marines from Huntington's battalion fight their way ashore at Guantanamo Bay. The captured position became a permanent American naval base.*

ness, not one case of yellow fever, and, after several months of garrison duty and skirmishing, returned home in fighting trim.

On 3 July the U.S. Navy destroyed Admiral Pascual Cervera y Topete's fleet, which had been holed-up in Santiago, and two weeks later the city surrendered to General Shafter. Skirmishing continued in Cuba, Puerto Rico, and the Philippines, the last shots being fired on 14 August 1898. Four months elapsed before the United States came to terms with Spain. Despite winning the war, the United States paid $20,000,000 for Guam, Puerto Rico, and the Philippines and forced Spain to relinquish her sovereignty over the island of Cuba.

For exemplary service the Marine Corps received its reward. On 3 March 1899 Congress defeated the Fullam clique and passed the Naval Personnel Bill, which provided for a permanent Corps of 201 officers and 6,062 enlisted men.

For the Marine Corps, the turning point had finally come.

Below: *On 11 June 1898, triumphant Marines hoist the first American flag on Cuban soil.*

CHAPTER THREE

THE NEW MARINE EXPEDITIONARY FORCE

(1899-1920)

▶ **1900**

18 MAY: The Boxer Rebellion begins.

31 MAY: The first Marines arrive at Peking.

13-14 JULY: Marines participate in the capture of Tientsin.

3-14 AUGUST: Marines help relieve the legations at Peking.

1901

28 SEPTEMBER: Major Waller's Marines destroy the Moros' force on the island of Samar in the Philippines.

Above right: In 1900, during the Boxer Rebellion, Marines poured into China. Relief parties marched 97 miles in five days to reach Tientsin.

Below: In 1905, Marines with full packs and ready to march form on the grounds below one of China's many temples.

General Smith, however, sent Marines on an ill-fated excursion through fifty-two miles of unexplored jungle to reconnoiter a telegraph route from Basay to Lanang. Boats foundered in treacherous rivers, provisions toppled overboard, and native bearers mutinied. Before the nightmare ended, ten of fifty Marines died of fever and exhaustion and one man became insane.

After emerging from the jungle, Waller formed a drumhead court martial that tried, convicted, and executed eleven Filipino bearers. After being relieved by a detachment of soldiers, Waller faced an Army court-martial for taking such drastic measures. Though he was acquitted, the shadow cast on Waller's career probably prevented him from becoming the Corps' future commandant. Nevertheless, his jungle march made him famous. After he took his men back to Cavite it became a custom to toast the surviving officers of Waller's battalion whenever any of them came into the brigade mess with, "Stand, gentlemen, he served on Samar."

MARINES CONFRONT BOXERS

In the summer of 1900, during the disturbance in the Philippines, the Western penetration of China provoked a violent xenophobic movement by the Righteous Society of Heavenly Fists. Foreigners mirthfully called them "Boxers." The Imperial Chinese government approved of the movement and sat quietly by as the rebellion spread from the country to the seat of foreign influence at Peking.

On 18 May 1900, U.S. Minister Edwin Conger cabled the Asiatic Squadron for help. Thirteen days later Captain McCalla arrived at the mouth of the Pei-Ho River and landed forty-eight Marines and five bluejackets. By 3 June an international force made up of some of 426 American, Austrian, British, French, German, Italian, Japanese, and Russians arrived.

While Marines protected American interests in the Far East, General Heywood retired on 3 October 1903 and passed the baton to fifty-seven-year-old George F. Elliot, a highly regarded veteran fighter. After becoming brigadier general commandant, he promptly left Washington to lead a brigade being formed for duty in Panama. His service in Central America marked the last time a

THE BOXER REBELLION

On 28 May 1900 the rebellion began when a horde of screaming Boxers went on a rampage and burned several railroad stations on the Belgian-built line running between Peking and Paotingfu. On the following day they destroyed Imperial railroad shops near Peking. A detachment of Marines and bluejackets from the USS *Newark* (C-1) and *Oregon* (BB-3) skirted through a howling mob and made their way to Tientsin, arriving there late at night. From Tientsin, Marine Captains John T. Myers and Newt H. Hall loaded their detachment on a train and headed for Peking. Arriving during the evening, they marched to the embassy through the streets of the city, watched by thousands of silent, staring Chinese who were intent upon killing all Westerners.

During the first eight days of June, Boxers shut off rail transportation to Peking, cut the telegraph lines, and isolated the legations. On 10 June an international relief force under British Vice Admiral Edward Seymour departed from Tientsin to repair the line but met stiff resistance and tried to withdraw. The Boxers cordoned off Tientsin, forcing Seymour to take refuge in the fortified Hsi-ku arsenal six miles outside the city. Toward the end of the month Major Waller arrived with 140 Marines from the Philippines and 440 Russian infantry. Waller's force failed to relieve Tientsin but managed to join forces with Seymour. Now 2,000 strong, the unified force fought its way back to Tientsin. By mid-July the international force had grown to 5,650 allied troops, including 1,021 men of the 1st Marines and 9th Infantry under Marine Colonel Robert W. Meade. On 13-14 July the allied force attacked and crushed 20,000 howling Boxers.

Above: *In 1900, Marines engage a horde of rebellious Boxers outside the Peking legation.*

'*I do not remember a more satisfying musical performance than the bugles of the American Marines entering the [Tientsin] settlement playing 'There'll be a Hot Time in the Old Town Tonight.* '

TWENTY-FIVE-YEAR-OLD MINING ENGINEER HERBERT HOOVER IN *YEARS OF ADVENTURE*.

The problem now shifted back to Peking, where on 20 June the legations came under siege. Almost every day the entire international community assembled to fight off attacks. Ammunition and supplies began to dwindle, and for the small force defending the Peking legations the situation became desperate. They did not know that on 3 August an International Relief Force of 18 600 men under Brigadier General Sir Alfred Gaselee began advancing from Tientsin. With him came a fresh regiment of Marines under Major William P. Biddle. For nine days the force shoved Chinese out of the way as they approached Peking. On the 13th they reached the outskirts of the city and attacked against strong Boxer opposition. Late afternoon Gaselee's force raised the siege and on the following day marched through the Imperial City. Marines remained in Peking until the end of September and then returned to the Philippines. For acts of heroism, thirty-three Marines received the Medal of Honor.

commandant would take the field, perhaps because commandants learned there were more skirmishes to fight at home than in distant lands. Elliott soon became involved in one – redefining the mission of the Marine Corps.

In 1900 the new General Board of the Navy, headed by Admiral George Dewey, had acknowledged that the Marine Corps was "best adapted and most available for immediate and sudden call" than any other branch of the service. Members of the board consisted of high-ranking officers of the Navy, the single exception being Marine Colonel George C. Reid, a permanent guest-member who served as Adjutant and Inspector of the Marine Corps. At the board's request, the secretary of the navy directed then-Commandant Heywood to select the personnel and develop the techniques for ensuring the Corps' mission of rapid deployment. In 1902, a year before he stepped down as commandant, Heywood placed the first battalion of the new Advanced Base Force in training.

Left: *Wearing the standard full dress uniform of the 1900s, a young Marine corporal in China takes his turn before the camera.*

Throughout the decade the Marine Corps built and perfected its capability for quelling disturbances on distant shores. On July 1910 Elliott established the first Advanced Base School in New London, Connecticut, which he later moved to Philadelphia. Though intended for the training of officers in advanced base concepts, the first class contained forty enlisted men. Along with this training the General Board also considered adding more foreign bases to those that had already been set up at Guantanamo and Grande Island in the Philippines.

Elliott assigned Marine officers to specialist schools conducted by the Army to learn skills helpful in implementing the advanced base concept. During this period Congress increased the Corps by more than sixteen percent. The secretary of the navy, now confident that the Marine Corps was on the right track, authorized Elliott to acquire the weapons and equipment necessary to carry out the advanced base mission.

President Teddy Roosevelt, however, confused everyone. In 1908 he issued an executive order defining the duties of the Marine Corps and omitted duty on board naval vessels. Roosevelt, a Navy man, thought Marines more decorative than useful and ordered their removal from ships. Days later, rumors circulated that Roosevelt intended to incorporate the Corps into the Army and make it part of the infantry. Elliott raised a ruckus with the Navy Department. The Senate saved the Corps in 1909 by adopting a Naval Appropriations Bill that stipulated that at least eight percent of enlisted men on board battleships be Marines. But other problems remained. The Navy wanted to make Marines responsible to naval officers on the premise that modern sailors were no longer mutinous, thereby making fleet Marines superfluous. Elliott balked because the Navy would be able to make coal-heavers and deck-swabbers out of his specially trained Marines. When Roosevelt left office, William Howard Taft became president and revoked all of Roosevelt's attempts to alter the duties of the Marines and restored the old regulations. The Corps escaped another effort to reduce its sea-land capability, but more battles were to come.

IMPROVED ORGANIZATION

In conjunction with the advanced base concept, the Corps established Marine-recruiting depots at the larger naval stations. For greater efficiency and consistency, the Corps also consolidated their training of recruits to two bases, one on each coast – Parris Island, South Carolina, and Mare Island, California, the latter moving to San Diego in 1923.

By 1913 the Marine Corps operated with a fixed defense regiment of 1,250 men on each coast with the prospects of organizing two more regiments of equal size as reinforcements in the event of war. Like his predecessor, Elliott instilled in the Corps the importance of marksmanship with all types of weapons. When William Phillips Biddle became commandant on 3 February 1911, he carried out Elliott's program of improving the artillery, adopting automatic rifles, adding more reliable machine guns, and increasing the overall firepower capability of the Corps.

Below: *The 1910 dress coat contains the chevrons of a sergeant and a single service stripe, designating five years of service. The dress coat comes with a white dress waist belt and a polished brass buckle. The matching dress trouser is striped in red along the seam, designating a noncommissioned officer.*

Right: *Group of artifacts attributed to Eugene E. Brong, including (left) his sharpshooter's certificate as gunnery sergeant (1908), (center) notification of promotion to sergeant major in 1916, and (right) a letter of commendation for training standard, 1 October 1918, when he was first lieutenant.*

On 13 December 1913 Biddle formed the first Advanced Base Force – a Marine brigade of two regiments – and placed it under the command of Colonel George Barnett. During fleet maneuvers in 1914 the Advance Base Force successfully "defended" the Caribbean island of Culebra, impressing naval observers and paving the way for an expansion of the Corps' amphibious mission during the next two decades.

As an Advanced Base Force, Marines began functioning as a combat-ready, brigade-sized, combined-arms command trained for assault or defense, depending upon the circumstances. All of these improvements occurred while Marine detachments confronted a host of problems in Latin America during the years leading up to World War I.

During 1901 and 1902, the Navy had landed Marine detachments on Panama to protect Americans and their property. During the following year, Marines went ashore at Honduras and the Dominican Republic because of civil unrest. In 1903 Teddy Roosevelt sent Marines back to Panama with instructions to prevent any other force from landing within fifty miles of the recently formed state. Commandant Elliott thought the mission important enough to take three more battalions and go himself. Colombian soldiers were no match for the Marines and the conflict soon ended. On 6 November the United States recognized the independence of Panama and twelve days later negotiated sovereign rights to a ten-mile wide canal zone across the isthmus. The deal included America's commitment to maintain the independence of Panama, thereby ensuring the presence of Marine activity during the ten-year construction of the canal. Congress was not quite sure what to do with Teddy Roosevelt's ditch, but that did not deter the president. "I took the Canal Zone and let Congress debate,"

▶ 1903

21 MARCH: A Marine peacekeeping force lands on Honduras.3

OCTOBER: Colonel George F. Elliott becomes 10th commandant of the Marine Corps.

5 NOVEMBER: Major John LeJeune's battalion secures Panama's independence from Colombia.

1904

7 JANUARY: Three Marine battalions are sent to Panama to keep the peace.

1906

28 SEPTEMBER: The 1st Provisional Marine Brigade – 2,800 strong – lands at Havana.

THE ADVANCED BASE FORCE IN MEXICO

In early 1914 tensions with Mexico reached the point of crisis. On 20 April Colonel John A. Lejeune (one of seven newly appointed colonels) waited off Vera Cruz for orders to land his force. The 1st Regiment, commanded by Lieutenant Colonel Charles G. Long, looked toward shore from the deck of the USS *Hancock* (AP-3). Lieutenant Colonel Wendell C. Neville stood by with the 2nd Regiment on the transport *Prairie*. Major Smedley Butler's Panama battalion, on board the cruiser *Chester* (CS-1), had been off coastal Mexico since the beginning of the year. Into this flotilla steamed the USS *New Hampshire* (BB–25), carrying the 3rd Provisional Regiment under Major Albertus W. Catlin. Every Marine wanted the opportunity to demonstrate his training under actual warfare conditions.

On 21 April President Woodrow Wilson ordered naval forces to land and seize the customs house at Vera Cruz. Lejeune sent Neville's 2nd Marines ashore, followed by Catlin's 3rd Provisional Regiment in support. The remainder of the brigade steamed south and landed from launches the next morning. More than three thousand bluejackets joined the Marines, wearing their whites dyed with ships' coffee. The three Marine regiments under Lejeune, together with the bluejackets, totaled some 6,429 officers and men, of whom 2,469 were Marines.

During the fighting, Lejeune proved the value of the Advanced Base Force concept. Neville's regiment stormed the city on 22 April and engaged in house-to-house fighting. When temporarily stopped by volley firing from the Mexican Naval Academy, Neville called for support from the guns of Commander William A. Moffett's cruiser *Chester*. Unlike the bluejacket battalions, Marines took to the rooftops and went into action against Mexican snipers. Butler's Panama battalion, thoroughly acquainted with street fighting, cleared the city block by block with machine gun and rifle fire. By nightfall Marines reached the edge of the city but had to withdraw to rescue a bluejacket battalion that had been pinned down and needed help.

With the exception of occasional sniping, the fight came to an abrupt end on 22 April. The weight of the American landing force, supported by naval gunfire, had been too much for the inexperienced Mexicans. The Marines lost only four killed and thirteen wounded in two days of erratic fighting. At the Army's request, Lejeune stationed a brigade at Vera Cruz for the next eight months while the Wilson administration negotiated with Mexico.

Nine Marines won Medals of Honor, among them Butler and Neville. The Corps' first amphibious landing under conditions of war worked with precision. Upon this model the Corps built and grew.

Below: *Not since the Boxer Rebellion had Marines been confronted with street fighting, but in Mexico in 1914 Colonel John A. Lejeune's leathernecks found themselves engaged in some rather hazardous work dodging snipers and clearing buildings.*

▶ **1908**

12 NOVEMBER:
President Theodore
Roosevelt removes
Marines from ships,
but incoming
President William H.
Taft restores them as
ships' guards.

1911

3 FEBRUARY:
William Phillips
Biddle becomes the
11th commandant of
the Corps.

1912

22 MAY: 1st
Lieutenant Alfred
Cunningham becomes
the first Marine pilot.

14 AUGUST: Major
Smedley D. Butler's
Marines intervene at
Nicaragua.

Above: *Cuba
continued to be a
restless country, and in
1906, when mobs took
to the streets, the
Marines moved in with
heavy artillery to quell
the unrest.*

Right: *Nicaragua
became another hot
spot for rebellions
against the
government, and in
1914 Marines moved
ashore, bringing with
them the new Benet-
Mercie machine guns
for use against
guerrillas.*

*Colonel Henry C. Davis tried to add a
fourth stanza to The Marine's Hymn. Though sung
for some years afterwards, it was dropped in 1929
when General John A. Lejeune copyrighted the
original three stanzas:*

*From the pest-hole at Cavite
To the Ditch at Panama,
You will find them very needy
Of Marines – that's what we are;
We're the watchdogs of a pile of coal
Or we dig a magazine.
Though he lends a hand at every job,
Who would not be a Marine?*

said Roosevelt, "and while the debate goes on, the
Canal does also."

In August 1906 mobs took to the streets to
protest fraudulent elections in Cuba. Roosevelt
watched the Cuban situation continue to deterio-
rate and in early September dispatched the USS
Denver (C-14) with a detachment of 120 Marines
and bluejackets. On 18 September Major Albertus
W. Catlin went ashore with a battalion of Marines

at Cienfuegos and reported that the conflict had
become a full-blown revolution. Elliott hurried
five more battalions to Havana and placed them
under the command of Colonel Waller. On 1
October Waller organized the units into a provisional brigade of 2,900 officers and men. Using an
armored train to reach and occupy twenty-four
strategic ports around the island, Waller began
disarming the insurgents. On 10 October the first
units of the Army of Cuban Pacification arrived.
With the situation already well in hand, Waller
kept the 1st Marine Regiment in Cuba and sent
the rest of the men home. Marines remained on
the island until 1909, withdrawing with the
Army in January.

In 1912 the Cuban dispute exploded again
when blacks staged a revolt. Commandant Biddle
hurriedly organized the 1st Provisional Marine
Regiment and shipped it off to Guantanamo. On 5
June, after a second regiment landed, Colonel
Lincoln Karmany combined the units into a
brigade and distributed the men in twenty-six
towns around Santiago and Guantanamo. In less
than a month the situation stabilized, Cuban
authorities took over the peacekeeping chore, and
most of the Marines returned home.

Between the years of Cuban strife, Nicaragua
became another boiling pot of violence and civil
war. Marines had landed there on seven occasions before 1910 to protect American citizens
and diplomats from warring factions. When in
1909 a revolution threatened to oust the
Nicaraguan government, a regiment of Marines
stood offshore for three months but was not
needed to quell the disturbance. Two months
later two companies of Marines came up from the
Canal Zone, occupied Bluefields on Nicaragua's
east coast, and for four months fended off rioters
and vandals circulating through the countryside.
In 1912 civil war erupted with a new intensity.
Rebels attacked the U.S. Legation at Managua,
threatening American lives and property.

Left: *Between 1912 and 1918, Marine combat uniforms consisted of a wool flannel shirt, topped by a standard issue campaign hat. In 1917, "Green" leggings gave way in 1918 to "Tan" leggings. Marines fighting in the Caribbean climes wore the standard issue khaki summer service trousers.*

Nicaraguan President Adolfo D az invited the United States to send more help, and on 4 August 100 Marines and bluejackets from the USS *Annapolis* (PG-10) landed at Corinto and marched to the legation in Managua. For the third time since 1909, Major Smedley D. Butler loaded his Panama battalion on a transport and on 15 August filed into Managua and set about establishing order. For several months a steady stream of Marines poured into Nicaragua. They fought rebel forces, guarded the railroad, occupied towns under attack, and rooted out guerrilla units hiding in the hills. Revolutionary activities brought the impoverished country to an economic standstill, preventing among other things the exportation of fruit, lumber, and minerals to America. Marine peacekeeping efforts during 1913 finally brought the crisis to an end. Commandant Biddle left a 101-man Marine guard in Managua and brought the rest of the men home. Civil wars in Nicaragua, however, did not end.

DOMINICAN REPUBLIC

While one Marine regiment served in Nicaragua, a second regiment sailed in 1912 to strife-ridden Santo Domingo, capital of the Dominican Republic, to protect American interests and preserve the country's government. For the better part of four years Marines came and went, staying on board ship and going ashore only when rebel activity intensified. In May 1916 the fighting again escalated. Marines would spend the next eight years skirmishing with rebels while training a native constabulary to perform a peacekeeping role.

Strife-torn Haiti, the Dominican Republic's neighbor on the western half of the island, suffered from a similar form of chaos. After stirring up trouble for many years, the Cacos, a lawless group of Haitian guerrillas, broke into open revolt. On 28 July 1915 a detachment of Marines and sailors debarked from the USS *Washington* (ACR-11) and landed at Port au Prince. The following day Colonel Waller and a company of Marines arrived from Cuba. When the 1st and 2nd Regiments reached Haiti in mid-August, Waller formed them all into the 1st Provisional Marine Brigade. Serving with brigade headquarters was Lieutenant Alexander Archer Vandegrift, a young Marine who would in later years indelibly etch his name on the history of the Corps.

Below: *During the summer of 1915, the Marines launched a campaign against Haitian Caco guerrillas, driving them back to their bastion at Fort Rivi re and, in a battle from all sides, captured the fort and suppressed the revolt.*

Right: *Lieutenant
Cunningham, hands
on the prop, cranks up
one of the early Curtiss
"flying machines" at
the Naval Aviation
Flying Camp near
Annapolis, Maryland.*

THE BIRTH OF MARINE AVIATION

Marines involved in the Caribbean missed some of the developments at home that would enhance the future of the Corps for generations to come – among them, Marine aviation.

On 22 May 1912, 2nd Lieutenant Alfred A. Cunningham reported to the Naval Aviation Camp at Annapolis for flight training, and became the Marine Corps' first flyer. Cunningham didn't actually fly until July, when he went to the Burgess Company plant at Marblehead, Massachusetts, and took hold of the controls of a Curtiss seaplane. On 1 August 1912, after receiving two hours and forty minutes of instructions, Cunningham made his first solo flight. Designated as Naval Aviator Number 5, he joined six Navy officers and became a member of the Chambers Board, an organization formed to draft "a comprehensive plan for the organization of a naval aeronautical service." Cunningham's efforts led to the

formation of the Aviation Detachment, Advanced Base Force. His career as a flyer took a temporary recess after he took off from a catapult on a moving battleship. His new bride forbade him to fly, and the Marine Corps' first pilot turned in his wings.

First Lieutenant Bernard L. Smith and Francis T. Evans took over from Cunningham and equipped two Navy seaplanes for aeronautical experiments. Smith successfully dropped a few small bombs from one seaplane while Evans successfully looped another.

Despite his wife's admonitions, Cunningham could not confine himself to the ground. After the honeymoon ended he retrieved his wings and continued experimenting with aircraft. At the outbreak of World War I, by this time major, Cunningham had a command of seven pilots – including Smith, Evans, and forty-three enlisted men – which formed the cadre for the Aeronautical Company of the Advanced Base Force.

Another Marine flyer, Lieutenant Harvey B. Mims, received his training at the first exclusively Marine Flying Field outside Miami, Florida. He described those days as: "...living in tents, housing the machines in canvas hangars, which are about to fall down, using a landing field which is made of sand so soft that no grass can...grow in it and which is so near sea level that there is a possibility at any moment of having the whole field flooded."

On 15 April 1918 the commandant split the 1st Marine Aviation Force into four squadrons – A,B,C,D and a headquarters company – and sent them to France.

Above: *In 1915,
Sergeant Dan Daly
won his second Medal
of Honor fighting
Cacos during the
uprising in Haiti.*

Right: *Daly earned his
first Medal of Honor
during the Boxer
Rebellion when he led
his men into battle at
Peiping.*

The task of Haitian pacification involved more than fighting the Cacos. While training Haitian officials in governmental functions and a local gendarmerie in peacekeeping methods, Marines also built roads, provided the country with communications, and established schools. As the all-native Haitian gendarmerie force emerged, coupled with needed reforms and the stabilizing influence of the Marines, conditions began to improve. However, although the Marines suppressed the Cacos in 1915, unrest continued for another nineteen years, making Haiti almost a second home for the Marines.

In 1915, while fighting in the hills against the Cacos guerrillas, Major Butler and Sergeant Dan Daly won their second Medals of Honor. Butler had earned his first the previous year for heroic action in Mexico. Daly's first medal dated back to the Boxer Rebellion, when he served with the China Relief Expedition.

What the Marine Corps needed was a real war, not the tinkering type of conflicts in Mexico and the Caribbean. On 26 August 1916 the new Navy Appropriations Bill became law and provided for an additional 5,000 enlisted men, bringing the

total to 16,000 Marines. The bill also raised the number of commissioned officers from 343 to 600. Eight months later the Marine Corps got their war without ever coming up to strength. Major A. S. McLemore, in charge of recruiting, conceived the slogan "First to Fight." The magnetic effect of those three words upon the young men of America overwhelmed McLemore and swamped his recruiting stations with the best-qualified applicants in the Corps' history. Having so many high-spirited young volunteers to draw from, Commandant General Barnett discontinued the practice of drawing officers from civilian life and filled the officer corps from the rich talent in the ranks. By rapidly expanding the bases at San Diego, Quantico, and Parris Island, and setting up temporary training stations at other locations, the Corps in December 1918 reached its peak strength of 75,000 officers and men, including members of the newly formed Marine Corps Reserve.

RESERVES, AND WOMEN MARINES

World War I marked the beginning of three additions to the Marine Corps that would play a significant role in the future: the Marine Corps Reserve, Women Marines, and Marine Corps Aviation. No authentic Marine Corps Reserve existed in a factual sense during the war, but the designation "Reserve" in the Navy Appropriations Act of 1916 allowed the Marine Corps to exceed its regular and wartime manpower ceilings. The Marines used the "Reserve" allowance judiciously, applying it to only 6,773 officers and men during the war. When the conflict ended, thousands of Marines returning to civilian life wanted to retain their connection with the Corps and the Reserves became a reality.

Under the "Reserve" clause, the Corps organized a Marine women's auxiliary force that

attracted 305 "Marinettes," as the first lady inductees were called. Most of them, like their Navy counterparts, performed clerical duties in cities like Washington, D.C. Though their purpose was to release men for combat, Marinettes received instruction in drill, served under military discipline, and wore an austere, long-skirted version of the enlisted man's green service uniform. *Leatherneck* magazine praised the Marinettes, writing, "Everyone is proud of the Marine girls. They carried themselves like real soldiers...and proved they were ready to go anywhere and conduct themselves with honor to the Marine Corps." After the war, nine Marinettes stayed with the Corps and worked for Chief Clerk Noble J. Wilson. Some became supervisors and stayed with the Corps for thirty years.

Above left: *Young Marine recruits train in bayonet combat on the specially designed World War I course at Quantico.*

Above: *In 1918 Marines went into battle armed with M1903 Springfield rifles and M1896 Krag rifles and bayonets. They carried either of the two cartridge belts shown above, a pack, canteen, and other supplies.*

Above: *Captain Robert G. Barnet, Assistant Paymaster, wears the 1919 standard officer's uniform.*

Left: *This view shows Captain Barnet's dress blue blouse with insignias on the collar, his captain bars, and his sharpshooter's medal.*

▶ 1916

15 MAY: Marines begin the occupation of Dominican Republic.

1917

6 APRIL: The United States declares war on Germany.

6 JUNE: The 5th Marine Brigade sails for France.

Right: *Young Marines being trained at Quantico receive instruction in firing the Lewis machine gun, which played a major role in World War I battles against the Germans in France.*

Below: *Directly below is the World War I Army overseas hat with Marine insignia, a trench knife, and a standard issue shaving kit. The steel helmet below bears the insignia of Headquarters Company, 5th Marines. To the right is the standard 1818 campaign cover with its distinctive rolled and stitched edge. Sergeant Arthur E. Hansen carried into France his personal duffle bag of dozens of items beside clothing, steel helmet, and a gas mask.*

The new 3,600-man Marine regiments were larger than and different from any regiment in the past. Each contained three infantry battalions 1,100 strong, a regimental machine gun company armed with Hotchkiss guns, and a headquarters and supply company. Transportation consisted of one automobile for the regimental colonel, three motorcycles, fifty-nine chargers for officers, and an assortment of wagons, water carts, and rolling kitchens, drawn by 332 obstreperous mules.

Marine uniforms and equipment also went through a transformation. While the typical rifleman carried less, probably no officer in the world was expected to lug onto the battlefield such an array of impedimenta:

1 bedding roll, pillow and mattress	4 towels, face
1 clothing roll	2 towels, bath
2 blankets	1 can opener and corkscrew
1 overcoat	1 pair Elliott ear protectors
1 coat sweater	1 flashlight with extra batteries
1 pair small rubber boots	2 toothbrushes
1 pair hip rubber boots	2 toothpaste, tubes
3 pairs shoes, with extra laces	1 cap
1 pair high lace leather boots	1 canvas leggings
1 pair puttees spiral	12 handkerchiefs
1 pair puttees, leather	2 wristwatches
1 pair leather gloves	1 note-book
1 Thermos bottle, unbreakable	2 pajamas, woolen
1 nest, aluminum cups	1 polished mirror
6 pairs socks, light	1 knife
6 pairs socks, heavy	1 compass
4 suits, underwear, heavy, woolen	1 whistle
6 suits, underwear, light, woolen	1 field glass
6 suits, underwear, light, summer	1 canvas bucket
1 jar, tobacco, with pipes, and watertight matchbox	1 rubber sponge
1 Romeo slippers	2 garters
	1 poncho
	1 housewife
	3 pillowcases
	4 sheets
	2 bellybands
	1 raincoat
	1 bathrobe
	2 soap, face
	2 soap, shaving
	1 set of brushes
	1 manicure set
	1 amber glass

When Marines arrived in France, the Army ordered them to shed their greens and wear olive drab. The Corps considered it an imposition but complied. Once back in the naval establishment they donned their greens again.

AMERICAN EXPEDITIONARY FORCE

The 5th Marines – 70 officers and 2,689 enlisted men – became the first regiment to form in the United States and contained the largest number of veterans. They sailed on 14 June 1917 and reached France in July. The 7th, 8th, and 9th

> '*When war was declared, I tendered, ready and equipped, two regiments of Marines to be incorporated in the Army. Some Army officers were not keen to accept them.*'
>
> SECRETARY OF THE NAVY JOSEPHUS DANIELS IN *THE WILSON ERA*.

Marines remained part of the Advanced Base Force while all the other regiments were slated to join the American Expeditionary Force (AEF) in France. Not all of them got there.

French soldiers took the 5th Marines under their wing and instructed them in the grim art of trench warfare. Fighting out of trenches did not impress the Marines. Seven months later the 6th Regiment and the 6th Machine Gun Battalion arrived. Under the command of Brigadier General Charles A. Doyan the three units became the 4th Marine Brigade and found work with the 2nd Army Division. The situation for the Marines began to improve when on 14 July 1918 Brigadier General Neville took command of the brigade and two weeks later Brigadier General John A. Lejeune took over the reins of the 2nd Army Division, becoming the first Marine officer to command an Army division in combat.

When the Marine Corps adopted the slogan "First to Fight," they meant it. One year after America entered the war the Marines had as many enlisted men in France as were in the Corps at the time Congress declared war. Before the conflict ended 30,000 Marines would serve with the AEF while another 1,600 men performed shore duty for the Navy.

The 4th Brigade, already formed, consisted of 258 officers and 8,211 enlisted men. When the Corps sent Colonel Alburtus W. Catlin and the 5th Brigade to France, it arrived with another 8,000 men. The Army liked Marine officers and detached them to command the doughboys. Not all the Marines went to France. During the war years the Advanced Base Force stood by in Philadelphia and responded to disturbances in Cuba, Haiti, and the Dominican Republic. Others

served on vessels of the Navy, garrisoned navy yards, and guarded naval stations in the United States and around the world.

During the winter of 1918, the 5th and 6th Marines began training in trenches near the front lines. The French deployed the regiments near Toulon, a quiet sector located on the heights above the Meuse River southeast of Verdun. Beginning on St. Patrick's Day, Marines filed into

Left: Airplanes made their first appearance during World War I, and Marines learned a new tactic – mounting machine guns to fire into the sky at aircraft while a spotter tries to direct the fire.

Left: On 18 June 1919 Brigadier General Smedley Butler (center) leads Major General John A. Lejeune (right) and Major General Charles P. Summerall on a post-Armistice visit to the 5th Marine Brigade at Pontanezen, France.

▶ **1918**

6 JUNE: The 4th Marine Brigade advances on Germans in Belleau Wood.

18 JULY: The 4th Marine Brigade engages in the battle for Soissons.

3 SEPTEMBER: In Haiti, the Cacos revolt against the Marines.

the trenches and sandwiched themselves between veteran French units.

Earlier, in 1917, soon after the United States declared war, Field-Marshal Paul von Hindenberg and General Erich F. W. Ludendorff had decided that Germany must defeat France before Americans began flowing into the country to tip the scales against them. On 21 March 1918 Ludendorff launched the massive Amiens offensive. He intended to drive a wedge between the British Army on the left and the French Army on the right, capture Paris, and defeat the two allied armies separately. On the Somme, the German Army penetrated to within 75 miles of Paris. Two offenses followed, one in the Lys-Aisne sector in April and May, and another in the Noyon-Marne sector in June and July. On 27 May, fourteen German divisions broke through on the Aisne and advanced at ten miles a day, a distance unequalled since the first days of the war. Thirty-six hours later the German spearhead reached Ch teau-Thierry, just forty miles from Paris.

MARINES IN THE TRENCHES

When Ludendorff launched the Amiens offensive, he forced France's Field Marshal Ferdinand Foch to pull reserves out of the quiet sectors along the front line to plug the gaps. Foch shifted the 5th Marines eastward to join a French regi-

ment taking over a sector vacated by an entire French division. The 6th Marines stayed near Verdun but expanded its front to cover trench lines formerly occupied by the French. Before the end of March, by an exchange with French units, the 6th Marines displaced eastward, rejoined the 5th regiment, and were once again together as a brigade and supported by their own 12th Field Artillery. For the next seven weeks Marines settled into the nerve-racking routine of trench life where raids, night patrols, box barrages, mud, cooties, gas attacks, and hungry rats were endured daily.

In early May, after losing 128 killed and 744 wounded during 53 days in the trenches, and having played an honorable but insignificant role in the Aisne defensive, the Marine brigade left the trenches and rejoined the 2nd Army Division near Ch teau-Thierry. Having had the taste of battle, they felt like veterans, but fighting from trenches seemed to Marines to be a poor way to win a war.

After the Marines came out of the front lines, Major General John J. Pershing placed the 4th Brigade under Brigadier General James G. Harbord, USA, and said, "Young man, I am giving you the best brigade in France – if anything goes wrong, I'll know whom to blame." At first Harbord did not know much about Marines, but he knew that the two regimental colonels in the brigade – Neville and Catlin – were both winners of the Medal of Honor.

Right: The manikin shows how a Marine looked in November 1918 with Army tunic, but retaining his Marine insignia on his helmet and wearing newly issued Marine collar disks, his sharpshooter badge, and his eighteen-month chevrons for overseas service.

Far right: The 1919 "mustering out" uniform of a Marine in the 1st Battalion, 6th Marines, consisted of a unit shoulder patch embroidered with "Army of Occupation" and an "A," the French Fouraguerre shoulder chord, and twelve months overseas stripes.

> 'They were losing a Regular brigadier of their own Corps to whom they were devoted [General Doyen]. They never failed me. I look back on my service with the Marines Brigade with more pride and satisfaction than on any other equal period in my long Army career.'
>
> MAJOR GENERAL JAMES G. HARBORD,
> THE AMERICAN ARMY IN FRANCE.

On 27 May 1918 Germany's General Luden-dorff launched his Chemin des Dames offensive against the Aisne heights, sliced the northern defensive line in two, and nearly reached Paris. Harbord soon learned what he needed to know about Marines when he sent the 4th Brigade into Belleau Wood. Ludendorff never intended it, but this sudden and successful German thrust set the stage for the future of the Marine Corps.

French reserves thrown in to stem the German advance could not hold the line, and Foch called in the U.S. 2nd and 3rd Army Divisions. Harbord sent the 4th Brigade of Marines into the Belleau Wood sector, which was located three miles north of Château-Thierry and at the apex of the German advance. Here 1,200 troops of the battle-hardened 461st Imperial German Infantry established a formidable defensive position in a square mile of rocky woods.

During the attack on Belleau Wood the 4th Brigade lost 112 officers and 4,498 enlisted men,

> 'The [Marines] looked fine, coming in there, tall fellows, healthy and fit – they looked hard and competent. We watched you going in, through those little tired Frenchmen, and we all felt better. We knew something was going to happen.'
>
> JOHN W. THOMPSON, IN FIX BAYONETS!

Below left: At Belleau Wood, the Marines wore any of three Indian head patches: Machine Gun Company, 5th Marines (top left); 1st Battery, 6th Marines (center); 6th Marines Machine Gun Battery (lower right); gunnery sergeant stripes, and an assortment of officers' and enlisted men's insignia and medals.

Far left: This uniform of the 5th Marine Brigade contains a patch for the 11th Regiment Supply Company, and the Marine insignia over the left coat pocket. On the sleeve is the short-lived crossed rifle insignia of a private first class.

Left: The 1918-1919 service tunic for the Headquarters Company, 6th Marines, contains a victory ribbon with one battle star. Also attached are two stripes on the lower sleeve indicating twelve months' overseas service. The collar lacks the new Marine collar disks.

Right: When the 4th Marine Brigade charged into Belleau Wood, they received their first harsh baptism of fire and eventually scattered some of the best veteran units in the German Army.

Below: The advance of the 4th Brigade into Belleau Wood marked one of the finest battles fought by Americans in World War I. The fight also marked the beginning of a new toughness and determination attributed to Marines.

BELLEAU WOOD

On the night of 5 June 1918 the 4th Marine Brigade trudged along the Paris-Metz highway, passing through throngs of retreating French infantry. A passing French officer suggested that *les am ricains* join the withdrawal. "Retreat, hell!" Marine Captain Lloyd W. Williams replied, "We just got here!"

The brigade turned off the road, trudged past the village of Lucy-le-Bocage, crossed a wheat field, and moved toward an ominous square mile of rocks and woods – the Bois de Belleau. The Marines did not know that they were about to encounter the largest single body of combat-seasoned regular troops since the 1814 Battle of Bladensburg.

The brigade spent an uneasy night holding the road to Torcy. At daybreak Major Julius S. Turrill led the 1st Battalion, 5th Marines, through a wheat field and struck Hill 142 west of Belleau Wood. By noon, after a bloody fight, the battalion captured the hill but in doing so suffered 410 casualties.

The second phase of the attack took the 3rd Battalion, 5th Marines, and the 2nd and 3rd Battalions, 6th Marines, directly into the tangled terrain of Belleau Wood. For a tenuous toehold on the southern edge of the woods and the occupation of the nearby village of Bouresches, the Marines lost 1,087 men. The attack would not have succeeded but for the individual heroism of two lieutenants – Charles B. Cates and J. F. Robertson – who fought off counterattacks, and of Sergeant John H. Quick, already a Medal of Honor winner, who drove an old Model-T Ford truck loaded with ammunition through a gantlet of machine gun fire to pinned-down troops under Major

Thomas Holcomb. War correspondent Floyd Gibbons went into the battle with Gunnery Sergeant Dan Daly's platoon. He remembered Daly swing his bayoneted rifle over his head with a forward sweep and yell at his men, "Come on, you sons-of-bitches. Do you want to live forever?"

For five days the 4th Brigade hammered their way through the woods, taking enormous casualties – among them Colonel Catlin, shot through the lungs. At nightfall on 12 June, Colonel Frederic M. Wise's 2nd Battalion, 5th Marines, broke through the last German line of defense and paused at the northernmost edge of the wood. At daybreak the German IV Corps counterattacked with artillery and mustard gas and streamed toward the woods. There they encountered a new experience. Marines, using their old 1903 Springfield rifles, began dropping the enemy at a distance of 800 yards. Still they came.

Division officers, watching from the distance, gave up for lost the village of Bouresches, but not the 1st Battalion, 6th Marines, under Major John A. Hughes. Despite 450 gas casualties, the Marines held fast, fighting at close quarters, attacking and counterattacking through stony outcroppings and shattered tree-stumps. General Harbord, by now a Marine despite his crossed sabers, reported to the division skeptics: "There is nothing but U.S. Marines in the town of Bouresches."

The final attack by the 3rd Battalion, 5th Marines, now commanded by Major Maurice Shearer, drove the last of the enemy out of the woods. Shearer, a terse man of few words, reported, "Woods now U.S. Marine Corps entirely."

The fight for Belleau Wood lasted twenty days. In the opinion of French Prime Minister Georges Clemenceau, the Marines "saved Paris."

TORCY

BELLEAU

Hunting Lodge

HILL 142

5th MARINES

Belleau Wood

BOURESCHES

LUCY-LE-BOCAGE

Wheat Field

5th & 6th MARINES

6th MARINES

Triangle Farm

VAUX

PARIS - METZ HIGHWAY

LE THIOLET

N

by all accounts half the brigade. The ecstatic French, amazed at the durability and pugnacity of the Marines, awarded the unit the coveted *Croix de Guerre.*

Other than skirmishes during the war of 1812, the Marines had spent most of their 142-year history in minor actions against enemies having no military training. At Belleau Wood they met a veteran force of professional soldiers equipped and supported with all the modern tools of war. The German IV Corps had been specifically instructed to inflict severe, punishing, and exemplary losses on Americans fighting their first big battle. The Germans were shocked by the ferocity of Marines, who by courage, discipline, and *esprit de corps* won the field. During those twenty days, thousands of Marine officers and men learned a lot about war.

> *'In view of the brilliant conduct of the 4th Marine Brigade…which in a spirited fight captured Bouresches and the important strongpoint, Belleau Wood, fiercely defended by the enemy in force, the Commanding General, VI Army, decrees that henceforth in all official papers, Belleau Wood shall bear the name, "Bois de la Brigade de Marine." '*
>
> STATEMENT OF GENERAL JOSEPH DEGOUTTE, FRENCH ARMY, QUOTED BY E. N. McCLELLAN IN "A BRIEF HISTORY OF THE FOURTH BRIGADE OF MARINES," *MARINE CORPS GAZETTE.*

On 14 July General Harbord received his second star and took command of the 2nd Army Division. Colonel Neville received his first star and became commander of the 4th Marine Brigade. Though the brigade had lost half its men as battle casualties, rugged old veterans still nursing wounds began stumbling back to their units.

As the German triple offensive began losing its head of steam, the advantage swung back to the Allies. Each month that passed brought another 300,000 American troops to France. In July 1918 Marshal Foch launched the first organized counterattacks – the British in the north, the French in the center, and the Americans on the right flank near Verdun – to drive the enemy out of three deep salients muscled into the Allied front during the spring offensive.

MARINES THE SPEARHEAD

On 15 July the German Army commenced its last offensive of the war, a thrust by 13 divisions under General von Hutier to capture Rheims and then Paris. To meet the attack Foch folded Harbord's 2nd Army Division into the French XX Corps and at General Pershing's urging determined to counterattack at Soissons, in the Aisne-Marne region. Harbord knew his Marines and made them the spearhead. At dawn on 18 July the massed artillery of the XX Corps opened on German positions, and the 5th Marines jumped off behind the barrage – the 1st Battalion on the left and the 2nd Battalion on the right. The men moved quickly against the rail center at Soissons, the northern shoulder of the Marne salient. On 19 July the 6th Marines, commanded by Colonel Henry Lee,

pushed through rapidly intensifying resistance, and, without realizing it, ran head-on into a counterattack by a German corps. The Marines had learned a trick while fighting in Belleau Wood. They scratched out shallow rifle pits whenever they hit the front lines. Someone called them "foxholes." A correspondent heard the name and reported it, and the era of the foxhole was born.

The German mincing machine went to work on the 4th Marine Brigade, but the men held. Typical of Marine tenacity were men like 1st Lieutenant Clifford B. Cates, who reported: "I am in an old abandoned French trench bordering on road leading out from your CP and 350 yards from an old mill. I have only two men left out of my company and 20 out of other companies. We need support but it is almost suicide to try to get it here as we are swept by machine gun fire and a constant artillery barrage is upon us. I have no one on my left and only a few on my right. I will hold." (Quoted from Andrew Geer, *The New Breed.*)

The Marines finally dug-in within rifle shot of the Soissons-Chateau Thierry road, the main artery for General von Hutier's salient. The brigade lost 1,972 men to get there. After nightfall a fresh division took over and the 2nd Army Division headed out of the lines with the surviving Marines. German intelligence questioned a few captured Marines and finally discovered something about this new breed of fighter. "The high percentage of Marksmen, Sharpshooters, and Expert Riflemen, as perceived among our prisoners, allows a conclusion to be drawn as to the

▶ **12 SEPTEMBER:** The 4th Marine Brigade begins the offensive against St. Mihiel.

3-4 OCTOBER: The 4th Marine Brigade begins the assault against Blanc Mont, the bloodiest fight in the Corps' history.

14 OCTOBER: Two Marine flyers, 2nd Lieutenant Ralph Talbot and Gunnery Sergeant Robert G. Robinson, win Medals of Honor.

Below: *One of the most severe battles at Belleau Wood involved the capture of Bouresches, which lay between two woods. Nobody believed the Germans could be driven out, but twenty Marines from the 1st Battalion, 6th Regiment, did just that.*

1 NOVEMBER: The 4th Marine Brigade enters the Meuse-Argonne battle and ten days later crosses the Meuse.

11 NOVEMBER: The Armistice is signed with Germany.

Above right: Artifacts from World War I include such items as the bugler's patch, the new crossed rifle patch for PFCs, various 5th Brigade patches, officer's dress collar insignia, collar disks, and overseas stripes.

Below: When the French refused to attack Blanc Mont Ridge, declaring it impregnable, General Lejeune went to the French commanding general and said the Marines would take it. On 3 October the 6th Marines hit Blanc Mont Ridge and swept into St. Etienne.

quality and training in marksmanship that Marines receive. The prisoners are mostly members of the better class, and they consider their membership in the Marine Corps to be something of an honor. They proudly resent any attempts to place their regiments on a par with infantry regiments." (*The Leatherneck*, November, 1957.)

After Soissons, the Marines lost General Harbord to promotion but gained Brigadier General Lejuene, who took command of the 2nd Army Division. Lejuene, on behalf of Commandant General Barnett, asked Pershing for permission to bring one or two full Marine divisions to France. Pershing rejected the idea, though he declared himself willing to have another Marine brigade provided that they filled rear-area jobs, such as provost guards and service troops. The 5th Marine Brigade reached France in September 1918 and Pershing spread it all over France. Disgusted, Lejuene found a few replacements for the 4th Brigade and took it back into the fighting.

During September the focus shifted to the German salient at Saint Mihiel, a bothersome position jutting across the Meuse between Nancy and Verdun that threatened Allied operations on the left. The salient also protected Germany's formidable Hindenburg Line – immensely strong defenses built along an arc tied together by Lens, Noyon, and Rheims. The fight would be the first battle of the war fought exclusively by the U.S. First Army. Lejeune could not fill the by now depleted ranks of the 4th Marine Brigade and held it in reserve.

The American attack caught the Germans in the middle of a tactical withdrawal. The I Army Corps under Lieutenant General Hunter Liggett achieved its secondary objectives but let all but 4,000 of the 50,000 retreating Germans slip through the closing ring. He had waited too long to call up the 6th Marines, which in sharp fighting had overrun positions held by a heavy force of the enemy, repelled four counterattacks, and reduced the fortifications that were screening the Hindenburg Line.

Field Marshal Foch now realized that the best troops in the Allied army were not the doughboys but Marines. He moved General Lejeune's division into the Fourth French Army, commanded by General Henri Gouraud. During the first few days of the Meuse-Argonne offensive, which began on 26 September, Gouraud put Lejeune's 2nd Division in reserve. Four days later the French offensive ground to a standstill, stopped by Blanc Mont Ridge, a precipitous massif occupied by the enemy since the beginning of the war.

"I WILL TAKE BLANC MONT"

For four years the ground before Blanc Mont had been chewed with shell and strewn with the wreckage and carnage of many battles. At this critical moment senior French officers suggested that Gouraud split up the 2nd Division and use its components as replacements to shore up battered French divisions. General Lejeune went directly to Gouraud and angrily objected, saying, in so many words: Keep the 2nd Division in one piece and I will take Blanc Mont. Gouraud did not believe him, but said, "Done!"

Lejeune put the Marine brigade on the left to spearhead the attack and seize Blanc Mont. Expecting the Marines to draw the heaviest fire, he put the 3rd Infantry Brigade on the right to disconcert the defenders. With both flanks of the enemy engaged, he intended to pinch-out the well-entrenched German strongpoint in the center. He held the French temporarily in reserve with instructions to follow the Marines on the left and hit the Essen Trench, an already battered German position. Instead of laying down the usual prolonged bombardment, which would have signaled an attack, Lejeune asked for only a five-minute barrage from 200 guns.

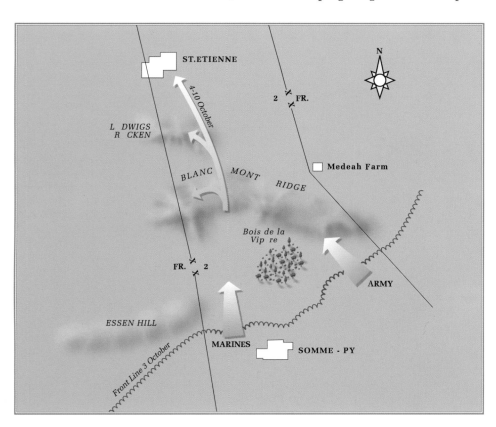

At dawn on 3 October 1918 the 6th Marines, followed by French tanks and the 5th Marines, hit Blanc Mont on the left and three hours later signaled Lejeune, "Objective taken." A single company of the 5th Regiment assaulted the machine gun studded Essen position after the French could not take it. Captain Leroy P. Hunt's 17th Company ousted the German defenders and handed it over to the French. A German counterattack drove out the French, and the 5th Regiment had to take it back.

The French could not keep pace with the Marines, who found themselves two miles deep into German territory with flanks unprotected all the way back to Essen Trench. Instead of withdrawing, they held their advanced position, fought on, and on 8 October captured St. Etienne. The French, still lagging behind, could not

Above: *The battle scene depicts "The Last Night of the War," when on 10-11 November the 5th Marine Regiment crossed the Meuse River.*

THE FINAL BATTLE

For the Marines, the war had not quite ended with the battle for Champagne. After the Meuse-Argonne offensive stalled in September, General Lejeune received a call from Pershing at First Army headquarters and was told to knock out two strongholds on the Hindenburg Line named Br nhilde and Freya Stellung. Lejeune turned to his Marines, the veteran 4th Brigade under Neville, and told them to capture Barricourt and drive the enemy across the Meuse.

On 1 November 1918 the 4th Marines took a position on the 2nd Division's left flank, and at 0520 the 1st Battalion, 5th Marines jumped off across "No Man's Land" and plunged forward. Supported by a rolling barrage, the rest of the brigade – Marine battalions from the 5th Marines on the right and the 6th Marines on the left – leapfrogged through Kreimhilde Stellung and Freya Stellung and gained five miles in one day. After taking Barricourt Heights, the Marines experienced a few anxious moments waiting for the infantry to catch up. When relieved by the 3rd Infantry Brigade, the Marines marched back to division headquarters with their bag of 1,700 German prisoners.

On 9 November the 2nd Army Division reached the Meuse River and regrouped for an assault crossing. Lejeune called once more upon his Marines to spearhead the attack. He picked the 6th Regiment to seize a bridgehead near Mouzon and sent the 5th Regiment to cross the Meuse at Villemontry.

After nightfall on 10 November, the 5th Regiment's assault battalions, beset by a vicious enemy shelling, attacked across fire-swept footbridges and gained a foothold on the other side of the Meuse. At Mouzon, enemy fire pinned down engineers constructing bridges, so the 6th Marines spent the night crouching in foxholes and waiting for the shelling to slacken.

At dawn, 11 November, the 5th Marines struck out against weak enemy resistance and desultory fire. At exactly 1100 they noticed an enormous burst of artillery fire from both sides,

and then sudden silence. A little later they learned the reason. Germany had surrendered. The men collapsed to the ground, built fires, and silently rejoiced.

But the Marines' service in France did not end with the war. When the doughboys went home, the 4th Brigade remained behind. They marched into Germany and became part of the army of occupation posted along the Rhine.

Left: *The Marines set up a machine gun nest against the Germans during the Meuse-Argonne offensive on 10-11 November 1918.*

Below: *When World War I came to an end, the Marines were still advancing through the bomb-shattered ruins of the Meuse-Argonne forest.*

Right: *A Curtis C-3 observation plane sits on its catapult on the USS North Carolina. With the prop in the back, the pilot squeezes into a seat above the nose of the aircraft and has a clear view of everything in front, above, and below him.*

Right: *The cloth patch of the 1st Marine Aviation Force contains the traditional globe and anchor, and because the pilots flew for the British it also contains the British bullseye. The coin-like disk is the aviator's early dogtag.*

believe that a single brigade of Marines could accomplish in five days what untold numbers of French divisions had been unable to accomplish during four years of war.

On 10 October, Army troops relieved Lejeune's battered 2nd Division, and for the Marines the battle for Champagne ended. The toll on Marine blood came high. Rifle battalions that had entered the fight with a thousand men marched to the rear with 300 or less. Blanc Mont cost the Marine battalion 2,538 casualties.

At Blanc Mont the 6th Marines won their third citation, the highest collective citation in the French Army. It entitled the brigade to carry the streamer of the *Croix de Guerre* on its colors. Individual members of the brigade won the honor of wearing the French *fourrag re*, which they irreverently called "the pogey rope."

Perhaps the greatest honor came from the Marshal of France, who said, "The taking of Blanc Mont Ridge is the greatest single achievement in the 1918 campaign."

1st Marine Aviation Force

Right: *Shortly after arriving in Belgium, Major Alfred Cunningham (right), Captain MacIlvaen (center), and Captain Roy S. Geiger present the first flag to the 1st Marine aviation Force.*

While Marines distinguished themselves on the battlefields of northern France, a new branch of the Corps made its debut in Europe – the 1st Marine Aviation Force. The Navy did not know what to do with the aviators and in 1917 sent the first Marine Aeronautics Company – 12 officers and 133 enlisted men – to the Azores to fly seaplanes on anti-submarine missions.

As more men became Marine pilots, the Corps in 1918 organized the 1st Marine Aviation Force and on 30 July sent three landplane squadrons to France, followed by a fourth in October. Marine flyers became the Day Wing of the Northern

> *'Surrendering wasn't popular at the time, and the only way to capture a Marine was to knock him senseless first.'*
>
> COLONEL ALBURTUS W. CATLIN,
> *WITH THE HELP OF GOD AND A FEW MARINES.*

Bombing Group near Calais. They flew British De Havilland D.H. 4s – Flying Coffins" to the men who piloted them – the best single-engined bomber of the war. Marine flyers made it into the war just in time to establish themselves as a viable weapon, flying missions in the Dunkirk area against U-boats and submarine bases at Ostend, Zeebrugge, and Bruges. When the Armistice took effect on 11 November 1918, the Marine Aviation Force had grown to nearly 2,500 officers and men flying 340 aircraft. They flew reconnaissance missions, shot down twelve enemy planes, and in fifty-seven raids dropped 52,000 pounds of bombs. They also recorded the first aerial supply-drop, delivering ammunition and provisions to a beleaguered French regiment cutoff on the battlefront.

The Marine Corps that evolved during World War I was quite different from anything experienced during their 143-year history. They had attained a top strength of 79,255 men and 269 Marinettes. Of that number, 32,000 officers and men served in France. After going into combat in March 1918, Marine units sustained more casualties than had been suffered during their entire existence. Only twenty-five Marines ever became prisoners of war.

Men of the 4th Marine Brigade won 12 Medals of Honor, 744 Navy Crosses and Distinguished Service Crosses, together with 1,720 other American and foreign decorations. They were no longer just an Advanced Base Force. They had become the toughest fighters in the AEF, the first to fight in any battle, the spearhead of the 2nd Army Division, and veteran flyers of distinction.

On 12 August 1919 the 4th Marine Brigade returned from Germany. En route to Quantico they passed through Washington, D.C. With General Neville at its head, the brigade marched past the White House, saluting President Wilson and his wife while the Marine Band played "Semper Fidelis."

President Wilson penned a brief note to General Barnett, writing, "We are intensely proud of their entire record, and are glad to have had the whole world see how irresistible they are in their might when a cause which America holds dear is at stake. The whole nation has reason to be proud of them." For the Marine Corps, a new beginning had begun.

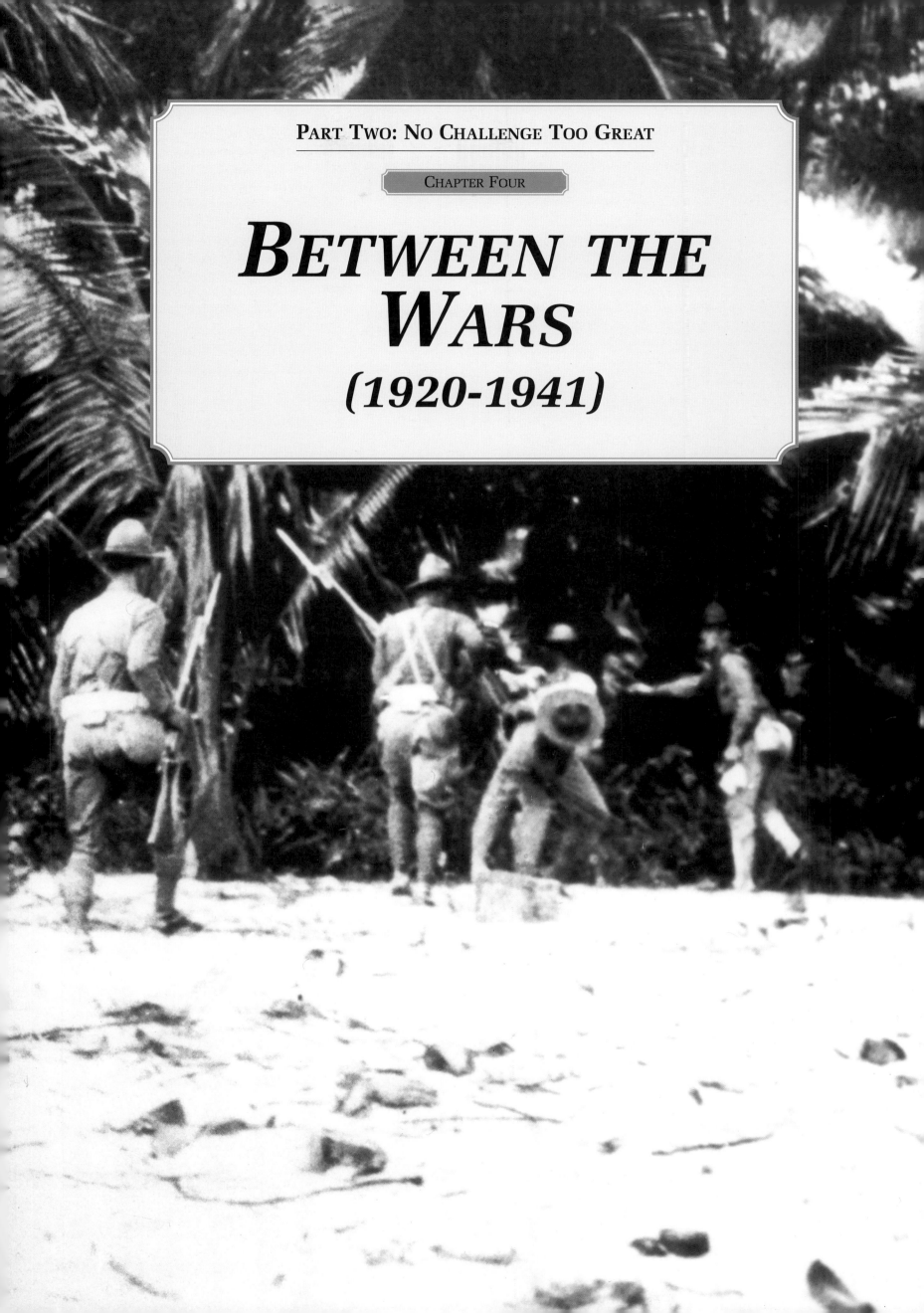

CHAPTER FOUR

BETWEEN THE WARS
(1920-1941)

Previous page: Marines from USS Sacramento *move inland at Socorro in support of Philippine Constabulary against the Colorum guerrillas, January 1924.*

Right: On 1 July 1920 Major General John A. Lejeune, who led the Marines in France during World War I, became the thirteenth commandant of the Marine Corps. His foresight contributed to preparing the Corps for war with Japan two decades later.

Peace in Europe produced rapid cutbacks in the U.S. armed services, and by July 1920 the Marine Corps had been sliced from its wartime strength of 75,000 to 17,165 officers and men. The men went home heroes, regardless of whether they had fought at Belleau Wood, France, spent the war as ships' guards, or battled the Cacos in Haiti. They settled back into civilian life, hoping the politicians who hailed the victory over the Axis as "the war to end all wars" were right. But just in case the Corps needed help in the future, many of the men joined the Marine Corps Reserves.

In 1914 Secretary of the Navy Josephus Daniels had chosen Major General George Barnett as the twelfth commandant of the Marine Corps. Daniels would have preferred John Archer Lejeune to serve the four-year term, but in those days seniority still counted more than ability, and Lejeune was only a colonel. In February 1918 Barnett's term expired, but with the war reaching its crescendo and Lejeune committed to France, Daniels had no choice and reappointed Barnett to a second term. He attempted to cajole Barnett into agreeing to retire as soon as the war ended but relented after Barnett angrily flushed at the sug-

JOHN ARCHER LEJEUNE

Major General John A. Lejeune, the 13th Commandant of the Marine Corps, came from humble circumstances. Born in Louisiana in 1867, he grew up surrounded by the poverty cast upon the South by the Civil War. He fought for everything in his life, including an education at tuition-free Louisiana State University. After graduation he accepted an appointment to the Naval Academy, completed his studies at the age of twenty-one, and went to sea for the obligatory two years as a naval cadet. He wanted to be a Marine and took his commission in the Corps.

Lejeune served during the Spanish-American War, took a battalion into Panama in 1903, fought in Cuba and the Philippines, and commanded the 1st Advanced Base Brigade at Veracruz. Before World War I Barnett made Lejeune his assistant and soon discovered that his understudy could deal with Congress better than anyone in the Corps. But Lejeune made his biggest mark in France, showing to the world the rugged toughness of the American Marine. In August 1919, during the victory parade in New York City, he marched at the head of his U.S. 2nd Infantry Division. Among the division were the valiant survivors of the 4th Marine Brigade.

On 1 July 1920 Lejeune became commandant of the Marine Corps. Not since Archibald Henderson had the Corps had such a man of strength, character, and vision. He prepared the Marines for a war with Japan and put a tactical team together to perfect the science of amphibious warfare. He improved the training of officers and enlisted men and organized company-grade and field-grade schools at Quantico. He also understood the value of public relations and fielded varsity-quality baseball and football teams. He entertained Congress and the public with Civil War reenactments, and became the impetus behind the organization of the Marine Corps League.

In 1929 Lejeune retired as commandant after serving nine years. His programs laid the foundation for victory in the Pacific in World War II. But instead of retiring to an easy chair, Lejeune carried on his work to improve the Corps, becoming superintendent of the Virginia Military Institute.

gestion and asked to see the president. After Germany surrendered, Daniels again tried to coax Barnett into retirement, but the wily commandant wanted something in return. So Daniels created a sinecure post and sent Barnett to San Francisco as the first commanding general of the Department of the Pacific. On 1 July 1920 Daniels replaced Barnett with Lejeune, a man the Marines would never forget.

In 1920, when Lejeune became commandant, big business and national revelry swept the country. Congress and the general public had little interest in building or maintaining a large and expensive military force. The election of Warren G. Harding to the presidency emphasized the preferences of America's voters – demilitarization and a return to isolationism – and the growing nation replaced statesmanship with incompetence. Antiwar films such as "What Price Glory" (1926) fueled the public's attitudes against the bitter losses suffered by Marines at Belleau Wood. A new society sprang from the ashes of the war, a young fun-loving society that wanted no burdens to shoulder, and their confidence in Harding soon turned to disillusionment.

U.S. MAIL ROBBERIES

The president had barely settled into his easy chair at the White House when the nation became engulfed in a crime wave capped by armed robberies of the U.S. Mail. Edwin Denby, the only former Marine ever to become secretary of the navy, called upon 53 officers and 2,200 enlisted men of the Marine Corps to keep watch on post offices, railway mail cars, and postal trucks across the country.

> 'You must be brave, as you always are. You must be constantly alert. You must, when on guard duty, keep your weapons in hand and, if attacked, shoot and shoot to kill. There is no compromise in this battle with the bandits.'
>
> TO THE MEN OF THE MAIL GUARD,
> EDWIN DENBY, 11 NOVEMBER 1921.

After the Marines reached their designated posts, mail robberies came to an abrupt halt. During the four months the Marines stood watch, not a single piece of mail was stolen. Five years later, when mail theft resumed, the Marines returned and put a sudden stop to the robberies.

Though Harding tried to isolate the United States from the problems of Europe and Asia, he could not ignore the strife infecting the western hemisphere. Marines had been trying to pacify the Dominican Republic since 1916.

Above: *The 1920 Gunnery Sergeant's tunic is fitted with medals of Croix de Guerre, World War I Victory, Good Conduct, and Expert Rifle.*

Left: *Marines wore the blue dress bell crown cap from about 1900 to 1920.*

Right: *In 1918 Marines not fighting in France found employment in the Dominican Republic when rebels attempted to destabilize the government. Unlike street fighting in modern cities, these were search and destroy missions in which Marines went from hut to hut.*

PACIFYING THE DOMINICAN REPUBLIC

Santo Domingo, the capital of the Dominican Republic, had a longer history than America's Old West for gunslingers feuding on the streets and assassins murdering law enforcement officials. Nor did the outlaws appreciate Americans mixing into their internal affairs. When a Marine battalion intervened in 1917, a band of gunmen shot two officers, killing one and wounding the other. The bandits took refuge in fortified positions in the hills and had to be rooted out by energetic patrolling led by hard-driving Lieutenant Colonel "Hiking Hiram" Bearss.

In 1918, when most Marines went to France, the 2nd Brigade, numbering 68 officers and 1,932 enlisted men, fought 44 engagements against hostile Dominicans. In late October Brigadier General Ben H. Fuller arrived to try his hand at pacification, only to be struck with a resurgence of banditry in 1919. The problem Fuller faced came from both factions – the elite as well as the bandits. The Marines built schools, improved sanitation, added roads, and brought honesty to financial institutions. However, the changes destabilized the politico-economic equilibrium and rekindled a resurgence of banditry.

Because the war in Europe had ended and the Corps had idle resources, Commandant Barnett

sent an additional regiment, the 15th Marines, and six Curtiss Jennies that had served in France as Squadron D, 1st Marine Aviation Force. The flyers carried mail and supplies, evacuated the wounded, and flew combat missions against the bandits. They experimented with a new kind of bombing by using the nose of the plane as a bombsight, diving at a 45-degree angle, releasing the bomb, and pulling-out at 250 feet. The experiments evolved into a new tactic: glide-bombing.

Pacification efforts continued through all the turmoil. Marines recruited, trained, and armed the "Policia Nacional," took them on patrols into the hills to subdue bandits, and brought the captives back to the city for trial and conviction in a court of law. By mid-1922, after a period of extended amnesty, the Marines declared Santo Domingo pacified. Lejeune brought all the men back to the United States except for the 2nd Marine Brigade and the 1st Air Squadron. This did not satisfy President Harding, who had decided that the occupation of Santo Domingo could not continue. On 16 September 1924 the rear echelon of the 2nd Brigade slung arms, filed aboard a ship, and sailed for home.

After nine years of pacification by a truly dedicated detachment of Marines, the occupation of the Dominican Republic ended.

During the years of turmoil in Santo Domingo, the Cacos of Haiti staged another revolt when the figure of Charlemagne Massena P ralte, a man of spirit and intelligence, organized the rebels. It seemed that no one but the Marines could stop the violence rippling across the island shared by Haiti and the Dominican Republic. Charlemagne struck at the strongholds of the Gendarmerie, assassinated its members, burned barracks, and sacked the towns. The Cacos guerrillas, especially selective in their attacks, avoided collisions with the Marines.

Lieutenant Colonel Alexander S. Williams, commanding the Gendarmerie, also commanded a reduced Marine brigade of 948 officers and enlisted men – too few to handle the national emergency. Four companies of reinforcements arrived from Cuba along with Squadron E, Marine Aviation, consisting of seven HS-2 seaplanes, six Jennies, eleven officers, and 138 enlisted men. Colonel Frederic M. Wise, overall commander of American forces, decided upon a plan to end the revolt by weeding out the insurgents. During the next six months Marines and gendarmes fought

> *'Near the Iron Market we saw a large number of Cacos coming down this street. We detrucked and opened fire. I had one man killed and six wounded in five minutes, but we mowed the Cacos down.'*
>
> FIRST LIEUTENANT G. C. THOMAS.

131 actions ranging from skirmishes to pitched battles, but the raids did not end.

As 1920 approached, the Marines killed Charlemagne and temporarily put the Cacos out of business. Another leader, Benoit Batraville, picked up the slack and renewed the revolt. Disguised in stolen Gendarmerie uniforms, the Cacos marched into Port-au-Prince to take the city. The Marines were ready and collided head-on with Batraville's mob.

The ensuing battle took the lives of 28 Marines and 70 Gendarmerie, but 2,000 Cacos lay dead among the streets of Haiti's capital.

For the next nine years Marines and Gendarmerie maintained a strained peace under the pacification policies and proconsulship of Brigadier General John H. Russell. By 1929 Marines had trained a local Gendarmerie of 2,700 men to keep the peace. As this force grew in size and stature, the Marines brigade diminished in strength. Haitian elite resented American interference, and the under-privileged peasants fomented occasional spats, but the country

remained remarkably peaceful. When in 1934 President Roosevelt called the last Marines home, they had been safeguarding the ailing country for sixteen years.

CHINESE CIVIL WAR

Though Harding had managed to skirt disturbances in Europe and the Far East, President Calvin Coolidge found the United States embroiled in another explosive situation in China. A new civil war erupted in 1927 and threatened to blossom into a second Boxer-style rebellion. Soviet Russia fueled the growing conflict by supporting the Cantonese army, led by Chiang Kai-shek, against the warring northern army led by Marshal Chang Tso-Lin.

Once again American lives and property in the region came under threat of attack, and in February Lejeune pulled Marines from Guam, Cavite, and the Asiatic Fleet to form a provisional battalion of 20 officers and 455 enlisted men under Major Julian P. Willcox. Two weeks later the 4th Marines – 66 officers and 1,162 enlisted men – arrived from San Diego under the command of Colonel Charles S. "Jumbo" Hill. Not satisfied with the force in China, Lejeune dispatched

Left: *During the fighting with the Cacos in Haiti, Captain Herman H. Hanneken disguised himself as a native, infiltrated the Cacos, shot their leader, and earned the Medal of Honor.*

Below left: *During 1922-1929, the dress blue uniform changed again. Pinned to the uniform are World War I Victory and Good Conduct ribbons, and Expert Rifle and Expert Pistol badges.*

Above: *Covers changed as often as uniforms. From top to bottom: the M1922 Dress Blue enlisted barracks cover; service enlisted barracks cover; and officer's barracks cover with a tan band.*

▶ **1922**

6 FEBRUARY: The Washington Naval Treaty is signed, the first Five-Power Treaty on naval arms limitations.

Right: *In 1927, when disturbances again erupted in China, General Lejeune decided to make a demonstration of strength and dispatched a number of Marine tanks from San Diego to Shanghai.*

Below: *During the disturbances in China, Marines wore a comfortable fur hat, which in 1941 would be seen again in Iceland.*

Right: *The summer khaki tunic worn in Nicaragua with collar insignia and a marksman qualification bar.*

Far right: *The khaki tunic gave way in 1927 to a slightly different pattern worn in China. This style remained in existence until World War II.*

Brigadier General Smedley D. Butler to Shanghai and brought the 3rd Brigade up to strength by adding the 6th Regiment, the 1st Battalion, 10th Marines. He augmented the force with engineers, tanks, and an aviation unit commanded by Lieutenant Colonel Thomas C. Turner, who had become the driving force of Marine aviation in the 1920s. Before the year 1927 ended, Butler's brigade numbered 238 officers, 18 warrant officers, and 4,170 enlisted men.

When the trouble center shifted to the north, Butler divided the 3rd Brigade. He moved all units except the 4th Marines to Tientsin, leaving a single regiment behind to keep the avenues of communication open with the American Legation at Peking.

Instead of picking a fight with the Chinese, Butler manipulated the political situation using noncombative techniques. On neighboring parade grounds, he put the Marines through a regular routine of drills, exercise, and demonstrations that sharpened the brigade and showed the American colors. The Chinese took particular interest in the novelty of Marine aviation. On one occasion they watched as a flyer performed a series of

aerial acrobatics, which Marine aviation historian Robert Sherrod described as having a remarkable ending: "During an exhibition of stunting, Captain James T. Moore zoomed over the crowds, went into a spectacular climbing roll, lost both wings off his plane and parachuted into a moat in front of the stands. 'Trust Smedley,' a lady spectator commented. 'He always puts on a wonderful show.'" (Robert Sherrod, *History of Marine Corps Aviation in World War II.*)

In 1928 Chinese Nationalist forces gained control over most of China, and on 10 October Chi-ang Kai-shek became president of the country. Political conditions rapidly improved, and in early 1929 the 3rd Brigade returned to the United States, leaving behind 1,150 men of the 4th Marines to protect Shanghai's International Settlement. The regiment would remain there for fourteen years (1927-1941). They became known as the "China Marines," witnessing the beginning of the Sino-Japanese War. Marines did not become involved in the fight when China and Japan went to war in earnest. Detachments at Peking and Tientsin were still at their posts, fac-

Left: *Corporal Richard Silvola, a China marine, presented this collection of artifacts, which included his shoes, helmet, Bible, Landing Forces Manual, NCO Club bar tab book, calling cards, a little money, letters, Good Conduct Medal, Marine insignia, corporal stripes, and a Legation Guard Newspaper listing him as being a Competition Rifle and Pistol Team member.*

Bottom left: *The* Walla Walla *Magazine, named after a town in Washington, was published for Marines serving in China during the 1930s.*

Below: *Marines of the 24th Company, 4th Marines, hunker down behind sandbags after being caught up in the Sino-Japanese conflict that began to escalate in 1934.*

Above: The soft officer's field (campaign) hat of post World War I vintage is still being worn.

Above right: On 6 June 1937, Marine Staff Sergeant Vincent John Buettner earned his "Shellback" certificate while aboard the USS Chaumont.

Right: During the 1920s-1930s, Marines serving as members of the U.S. Legation guard in North China wore emblem plates of different colors: headquarters Peking, green; headquarters Tientsin, white; A Company, red; b Company, light blue; C Company, dark blue; and D Company (mounted detachment), yellow.

ing one crisis after another, as Japan swept across China and fortified the islands of the Pacific. Prior to the Japanese attack on Pearl Harbor, most of the Marines at Shanghai withdrew to the Philippines.

FIVE POWER NAVAL TREATY

To avoid future wars elsewhere in the world, Britain, Japan, France, Italy, and the United States adopted at the close of 1921 the Five Power Naval Treaty. The accord placed limits on future naval ship construction and tonnages among the five war powers. A second part of the treaty contained an agreement not to fortify the islands of the Pacific. Japan, having received a mandate over the Marianas (except for Guam) and the Caroline Islands, generally agreed to the terms but did not like them. The U.S. Navy, knowing that Japan had designs on the Pacific, also did not like the terms because they prevented the United States from fortifying the Philippines, Guam, Midway, and Wake Island while Japan fortified, without restriction, the Imperial homeland. The General Board of the Navy began developing contingency plans for possible warlike acts because they believed that Japan would ignore the pact and continue to strengthen its navy in the Far East – a suspicion substantiated twenty years later.

Lejeune recognized that the Marine Corps would not survive by duplicating the mission of the Army. He also recognized that while the Navy needed a trained and ready strike force, it no longer needed ships' guards to maintain discipline over professional sailors. It became essential for the Corps to develop a mission of its own – and this he proceeded to do, using as his nucleus the Advanced Base Force concept.

First he needed a staff organization that worked like the one developed by the Army. Barnett had

introduced a system in 1918 and filled it with officers who had learned the basics of staff work while serving with the Army during the war. The staff included a Planning Section devoted to "all matters pertaining to…operations and training, intelligence, ordnance supplies and equipment." The section consisted of three officers who were placed under the direct supervision of Barnett's assistant. When Lejeune took command of the Corps he reformed the Planning Section, renaming it the Division of Operations and Training. He then expanded the division to include sections for Military Education, Military Intelligence, and Aviation. He put Brigadier General Logan M.

Feland in charge of the division and soon had it running much like it does today – a smaller version of the General Staff of the Army and the Office of the Chief of Naval Operations.

The Navy and the Marine Corps maintained a much closer vigil on world affairs than did the Army. Major Earl H. Ellis, one of the Marine officers concerned with planning during the 1920s, recognized the Japanese threat in the Pacific and made it his lifelong obsession. He predicted a future war with Japan and stated that the outcome would hinge on the possession of the islands of the trans-Pacific. Unlike other planners, Ellis believed that the Marines might first have to seize a defended island before it could become an advanced base. He scuffled over the issue with colleagues, arguing that the Corps was not responding to his perception of its new mission – an advanced force capable of defense or assault. Lejeune supported Ellis's concepts and became the driving advocate in reshaping the Corps to its future mission. When the Office of Naval Intelligence launched a study concerning the possibility of war with Japan, the Marine Corps contributed to what eventually became the "Orange Plan." Ellis made a major enhancement to that portion of the plan dealing with advanced base operations, adding his own revolutionary thoughts on amphibious warfare. He never lived to see the fruits of his efforts. Ellis died mysteriously while playing the role of tourist during a visit to Japan's Palau Islands.

CHANGES IN STRATEGY

Why the Marine Corps seemed to be shoved aside during the 1920s can be attributed to a number of factors. Colonel William "Billy" Mitchell argued that air power, and especially massive forces of strategic bombers, would become the single most important element in the next war, rendering other armed services obsolete. In Europe, new revolutionary theories evolved on armored warfare that caught the attention of the U.S. Army, such as those of one young German Army officer, Heinz Guderian, who became the architect of the *blitzkrieg*.

The Washington Naval Treaty of 1922 established a worldwide ratio of battleships and allotted the United States and Great Britain five each and Japan three. The treaty also limited capital ships to 35,000 tons and 16-inch guns and created other restrictions in the building and armament of secondary vessels. When Major Ellis presented his 50,000-word Operations Plan 712D, titled "Advance Base Operations in Micronesia," Captain Fullam, never an advocate of the Marine Corps, did not want to hear about Ellis's appeal for new weapons and new techniques such as reef-crossing vessels and fleets of specially designed landing craft.

> *'To effect [an amphibious landing] in the face of enemy resistance requires careful training and preparation . . . and this along Marine lines. It is not enough that the troops be skilled infantrymen or artillerymen of high morale; they must be skilled watermen and jungle-men who know it can be done – Marines with Marine training.'*
>
> EARL H. ELLIS TO LEJEUNE, 23 JULY 1921.
> OPERATIONS PLAN 712, DIVISION OF OPERATIONS AND TRAINING, HQMC.

While the Army and Navy haggled over their missions of the future, General Lejeune accepted Ellis's Operation Plan 712D and proceeded, with limited appropriations, to find a way to implement it. He completely agreed with Ellis and disagreed with Fullam on the concept of the role of the Advanced Base Force. Because of the spread of Japanese imperialism in the Pacific, Lejeune accepted Ellis's premise that during the next conflict Marines must have the resources to seize heavily fortified enemy bases and then defend them against counterattack.

Cutbacks in funding and the inability to staff the planning function with experienced officers created problems for the Corps. Lejeune feared that the Marines would be left out of joint plans being developed by the Army and the Navy. To get a voice inside the Army-Navy planning conferences, Lejeune established a War Plans Section responsible directly to himself. He did not expect to get much satisfaction from the Army and made his arguments with the Navy, projecting the primary war mission of the Corps as a mobile land

▶ **11 FEBRUARY:** Brigadier General John H. Russell becomes U.S. High Commissioner for the administration of Haiti.

28 APRIL: The first Marines land in China to protect the American legation during China's long civil war.

Below: *During the years of World War I and through the 1930s, the Marine Corps used many recruiting posters and material, such as those below. The theme "Soldiers of the Sea" became the title of one of the fine histories of the Marine Corps.*

1924

9 MARCH: Marines land to protect Americans in Honduras.

18 SEPTEMBER: Marines withdraw from the Dominican Republic.

1925

1 AUGUST: Marines are called home from Nicaragua.

1926

7 MAY: Marines return to Nicaragua to suppress internal strife and protect American interests.

20 OCTOBER: President again calls upon Marines to protect the U.S. Mail.

Below: *On 24 January 1924, First Lieutenant Orrel A. Inman directs the deployment of Marine machine gunners in support of the constabulary attack on the Colorums at Socorro in the Philippines.*

force to accompany the fleet for *offensive and defensive operations in support of the fleet.* On 14 December 1923 Lejeune put his force-in-readiness concept before the Naval War College, explaining:

> "…on both flanks of a fleet crossing the Pacific are numerous islands suitable for utilization by an enemy for radio stations, aviation, submarine, or destroyer bases. All should be mopped up as progress is made…The presence of an expeditionary force with the fleet would add greatly to the striking power of the Commander-in-Chief of the fleet. The maintenance, equipping, and training of its expeditionary force so that it will be in instant readiness to support the Fleet in the event of war, I deem to be the most important Marine Corps duty in time of peace."

Much work needed to be done before the Advanced Base Force concept of the time could be shed and the amphibious warfare mission described by Lejeune to the Naval War College could be adopted. His proposal augmented the Orange Plan – a work that was still in progress – by providing a ready strike-force. Lejeune's and Ellis's hypothesis established the foundation for what would become the Fleet Marine Force.

The Orange Plan, finally adopted in 1926, stipulated that the Marine Corps be prepared for "land operations in support of the fleet for the initial seizure and defense of advanced bases and for such limited auxiliary land operations as are essential to the prosecution of the naval campaign." When Lejeune retired in 1929, the Marine Corps lost its champion. In 1935 – three commandants later – all references to a separate Marine Corps mission were dropped. Only a small passage under "General Function of the Navy" indicated an "auxiliary" Marine role in landing operations: "To seize, establish, and defend, *until relieved by Army forces,* advanced naval bases;

and to conduct such *limited auxiliary land operations* as are essential to the prosecution of the naval campaign." The Joint Planning Committee of the Joint Board of the Army and Navy badly underestimated the vital importance of the Marine Corps mission in the Pacific during World War II.

EXPERIMENTAL LANDINGS

In 1922, Lejeune's staff was already at work conducting landing exercises at Guantanamo, Cuba, and Culebra, an island east of Puerto Rico. The real purpose of these primitive maneuvers was to allow mistakes to be made so that methods could be developed to correct them. There were plenty of mistakes, and Lejeune pressed his Marines to find solutions through constant experimentation. Perhaps as an incentive, he raised the monthly pay of enlisted men, bringing it closer in line with Navy pay:

1st Grade: Sergeant major/ Quartermaster sergeant.	$74
2nd Grade: First sergeant; Gunnery sergeant	$53
3rd Grade: Staff Sergeant (1923)	$45
4th Grade: Sergeant	$45
5th Grade: Corporal	$37
6th Grade: Private first class	$35
7th Grade: Private; drummer; trumpeter	$30-$21

In 1923 the term Marine Corps Expeditionary Forces replaced the term Advanced Base Force. The new designation encompassed permanent or provisional units of the Corps intended for overseas service with the fleet. From December 1923 through February 1924 a Marine Corps Expeditionary Force of 3,300 officers and men under the command of Brigadier General Eli K. Cole participated in fleet exercises at Culebra and the Canal Zone. The exercise included both offensive and defensive training while conducting ship-to-shore operations. The Marines discovered two important deficiencies. The first, to unload a cargo ship with Marine equipment efficiently depended upon how the ship was loaded. Later, Marines on board vessels and combat cargo officers would eventually become responsible for this task. The second problem concerned suitable landing craft. Conventional ships' boats failed to perform the task and the Marine Corps began serious experimentation with landing craft.

In 1925, when joint Army-Navy war games moved to Oahu in the Hawaiian Islands, the only beneficiaries of this highly theoretical exercise were the 1,500 officers and men of the Corps who successfully simulated a 42,000-man Marine landing force. They made successful landings against an opposing force, tested more equipment, and improved landing tactics. For the

Left: *In 1927, with trouble from Sandino's guerrillas threatening to destabilize Nicaragua, Marines under the command of Lieutenant Colonel James J. Meade arrive at Bluefields and Corinto.*

remainder of the decade, however, disturbances in Latin American and China interrupted the Corps' participation in fleet exercises.

Following the end of World War I, Haiti, Cuba, Santo Domingo, and Nicaragua continued to be trouble spots requiring small detachments of peacekeeping Marines. When civil war threatened to consume Nicaragua in May 1926, Marines from the USS *Galveston* landed at Corinto and worked their way to Managua. Three weeks later the 2nd Battalion, 5th Marines, commanded by Lieutenant Colonel James J. Meade, after settling a disturbance at Bluefields on Nicaragua's east coast, transited through the Panama Canal and also landed at Corinto. When insurrectionists fired into Managua and swarmed through central Nicaragua, Rear Admiral Julian L. Latimer called for more Marines. On 26 February 1927 the first reinforcements arrived from San Diego – Observation Squadron 1 (VO-1-M) and a rifle company under Major Ross E. "Rusty" Rowell. Rowell, who would become the first Marine aviator to wear stars, disembarked at Corinto and hauled his six De Havilland D.H.4s to Managua on flatcars.

Brigadier General Feland, who had commanded the 5th Marines in France, set up 2nd Brigade headquarters at Managua. The affair had worked itself into an expedition-size operation. Feland now had 2,000 Marines in Nicaragua distributed through fourteen different towns and two air observation units, which he combined into an aircraft squadron under Rowell. Future Secretary of War Henry L. Stimson negotiated an armistice, the liberals laid down their arms, and the process of troop withdrawals began. The ink on the armistice had barely dried when charismatic leader Augusto Cesar Sandino disrupted the accord. He refused to accept the settlement, moved into the mountains, and began to wage a guerrilla campaign against the Marines and the newly formed government of Nicaragua.

One of the important aspects of the Nicaraguan expedition was the experience it provided to young Marine officers like Lewis B. "Chesty" Puller, Evans F. Carlson, and Merritt A. Edson, all of whom would face similar jungle conditions during World War II. The officers established numerous outposts and garrisoned villages in the

Below left: *A Marine mounted patrol in Nicaragua heads into the highland jungles after receiving intelligence that on 27 February 1928 a pack train escorted by 35 Marines had been attacked by 600 Sandinistas near Bromaderos.*

Below: *The Banana War against the Sandinistas in Nicaragua provided the Marines with a taste of the fighting a decade later on Guadalcanal, where ambushes from concealed positions in the jungle became a daily occurrence.*

jungle lowlands in an attempt to contain Sandino in the highlands, but the strategy did not work. The guerrillas knew the terrain, and the local inhabitants proved hostile.

The Marines never had enough men or aircraft in Nicaragua to score a decisive victory against the rebels. By 1933 the war had spread to ten of Nicaragua's sixteen provinces. Under pressure from Congress to end American involvement, the Marines came home. A year later assassins killed Sandino but not his movement. In the 1980s it sprang back to life in the form of Nicaragua's Sandinista revolt, once again involving the United States in another Latin American imbroglio.

REVISING THE CORPS' EDUCATION

Commandant General Lejeune may have saved the Marine Corps from virtual extinction because of the proactive measures he took to preserve and redefine the Corps' mission. He received help from Congress and the secretary of the navy, both of whom had confidence in Lejeune's vision and professional competence. One of the significant changes he made in the early 1920s was to change the Marine Corps Schools' (MCS) curriculum.

AIR OPERATIONS IN NICARAGUA

The development of Marine air-ground cooperation and close-air support during World War II began in the jungles of Nicaragua. On the night of 15 July 1927, guerrilla leader Augusto Sandino launched a surprise 600-man attack against a small Marine outpost located at Ocotal. Sixty-two Marines under Captain Gilbert D. Hatfield and 48 poorly trained National Guardsmen under a Marine NCO beat off the attack. Sandino's men surrounded the village, leaving Hatfield with the choice of remaining under siege at Ocotal or cutting his way to the nearest friendly outpost 125 miles away.

On 17 July two D.H. 4s from Major Ross E. "Rusty" Rowell's squadron made aerial contact with Hatfield and strafed Sandino's guerrillas before returning to base. Having observed Hatfield's plight, Rowell loaded each of his five D.H. 4s with four 25-pound fragmentation bombs and all the machine gun ammunition they could carry. Having been a postwar pioneer of dive-bombing, Rowell taught the technique to his flyers. The time had come for the training to be put into practice.

At 1,500 feet Rowell approached Sandino's base, keeping one eye on the ground and the other on a tropical storm brewing ahead. Sandino's men watched as the planes circled and climbed back to 1,000 feet. The guerrillas had never been struck by a serious air attack

'After the second pass of the planes the enemy began pouring out of town and ran wildly to cover, horses were dispersed, and in general there was a wild scramble. This afforded an excellent target for the planes with their machine guns, and bombs were reserved for large groups.'

MAJOR ROSS E. "RUSTY" ROWELL, *MARINE CORPS GAZETTE*, MARCH 1928.

Below left: *Major Ross E. "Rusty" Rowell prepares to step into the cockpit.*

Below: *In 1929, First Lieutenant Christian F. Schilt received two of the new O2U-1 Corsairs at Quilai.*

and did not take cover. Major Rowell led the squadron down, leveling off at 300 feet, and plastered the guerrillas.

After forty-five minutes the D.H.4s began running low on fuel and returned to base. With Sandino's force dispersing in different directions, Hatfield mopped-up the guerrillas, but this did not end the war. Although aerial bombing dated back to World War I, Rowell's air attack was the first instance of dive-bombing, coordinated by ground signals, used in conjunction with troops in combat.

Air-ground support came into use in other ways. In early January 1928 Major Rowell had to fly his planes into Quilali to take out the wounded, but the town had no airstrip. Flyers dropped engineers' tools from the sky and the bottled-up Marine garrison set to work under fire building an airstrip. By 6 January they had converted Quilali's main street into a strip 100 feet wide and 500 feet long. First Lieutenant (later General) Christian F. Schilt volunteered to test the field in a jury-rigged Vought O2U-1, which had no brakes. Marines on the ground agreed to be the brakes and, as the plane landed, they grabbed the wings to keep the plane from going into a ravine. Schilt made ten flights over a period of three days, flying in 1,400 pounds of emergency medical supplies and flying out eighteen casualties who would not have lived if evacuated by mule.

Most of the books used by MCS had been written by the Army. Also, a number of senior Marine officers had attended the Army War College and received additional indoctrination into the Army's mission, a mission that did not conform to Lejeune's vision of the future Corps. To imitate the Army invited absorption into it, he believed, so Lejeune set about revising the Corps' military education program.

With the establishment of the new Marine Corps Institute in November 1920, the school organized its own staff of instructors and initiated a correspondence program for all those who wished to enroll. By 1924 one-third of the men were studying different subjects under the Institute's guidance.

Throughout the decade instructors made changes and improvements to the curriculum to keep pace with the changing mission of the Corps. After the fleet exercises in 1925, Lejeune directed that the subject of overseas expeditions and ship-to-shore operations be added as a tactical course of study for both the Field Officers' School and the Company Officers' School. By 1926 landing operations totaled forty-nine hours of instruction compared with just five the previous year.

On 28 February 1925 Congress passed the Marine Corps Reserve Act, providing for two classes of reserves: the Fleet Marine Corps Reserve and the Volunteer Marine Corps Reserve. The Act gave the Corps an opportunity to organize a reserve to reinforce the regulars during times of crisis. Basic training at Quantico during the summer could not fulfill the requirements of providing a military education for reservists. The Marine Corps Schools organized a special correspondence branch for the reserves, added additional courses written by Marines, and over the decade eventually phased out Army courses. The new courses included such subjects as operations with the fleet, overseas operations, and small wars. In 1927, when Marines intervened in Nicaragua, many of the students and instructors served with the regulars for on-the-job training.

In August 1930 Commandant General Ben Fuller, furthering Lejeune's mission of education, appointed Brigadier General Randolph C. Berkeley Commandant of the Schools. Berkeley had served in the Philippines, China, and Nicaragua, and he understood the importance of the new Marine mission. He kept instruction at the schools up to date and introduced more emphasis on landing force operations.

On 7 December 1933 the Navy redesignated the East Coast and West Coast Expeditionary Forces of the Marine Corps as a Fleet Marine Force (FMF), thereby eliminating the old term "expeditionary." The Navy assigned one FMF to the Atlantic Fleet and the other to the Pacific Fleet.

The designation Fleet Marine Force gave the Corps new meaning. They now thought of themselves as a unique force specializing in amphibious operations and began changing all their courses of instruction to fit the mission. The staff that prepared *The Tentative Manual for Landing Operations* became so anxious to introduce it that they printed the first edition in mimeograph form. The document eventually evolved into the *Manual for Naval Operations Overseas* and became one of the most important single contributions of the Marine Corps toward the art of warfare. Designated in 1938 as *FTP-167*, the manual became the basic doctrine for carrying on the war in the Pacific, and the major guide that was followed for American amphibious landings in Africa and Europe.

From 1935 through 1940 Marine schools continued to grow and expand in popularity. New buildings housed the growing needs of the schools at Quantico. In 1935 the Corps established a Platoon Leader's Class to enroll and train new lieutenants. The expanded Basic School drew students from the Naval Academy, the Reserves, the ranks, and from colleges and universities. In 1939, as war threatened in Europe, the Corps introduced advanced training for reserve officers, and during October the First Reserve Officers' Course, composed of first and second lieutenants, convened at Quantico.

When President Franklin D. Roosevelt declared a state of limited national emergency on 27 June 1940, the Marine Corps began its expansion at break-neck speed. They had a tradition to maintain – The First to Fight.

> *'It is desired that the service be alive to the significance of the authorized designation [Fleet Marine Force] and avoid obsolete, less-inclusive terms [such as Expeditionary].'*
>
> Brigadier General David D. Porter
> to all commanders, 3 January 1935.

▶ **1927**

6 January: Marines begin a second Nicaraguan intervention to fight guerrilla leader Ernesto Sandino.

16 March: The 4th Marines (China Marines) land at Shanghai and garrison the International Settlement until 1941.

16 July: Major Ross E. Rowell, USMC, leads the first dive-bombing attack in history at Ocotal, Nicaragua.

1928

January 6-8: Lieutenant F. Schilt earns the Medal of Honor for making ten flights to an emergency airfield laid out on the streets of Quilali, Nicaragua, by besieged Marines.

8 March: Captain Merritt A. Edson begins an epic Coco River patrol to hunt for Sandino.

Below: *During operations in September 1932, and after a ten-day patrol that destroyed thirty enemy camps, Marine Lieutenant Lewis B. "Chesty" Puller holds the staff of a captured rebel battle flag.*

Right: *During exercises in Wellington Harbor, New Zealand, a column of Higgins boats make their way across the bay as they shuttle Marines to their landing site.*

Right: *During the 1920s, when the Marine Corps sought ways to find a permanent niche in the armed forces, they developed the concept of amphibious warfare, but did not have landing craft so experimented with various designs. This one, used during maneuvers at Culebra, Puerto Rico, in 1924, proved wholly inadequate compared with the Higgins boats that came later.*

ALLIGATORS AND EUREKAS

During the many joint Army and Navy exercises in which Marines participated, the Corps never possessed a satisfactory landing vessel because none existed. By 1933 Commandant Fuller had seen enough landing fiascos, so he established the Marine Corps Equipment Board at Quantico. The board spent long hours testing and developing material for landing operations and in 1937 initiated military trials on retired manufacturer Donald Roebling's "Alligator," an amphibian tractor used for rescue missions in Florida's Everglades. His design consisted of an aluminum hull fitted with tracks that served as paddlewheels and enabled the contraption to both move through the water and over land.

The Alligator proved too complicated and underpowered for military use, but Roebling had a concept worthy of expansion. The developers plunged into the work of improving the vehicle's performance by increasing its speed in the water and its ability to crawl over reefs. An overly eager Equipment Board created a few doubters by prematurely giving Navy admirals and Marine generals short, wet rides during the early tests. Fueled by the needs of the Fleet Marine Force, Roebling's awkward Alligator grew in dimensions and durability to become in 1941 the Marine Corps' troop carrier, the Landing Vehicle Tracked (LVT).

While one group worked on improving the Alligator, another group meddled with modified fishing boats in an effort to find a vehicle fit for beach assault. The task seemed hopeless until they rediscovered the "Eureka," a contraption that civilian designer Andrew J. Higgins of New Orleans had proposed to the Navy in 1926. Developed for use in bayou waters by fur trappers, Eureka contained all the elements of a landing craft – a shallow draft, a broad, flat bow for landing and retracting, and a protected propeller. Higgins kept pestering the Navy, and in 1938 they gave him enough money to lengthen the craft, add a troop compartment, and increase the craft's horsepower. The Equipment Board liked the results, but Eureka still lacked the means for rapidly disembarking troops. Brigadier General Franklin J. Moses, head of the Corps' Equipment Board, persuaded Higgins to add a retractable bow ramp, and the results proved to be remarkable. The modified Eureka became the Navy's Landing Craft Vehicle Personnel (LCVP) – the "Papa" boat that landed thousands of Marines on beaches during the next forty years.

Higgins emerged as the Navy's foremost designer of landing craft, including boats for transporting tanks, wheeled artillery, and trucks to the beach. As Army tanks became bigger than the lighters that carried them, Higgins designed the 50-foot Landing Craft Mechanized (LCM) or "Mike" boat to carry 30-ton Sherman tanks. For the Marine Corps, finding the right landing craft had been a race against time. Now they could go to war.

During the troubling times between the wars, keeping the Marine Corps in a state of readiness developed into a full-time job for commandants trained in the fine art of juggling. For ten years Lejeune had reformed the Corps and kept it active. When he retired he virtually handed the reins over to Wendell C. "Buck" Neville, who had followed Lejeune from Veracruz to France. On 5 March 1929 Neville became the fourteenth commandant of the Marines Corps. He died sixteen months later, riding through his brief administration on the momentum built by his predecessor.

On 9 July 1930, Ben H. "Uncle Ben" Fuller stepped into the vacancy created by Neville's death. Another disciple of Lejeune, Fuller served as acting commandant during Neville's brief tenure. The Great Depression shaped his lackluster administration, aided by President Franklin Roosevelt's so-called "Good Neighbor" policy, which brought the Marines home from Nicaragua in 1933 and from Haiti in 1934. Fuller served the traditional four-year term and on 28 February 1934 stepped down.

On 1 March 1934 John Henry Russell, the sixteenth commandant, succeeded Fuller. When he had become Fuller's assistant in February 1933, he also became the virtual commandant, running the office with far more effectiveness than his mentor. He had missed the war in Europe but had spent nearly fifteen years serving in Santo Domingo and Haiti. While acting as assistant commandant to Fuller, he became the main driving force in converting the Marine Corps from an expeditionary force to the Fleet Marine Force. As commandant he began upgrading the landing force capabilities of the Corps, and on 30 November 1936 passed the baton to Brigadier General Thomas Holcomb, who would lead the Corps through the early years of World War II.

Five commandants – Lejeune, Neville, Fuller, Russell, and Holcomb – served the Corps during its most important transition from an expeditionary force to a fully capable Fleet Marine Force, and they did it in the face of opposition and a lack of funding.

MARINE AIR-GROUND TEAM

Between World Wars, the only American ground and aviation units engaged in combat were Marines. Young Marine flyers grew in experience and stature around the world, serving in the Dominican Republic from February 1919 to July 1924; in Haiti from March 1919 until August 1934; and in Nicaragua from 1927 until 1933. They became daring brush pilots, flying over jungles, landing and taking off from short, improvised airstrips, and performing a multitude of missions from search and rescue to strafing and dive-bombing. In the process they developed new tactics that would later revolutionize both air and ground warfare – the Marine air-ground team.

In 1919 Lieutenant Lawson H. M. Sanderson, one of the first to experiment with dive-bombing, discovered that he could strike a target with more accuracy by pointing his plane at it. He released the bomb from a makeshift rack after diving at a 45-degree angle from 2,000 feet to 250 feet. The technique, known as glide-bombing, would be used by far different aircraft during World War II.

In 1927 Major Ross E. Rowell took a group of Marine pilots to Nicaragua where he continued performing experiments under combat conditions. All of his flyers became proficient dive-bombers, using the technique for air support missions in cooperation with ground troops. In the days before air-to-ground radio communication, Marines on the ground laid out panels of cloth to indicate the direction and range of the enemy, pointing the way for an air attack. This technique, first used in Nicaragua, later probably saved hundreds of Marine units pinned down by Japanese fire on the islands of the South Pacific.

The small biplanes used by Marines during the 1920s could carry few bombs, few supplies, and few passengers. When in the late 1920s Major

Above: Lieutenant Lawson H. M. Sanderson, flying a D.H. 4, experimented with dive-bombing and discovered that, by pointing the plane at the target, he could usually hit the target. The technique developed into the tactic known as glide-bombing.

Below: Scouting planes became an integral part of the Advanced Base concept, as well as light aircraft that could be catapulted from cruisers and recovered played a major role in maneuvers.

▶ 1934

JANUARY: *The Tentative Manual for Landing Operations* is published, forming the basis for future amphibious operations.

1 MARCH: Major General John H. Russell, Jr., becomes the sixteenth commandant of the Marine Corps.

15 AUGUST: The 1st Marine Brigade ends intervention of Haiti after nineteen years of occupation.

18 NOVEMBER: Northrop Corporation receives a contract for the development of the Dauntless dive-bomber.

Above right: *Major Edwin H. (Chief) Brainard leans against his Wasp-powered F6C-4 Curtiss "Hawk" at Quantico. Brainard was officer-in-charge of Marine Aviation from 1925 to 1929.*

Right: *In 1929, a Fokker transport comes in low to drop supplies to a Marine patrol waiting at a clearing in the Nicaraguan jungle.*

Right: *Lined up for inspection at the San Diego airfield in 1933 are Marine SU-2s (two-seat scout planes) and F-4B3s (single-seat fighters), with a trimotor transport in the background.*

Edwin H. Brainard delivered the first of three tri-motor German Fokkers to Nicaragua, tactics again changed. Marines established new "firsts" by using the seemingly giant aircraft to transport troops and supplies by air to hurriedly con-structed airfields.

During the years between the world wars, no branch of the services developed their flight skills under combat conditions more than the Marines. Aviators flying the old cranky D.H. 4s evacuated the wounded from Haiti, Nicaragua, and the Dominican Republic. They performed the same type of rescue missions as did helicopter pilots in Korea thirty years later. During the Chinese civil war, Marine pilots flew 3,818 reconnaissance sor-ties around Tientsin over a period of eighteen months to keep a watch on potentially hostile troop movements.

At home, Marines tried to keep pace with the rapid developments in aviation technology. The old Liberty-engined De Havilland D.H. 4 bombers, the Vought O2U Corsairs, and the Curtiss JN-4HG Jennies gave way in the 1930s to the Chance Vought SU-2 two-seat scout planes and the Boe-ing F4B-3 single-seat fighters. Marine pilots engaged in record-breaking flights and won safety awards while at the same time dispatching medi-cines and supplies to areas stricken by floods, hurricanes, and earthquakes. They experimented with blind flying, aerial cartography, and photog-raphy. Lieutenant Frank Akers, a Marine dare-devil, made the first blind landing on a carrier, setting down an OJ-2 observation plane on the deck of the USS *Langley* (CV-1).

Naval tactics began to change on 18 January 1911 after Eugene B. Ely, a civilian pilot, flew a Curtiss pusher off the deck of the USS *Pennsyl-vania* (ACR-4). Eleven years later the Navy com-missioned the first carrier, the USS *Langley*, and

When in 1940 Holcomb's four-year term ended, Roosevelt would not consider another man for the job and cajoled the commandant into serving another term.

WORLD WAR II BEGINS

Japan, after invading China in 1937, had continued to press south, capturing territory that would lead the Imperial Japanese Army to the oilfields of the Netherlands East Indies. On 1 September 1939, Germany invaded Poland, bringing France and Great Britain into a new world war. Ten months later, on 14 June 1940, the German Army entered Paris, and Britain stood alone against Hitler's mincing machine.

Meanwhile, high-pressure expansion of the Marine Corps had already begun. In mid-1940 there were 26,568 officers and men in the ranks. Twelve months later that number doubled, but more than 18,000 members of the Corps were spread around the world – from the Panama Canal to American Samoa and China. The only unit completely together and deployed was a reinforced brigade sent to Iceland in July 1941 to relieve a British garrison and prepare a staging area for an influx of U.S. Army troops.

The build-up of the Fleet Marine Force was already underway. The Marine Corps purchased and leased 111,710 acres of water, coastal swamp and plain, scrub pines and sand flats, along the New River near Morehead City, North Carolina. In the bargain they acquired an infestation of sandflies, ticks, chiggers, and snakes. Holcomb gave the tract a distinguished name – Camp Lejeune. The 1st Marine Division found its new home a Southern wasteland. As the division trained for warfare,

> '*I am still concerned over the widespread scattering of the Marines into small groups in hundreds of places. I think Tommy Holcomb ought to make a No. 1 priority effort from now on to build up his [Fleet Marine] Force.*'
>
> PRESIDENT ROOSEVELT TO SECRETARY OF THE NAVY FRANK KNOX, 10 AUGUST 1941.

one officer remarked, "This division won't be fit for anything but jungle warfare." Whether by prescience or accident, the men of 1st Marine Division would soon be staring over the bulkheads of LVTs heading toward the beaches of Guadalcanal.

The 2nd Division trained near San Diego on the West Coast. As part of their routine they made movies, participating in such 1942 film releases as "To the Shores of Tripoli" and "Wake Island". The so-called "Hollywood Marines" eventually moved to two new and expanded bases, Camp Elliott or Camp Pendleton. They continued to play minor roles in dozens of war productions starring such film icons as John Wayne William Bendix, John Payne, and Robert Ryan.

On 7 December 1941 the Marine Corps had grown to 65,000 officers and enlisted men. Twenty thousand were still in training in the United States, and 4,000 were serving on Navy ships or at naval stations. Others were still scattered all over the world. Of that number only 4,500 Marines served at the important naval center on the Hawaiian island of Oahu – Pearl Harbor. For those Marines, the first day of the war in the Pacific would etch unforgettable memories of death and destruction.

For the Marine Corps, the supreme test was about to begin.

▶ **1935**

30 JULY: Lieutenant Frank Akers, flying an OJ-2, makes the first blind landing on a carrier.

1936

1 DECEMBER: Major General Thomas Holcomb becomes seventeenth commandant of the Marine Corps.

1937

7 JULY: Japan invades China.

1939

1 SEPTEMBER: Germany invades Poland and World War II begins.

1940

14 JUNE: France surrenders to Germany.

1941

1 FEBRUARY: The 1st Marine Division is created.

22 JUNE: Germany attacks USSR along 2,000-mile front.

7 JULY: 1st Provisional Marine Brigade lands at Reykjavik, Iceland.

27-28 NOVEMBER: The 4th Marines leave Shanghai after fourteen years' service in China.

Above left: *On the verge of the United States entering World War II, the reliable Marine two-seat Douglas Dauntless SBD bomber was just going into production.*

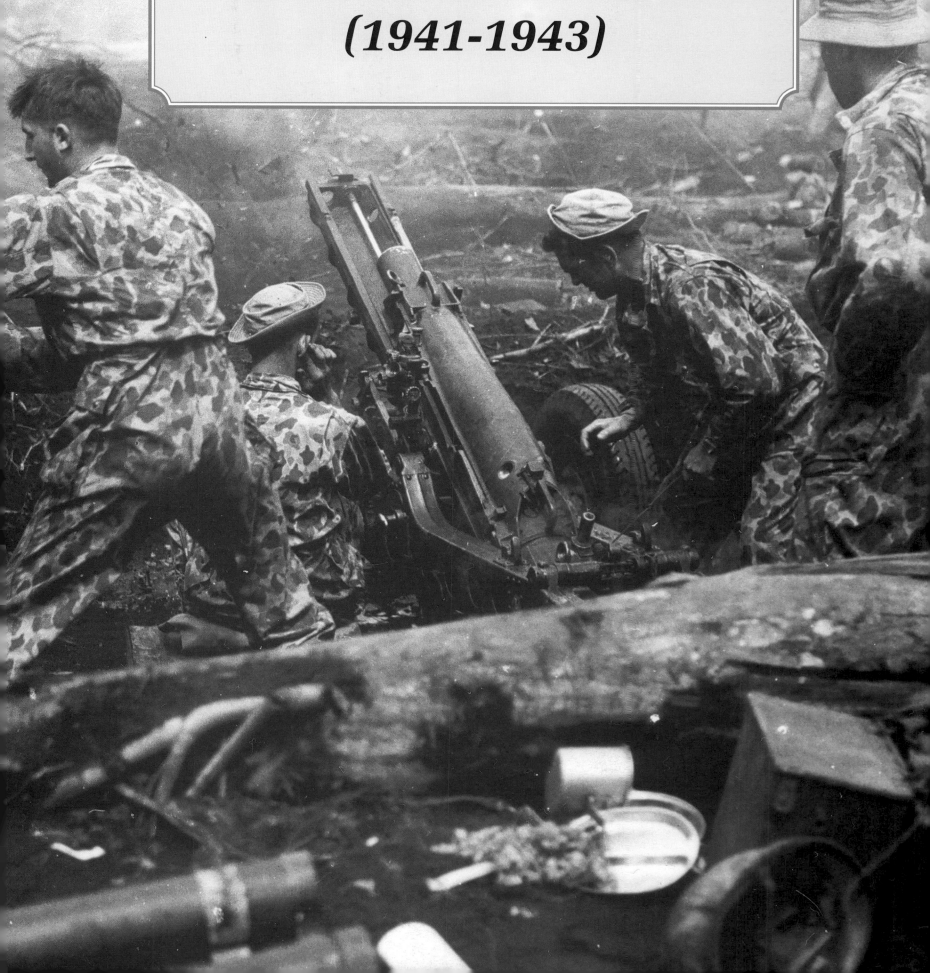

CHAPTER FIVE

THE CRISIS IN THE PACIFIC

(1941-1943)

Previous page: *Marines pass shells to the two artillerymen manning a 75mm pack howitzer aimed at Japs defending the Cape Gloucester airfield, 29 December 1943.*

Above right: *On the morning of 8 December 1941, the newspapers of the nations ran extra editions announcing the Japanese attack on Pearl Harbor. The next day thousands of young Americans poured into recruiting stations.*

Right: *On the morning of 7 December 1941, two waves of Japanese bombers struck American battleships anchored off Pearl Harbor's Ford Island and swept across the Marine airfield at Ewa, destroying aircraft on the ground and blowing up fuel dumps.*

At dawn on 7 December 1941, a Japanese task force composed of six carriers, two battleships, three cruisers, and nine destroyers turned into the wind 230 miles north of Honolulu. At 0600 Vice Admiral Chuichi Nagumo, commanding the Japanese strike force, signaled from the flagship HIJMS *Akagi* to launch the attack. Sixty seconds later the first wave of Japanese aircraft – 43 Mitsubishi A6MZ Zero-Sen fighters, 89 Nakajima B5NA "Kate" level-altitude bombers, and 81 Aichi D3A2 "Val" dive-bombers – began assembling in the sky for a surprise attack on the U.S. Pacific Fleet anchored at Pearl Harbor. As the Japanese pilots flew off the decks of the carriers *Akagi, Hiryu, Kaga, Shokaku, Soryu,* and *Zuikaku,* they gave a cheer, for their presence off Oahu had not been discovered. As the first wave disappeared from sight, a second wave of 171 bombers and fighters moved onto the carriers' flight decks.

A lone U.S. radar station on Oahu picked up the approaching aircraft, but the sleepy communications center in Honolulu ascribed the blips to a squadron of bombers expected from the mainland and did nothing.

The lovely, clear Sunday morning promised a quiet day of rest for the men enjoying breakfast on the eight American battleships anchored off Ford Island and the eight cruisers lying nearby. Around the harbor lay three air bases – one for each of the U.S. services – with planes standing unattended in neat order on the grass. Antiaircraft guns remained unmanned with ammunition under lock and key.

Ashore, Marines prepared for a day of ease. Men of the Marine Air Group 21 (MAG-21) at Ewa airfield went to breakfast after a night on the town. Men billeted at the Marine Barracks and at Camp Catlin loitered outside the mess hall, smoking cigarettes and chatting with members of the 3rd Defense Battalion and the 4th Defense Battalion (just arrived from Cuba). Scattered among them were members of the rear echelon of the 1st Defense Battalion, whose units were already on Wake, Johnston, and Palmyra Islands, and a detachment from the 2nd Engineer Battalion.

The Japanese air attack on Oahu began at 0755 and continued, with a brief lull between the first and second waves, for two hours. Armed with torpedoes and armor-piercing bombs, the Japanese warplanes inflicted the most

damage during the early minutes of the attack. Ten minutes into the strike, antiaircraft guns opened, resistance stiffened, and smoke from burning vessels obscured the targets. Four battleships – *Arizona* (BB-39), *Oklahoma* (BB-37), *California* (BB-44), and *West Virginia* (BB-48) – went to the bottom. Through a Herculean effort, the crippled *Nevada* (BB-36) got underway. The three remaining battleships, though severely damaged, limped out of Pearl Harbor and steamed to the West Coast of the United States. Much to the chagrin of the Japanese, the carriers of the U.S. Pacific Fleet – *Lexington* (CV-2), *Enterprise* (CV-6), and *Saratoga* (CV-3) – were not at Pearl Harbor. Two of them were carrying planes to Marines on Midway, Guam, and Wake. Six months later the Japanese would pay a heavy price for missing the carriers.

MAG-21 at Ewa lost all except one of its forty-eight planes, but the heroic action of its Marines kept the airfield open throughout the attack, enabling Army and Navy aircraft to use the field for servicing. The Marines lost 112 men killed and 64 wounded, most of them among those posted on ships.

Simultaneous with the hammer-blow delivered at Pearl Harbor, the Japanese brought forces up from Truk in the Carolines to seize American outposts at Guam and Wake Island. American strategists never considered Guam – a 225- square-mile island of jungle – defendable. The island lay among the southern Marianas, surrounded on all sides by fortified Japanese possessions. Along with a few Navy personnel and the local militia, a small detachment of 153 Marines armed with nothing larger than .30 caliber machine guns withstood a two-day air offensive. Invaded by 6,000 enemy troops, the island commander, Captain G. J. McMillan, USN, had no option but to surrender to prevent the Japanese from taking reprisals against the native population.

With the fall of Guam, the Japanese secured the first American outpost. They would not find the going so easy when they attacked Wake Island, a bleak atoll of three islands 2,000 miles west of Hawaii and 600 miles from the nearest Japanese base.

December 8 continued to be a day of brilliantly coordinated attacks by the Japanese. One of the most powerful invasion forces ever formed by the Japanese prepared to strike the Philippines. Bombing raids against Clark Field destroyed 103 American planes, most of them on the ground. On 10 December Lieutenant General Masaharu Homma's Fourteenth Army landed unopposed on the northern tip of Luzon. Two days later a Japanese force from Palau captured Legaspi in southern

> *'I don't know what the time interval was between these attacks, but between the first and second was long enough for me to get from our house at Ewa Beach into my pants and out to the field in time to see my planes destroyed in most expert fashion... And I got a bullet through my erstwhile best Saturday morning inspection pants – but without touching me.'*
>
> MAJOR GENERAL RICHARD C. MANGRUM IN
> *SOLDIERS OF THE SEA*, BY ROBERT DEBS HEINL.

Below: *A squadron of twelve Grumman F4F Wildcats arrived at Wake Island a few days before war with Japan began. On 8 December Japanese bombers struck Wake and destroyed seven of the planes before they could get off the ground.*

THE MARINES ON WAKE

On 8 December 1941, thirty Japanese bombers struck Wake Island, dropping a dense pattern of bombs on the airfield, and destroying seven of the twelve Grumman F4F Wildcats that had been delivered to the atoll by the carrier *Enterprise* four days before. The attack blew up the squadron's 25,000-gallon fuel tank and left Major Paul A. Putnam's Marine Fighting Squadron (VMF-211) in dire straits. Putnam lost his planes because the Marines had no radar warning system (it was still in a box at Pearl Harbor), just lookouts stationed atop two 50-foot water towers. On 9 December twenty-seven enemy bombers returned, and Putnam's four patrolling Wildcats shot one down. When the bombers reappeared on 10 December, Captain Henry Elrod shot down two. The others returned with heavy flak damage. The softening-up raids laid the groundwork for the enemy's 11 December amphibious attack.

Major James P. Devereux's 1st Defense Battalion of 388 officers and men, aided by the pilots of Putnam's squadron, repulsed a Japanese sea-borne assault of three light cruisers and six destroyers that cost the enemy 700 casualties. Seacoast guns sent one destroyer to the bottom and Captain Elrod sank another. The cruiser *Yubari* limped away, spewing smoke. Wildcats damaged two more destroyers, and shore batteries crippled two transports. To the enemy, the first reverse of the war came as an unexpected shock.

Devereux had good guns but too few veterans to man them. Ground defenses on Wake consisted of six 5-inch seacoast guns, twelve 3-inch antiaircraft guns, and dozens of machine guns, more firepower than the severely under-strength 1st Defense Battalion could man.

To complete their Pacific defensive perimeter, the Japanese needed to capture Wake. To keep Japan from securing a base from which to attack

Above: For fifteen days the Marines on Wake fought valiantly to keep the Japs off the island.

Above: Marines on Wake Island wore steel helmets with the traditional globe and anchor emblem.

Below left: Wake Island, because of its shape, was extremely difficult for so few Marines to defend.

Below right: The Wake Island Memorial is dedicated to the Marine, Navy, Army, and civilian personnel who defended so resolutely.

Midway, the Americans needed to hold Wake. Admiral Husband E. Kimmel, the Navy commander who had been caught asleep at Pearl Harbor, reacted too slowly in reinforcing Wake, and forces on their way to the island were inexplicably recalled. Apparently, Devereux's force was expendable.

Pounded every day by Japanese bombers, Putnam's five flyable Wildcats eventually ran out of parts and became inoperable. On 20 December, in preparation for a final assault, forty-seven carrier-based enemy bombers and fighters attacked Devereux's batteries. Shortly after midnight on 23 December, 1,000 Japanese troops came ashore at four landing points and infiltrated Marine positions. With ferocious hand-to-hand fighting, Marines resisted the attack at the water's edge. After several hours of increasingly hopeless fighting, Commander Winfield Scott Hamilton, the island commander, told Devereux to surrender.

After sinking four Japanese warships and inflicting more than 1,000 casualties on the enemy, the Marines reluctantly laid down their arms. Their heroic example served as a rallying point in America. In 1942 William Bendix and Robert Preston starred in the movie "Wake Island." The film drew thousands of young men into the Marine Corps.

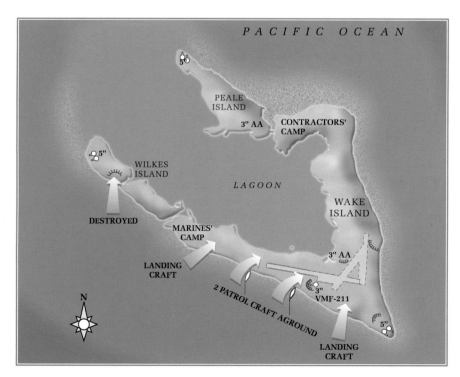

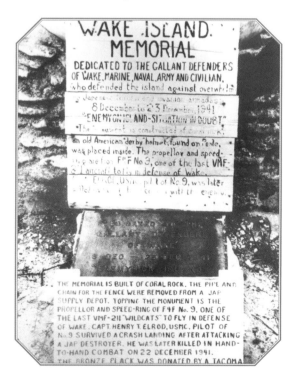

Luzon. Homma began closing the pincers, moving toward Manila against scattered pockets of stiff resistance.

Colonel Samuel L. Howard's 4th Marines, after fourteen years in Shanghai, had joined the forces of General Douglas MacArthur, commanding the Philippines. Had they stayed in China much longer, they would have shared the fate of 500 Marines taken prisoner at Peking and Tientsin. MacArthur attached the Marines to Howard's regiment and sent them to Corregidor, a rocky lizard-shaped island at the entrance to Manila Bay. A few detachments of Marines remained on Bataan to slow the advance of the enemy.

On 9 January 1942 Japanese struck the Bataan peninsula in force. Both sides suffered heavy losses, and by the end of the month the combined forces under MacArthur fell back to the reserve line running across the neck of the peninsula from Orion to Bagac. MacArthur's dwindling army dug in, and despite savage air attacks, continuous shelling, and constant pressure, held the line for two months.

U.S. TROOPS SURRENDER

On 12 March, under orders from President Roosevelt, MacArthur departed on a PT-boat for Australia and transferred the command to Lieutenant General Jonathan M. Wainwright. Before leaving, MacArthur awarded the Army's Distinguished Unit Citation to all the units on the Philippines except for the Marines. General Wainwright rectified the oversight the day he took command. Four weeks later Wainwright gave up Bataan, surrendering 80,000 U.S. and Filipino troops, including 1,500 Marines. After the surrender, only 2,000 American and Filipino troops escaped and made their way to Corregidor.

In late March the Japanese targeted Corregidor with every weapon in their arsenal. As each day passed the bombardment increased in intensity. As one Marine recalled, it was like "living in the center of a bullseye." The shelling reached a crescendo on 29 April when Japanese siege batteries celebrated Emperor Hirohito's birthday with a salute of 10,000 rounds that enshrouded the island in a pall of smoke and dust.

On 4 May Japanese artillery dropped another 16,000 shells on Corregidor, and at nightfall Homma sent 2,000 men in assault boats against the island. The boats missed their landing point by a mile. They came ashore near the 1st Marine Battalion and were cut to pieces in the moonlight by enfilading fire. But the Japanese established a beachhead, captured Battery Denver, and forced Howard to commit his last reserves – Marines from headquarters and service companies.

In the morning ten percent of the 4th Marines lay dead or wounded. Few batteries still operated; among them two 14-inch turrets on Fort

> *'Most of the beach defenses – the barbed wire, the foxholes – were wiped out. Nearly all the beach defense guns were destroyed, and all of the Rock's great batteries were silenced – the mortars, the 12-inch rifles, the 8- and 10-inch disappearing guns, the 155s. The star shells were burned, the searchlights – except for one or two – were wrecked; of the AA guns a few remained, but the fire-control instruments were destroyed.'*
>
> HANSON BALDWIN, IN
> "THE FOURTH MARINES AT CORREGIDOR,"
> *MARINE CORPS GAZETTE.*

Drum manned by the Marines. The Japanese landed tanks and in overwhelming numbers began the sweep of the island, knocking out the water supply. At noon on 6 May General Wainwright notified Homma of his intention to surrender, but sporadic fighting continued.

When Colonel Howard received word of Wainwright's decision, he turned to his adjutant and with tears in his eyes ordered the regiment's colors and battle standard burned. Then reality struck. Horrified, he gasped, "My God...I [am] to be the first Marine officer ever to surrender a regiment." Howard had little to surrender in the way of men. Of 66 officers and 1,364 enlisted Marines on Corregidor, Howard's force sustained 668 casualties. Two hundred and thirty-nine more would die in prison camps.

The five-month fight for the Philippines took much longer than the Japanese anticipated, but it did not slow the enemy's game plan. Imperial forces overran the Dutch East Indies, Singapore, and Malaya, and drove the British out of Burma. China became isolated from her allies; India faced a threat along her borders; and the north coast of

▶ **20 DECEMBER:** Admiral Ernest J. King becomes Commander-in-Chief, U.S. Fleet.

23 DECEMBER: Wake Island falls to the Japanese after a stubborn defense.

28 DECEMBER: The 4th Marines move from Bataan to Corregidor.

31 DECEMBER: Admiral Chester W. Nimitz takes command of the Pacific Fleet.

Below: *In April 1942, General Wainwright surrendered 80,000 American and Filipino troops and 1,500 Marines to the Japanese. During the next few days, the infamous Bataan Death March began to prison camps in the jungle.*

▶ **2-6 JUNE:** Marine air groups participate in winning the Battle of Midway.

7 AUGUST: The 1st Marine Division lands on Guadalcanal.

17 AUGUST: Lieutenant Colonel Evans F. Carlson's 2nd Raider Battalion raids Makin Island in the Gilberts.

Right: *On the morning of 7 August 1942, Colonel Clifton B. Cates prepares the 1st Marine Regiment for the landing of the second wave on Guadalcanal. To the surprise and relief of all, the Marines met no enemy resistance.*

Above: *Early in the war, Samoan Marines formed a defense battalion, along with their own style of hat. In 1942 they all became enlisted members of the U.S. Marine Corps.*

the enemy, nor did they want to give Japan any rest. Consistent with RAINBOW 2, they mobilized the Marine Corps, created six divisions and five aircraft wings, and thrust them one by one into the battle for the Pacific.

On 2 July 1942 the Joint Chiefs of Staff (JCS) approved Operation Watchtower, a wild stab at Guadalcanal. The island had never been accurately mapped and little was known of its tides or reefs. Japanese were building an airfield, but the U.S. planners knew nothing about the enemy's strength or dispositions. General MacArthur, commanding Allied forces, and Vice Admiral Robert L. Ghormley, commanding the South Pacific Fleet, objected to the plan on the grounds of having inadequate resources. The operation came as a complete surprise to Major General Alexander A. Vandegrift, who on 25 June had just begun assembling the 1st Marine Division in New Zealand and Western Samoa for six months of training. He had not expected to go into battle until 1943, but Ghormley ordered him to be ready in six weeks. As the less experienced units of the 2nd Marine Division began arriving, Vandegrift placed them in reserve. Neither division had participated in any large-scale exercise involving amphibious maneuvers.

The JCS set 7 August as D-Day for the assault on Guadalcanal, Tulagi, and Gavutu-Tanambogo. During the month of July the 1st Marine Division assembled in the Fijis. Vandegrift still doubted whether he could pull his command together on such short notice. Complications continued to mount. Naval forces assigned to Operation Watchtower were no more experienced than the Marines, and a dress rehearsal conducted in the

Fijis on 26 July resulted in a fiasco. Assault craft lodged on reefs, naval gunfire went wild, and supporting aircraft missed their marks. Admiral Fletcher balked at leaving his flattops off Guadalcanal for four days (he promised two) to protect transports unloading supplies and munitions. Rear Admiral Richmond Kelly Turner, the naval attack force commander, demanded that the 2nd Regiment be retained on his vessels "for future operations," though none ever materialized. The posturing in the upper levels of the Navy never filtered down to the men. The Marines wanted to grt on with what they were trained to do – fight.

As night fell on 31 July, the 1st Marine Division sailed for the Solomons to lead the first American offensive ground assault in World War II. To every Marine in the division the designation "First to Fight" gave new meaning to their long history, for they had been chosen to take the point position on the long road back to victory.

At daylight, 7 August, thousands of sleepless, grim-faced Marines scrambled down cargo nets slung over the sides of transports and tumbled into the landing craft waiting below. For thirty minutes they nervously listened as the guns of the Navy pounded the area designated as Red Beach. They felt queasy as their boats moved across the calm waters of Sealark Channel and into assault formation. Then the engines roared and the boats sprinted toward the white sand beaches of Guadalcanal, a shimmering jungle-covered island 90 miles long and 25 miles across in the southern Solomons.

At 0910 the landing craft carrying the first wave of the 5th Marine Regiment scraped the sandy shallows and came to a stop. Thousands of wide-eyed Marines splashed through the tepid green water and raced for cover. From the dense coconut grove ahead not a sound could be heard but the whoosh of Navy shells whistling high overhead and thumping among the coconut grove inland. The assault took the shocked enemy by surprise. They had been building an airfield on the island from which to attack the sea supply routes between the United States and Australia. Marines darted through the brush and coconut groves behind Red Beach and established a 600-yard defensive perimeter. They sweated, swallowed salt tablets, and cursed the insects and steaming jungle that had so rapidly reduced them to a state of exhaustion.

General Vandegrift came ashore and sent a detachment forward to reconnoiter the near-complete airfield at Lunga Point. The first morning salvo had chased 2,230 ill-prepared Japanese — mostly construction workers — into the jungle. He halted the regiment for the night, set up a temporary command post, and sent skittish patrols into the jungle. They fumbled through the unfamiliar terrain firing at noises made by land crabs and night creatures.

LOGISTICAL PROBLEMS

On the beach the 1st Pioneer Battalion worked day and night to prevent the mountain of supplies coming ashore from turning into a logistical shamble of randomly dumped material having hundreds of different uses. In Admiral Turner's anxiety to get everything ashore, he had scores of LVAs roaming up and down the beach looking for space to dump their loads. Had the Japanese been more vigilant, they would not have missed the opportunity to hit the congested beaches and cripple Operation Watchtower in a single blow.

On the afternoon of 8 August Marine patrols reached the airfield and found it deserted. When the Japanese construction workers fled, they left behind their equipment, fuel, and large quantities of food. After all the hours of trepidation on the transports, the Marines congratulated each other for completing the first phase of their mission in record time.

Twenty miles across Sealark Channel, soon to be renamed Ironbottom Sound as a graveyard for shipping, the 2nd Marine Regiment and the 1st Parachute Battalion landed at Tulagi and Gavutu, small islands off the southern coast of Florida Island. Fortunately for the Marines, the early morning attack on 7 August caught the enemy off guard and carrier aircraft wiped out all the Japanese planes at Tulagi. Unlike the defenders of Guadalcanal, the aroused Japanese fought back, giving the Marines a dose of fighting on ridges concealed beneath dense foliage and pockmarked with caves — a portent of things to come. One captain, anxious to demonstrate the technique for

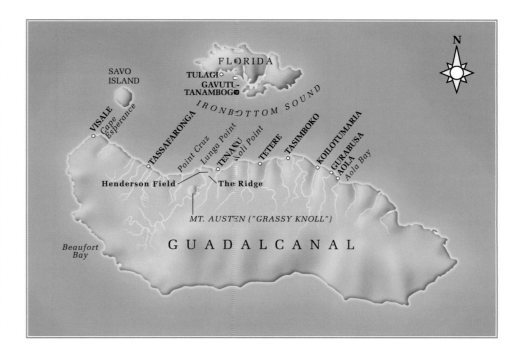

disposing of Japanese hidden in caves, overestimated the amount of dynamite needed for the job and blew off his trousers.

Marines on Tulagi and Gavutu-Tanambogo soon discovered another Japanese tactic: night attacks interspersed with enemy infiltration.

To clear out enemy positions, Marines called upon the Navy for attack preparation, which was probably the first call-fire naval gunfire support action performed by a U.S. ship in World War II. Some of the air support strikes from poorly briefed flyers fell indiscriminately on both sides. For three small islands across from Guadalcanal, the Marines paid with 108 dead and 140

> 'The first night on Tulagi set the pattern for many nights in the Pacific War.'
>
> JOHN L. ZIMMERMAN,
> THE GUADALCANAL CAMPAIGN.

Above: *On 7 August 1942 the 1st Marine Division began wading ashore near Lunga Point on Guadalcanal while the 2nd Marine Regiment and the 1st Parachute Battalion attacked Tulagi and Gavutu, twenty miles across the sound at Florida Island.*

Below: *The 1st Marine Division landed at Guadalcanal with a company of 15-ton M3A1 Stuart light tanks armed with a 37mm gun and two machine guns. As the war progressed, M4 medium Shermans became the tank of choice.*

▶ **1943**

9 FEBRUARY:
Guadalcanal is
secured.

13 FEBRUARY:
Women's Reserve
Program is announced.

21 FEBRUARY: Army
and Marine assault
battalions capture the
Russell Islands.

18 APRIL: Admiral
Yamamoto is killed by
aircraft from
Henderson Field.

*Right: One year after
the American invasion
of Guadalcanal,
Lieutenant General
Alexander Vandegrift,
now the commander of
the I Marine
Amphibious Force
(IMAC), paid a return
visit to the scene of the
battle to confer with
Major General Charles
D. Barrett. Though the
subject of the
conversation is not
known, Barrett took
command of IMAC
two months later and
helped to plan the
attack on Bougainville.*

of Ichiki's force, the Cactus flyers pounced on the flotilla, set a transport and the cruiser *Jintsu* on fire, and forced the entire squadron to retire to the Shortland Islands. Tanaka changed his method of reinforcing the island. Instead of bringing troops and supplies by transports, he carried them on fast destroyers. Marines called his nocturnal efforts "Rat Runs" of the "Tokyo Express."

By the end of August, Vandegrift needed every half-starved, walking-wounded Marine on the island to hold Guadalcanal. To reconnoiter the extent of the Japanese build-up east of Henderson Field, he moved Colonel Merritt A. "Red Mike" Edson's 1st Raider Battalion and the Parachute Battalion from Tulagi to Guadalcanal. Vandegrift had in mind a mini-amphibious raid behind enemy lines where Marine scouts reconnoitering Tasimboko reported several hundred enemy and large stocks of supplies. Supported by two World War I destroyers and Cactus Air, Edson's 850-man force hit the beach near Tasimboko and collided with more than 1,000 Japanese equipped with artillery. Edson reformed and circled through the

jungle, struck the Japanese flank, and entered Tasimboko. He found tons of supplies and ammunition, a poncho filled with top-secret documents, and – most valuable – the first accurate maps of Guadalcanal.

JAPANESE PLANS REVEALED

From Edson's haul of documents, Vandegrift correctly surmised that Major General Kiyotake Kawaguchi, commanding Japanese units on Guadalcanal, had taken the main force into the jungle with the intent of striking Henderson Field from a low 1,000-yard ridge extending south from the airstrip and running parallel to the Lunga River. To bolster the southern front, he placed Edson's Raiders and the parachutists in the forward sector and supported them with 105mm howitzers and two detachments of Marines.

Kawaguchi intended that his three-jawed envelopment of Vandegrift's position, coordi-

THE QUINTESSENTIAL MARINE

Fifty-five-year-old Major General Alexander Archer Vandegrift received his commission in the Marine Corps in 1909 and spent most of the rest of his early career chasing bandits in Central America and protecting Americans from revolutionaries in China. When he took command of the 1st Marine Division in 1942, he had experienced jungle warfare and the problems of disease and sanitation associated with fighting in the tropics.

Under the worst possible conditions, and left to his own devices by less courageous Navy commanders, Vandegrift pulled his force of 12,000 greenhorns together and made them the toughest fighters in the Pacific. Using a combination of personal stamina, wit, and rugged determination, he made believers out of JCS planners who had sent him on the hasty, poorly prepared, and perilous mission to Guadalcanal. To take an island that would become the springboard for future operations in the Solomons, he had to fight MacArthur and his own comrades in the Navy. When he finally declared Guadalcanal secured, his robust physique had shrunk to a skeleton.

At the end of 1943 he returned from triumph in the Pacific wearing three stars and the pale blue ribbon of the Medal of Honor. On 1 January 1944 he replaced Thomas Holcomb and became the eighteenth commandant of the Marine Corps.

Perhaps his greatest contribution to the Marine Corps came in 1946 when "Tri-elementalists" on Capitol Hill tried to repackage the forces of the United States into land, sea, and air components and tried to eliminate the Marine Corps, which used all three. Never a man of verbal flamboyance,

Vandegrift set the record straight on 6 May 1946 when he tersely testified before the Senate Naval Affairs Committee and said:

"Sentiment is not a valid consideration in determining questions of national security, but we do not rest our case on any presumed ground of gratitude owing us from the nation. The bended knee is not a tradition of our Corps. If the Marine as a fighting man has not made a case for himself after 170 years of service, he must go. But I think you will all agree with me that he has earned the right to depart with dignity and honor, not by subjugation to the status of uselessness and servility planned for him by the War Department."

With Vandegrift at the helm, the Marine Corps passed another test of survival. Congress passed the National Security Act of 1947 and preserved the Marine Corps as an integral part of the Navy.

2100 an enemy plane dropped a flare over Henderson Field. Moments later a Japanese cruiser and three destroyers began shelling the Marine perimeter, a signal for Kawaguchi to begin moving 3,450 assault troops down the right bank of the Lunga River. Edson's thin line stopped two attacks before being pressed into the spurs of "Bloody Ridge." At dawn Edson counterattacked, but the Japanese were too strong, so he pulled his force back to the ridge and dug in, forming one line to the front, the other to the rear. All day Japanese fighters screamed overhead, strafing the ridge and dropping fragmentary bombs.

At nightfall on 13 September, Kawaguchi struck the center of Edson's line and the parachutists on the left. The parachutists buckled, fell back on the Raider's line, and held. The 105mm howitzers of the 5th Battalion, 11th Marines, roared into action and shells began bursting near Edson's position. He used the barrage to pull back to his main line of defense. Before the fight ended, 1,992 rounds of 105mm projectiles fell upon the enemy.

Left: *One of the most popular war books and movies of 1943-44 was* Guadalcanal Diary, *written by war correspondent Richard Tregaskis and starring some of the best known actors in Hollywood.*

nated with naval and air support, would not be detected. He overlooked two factors: the jungle would severely fatigue his troops before they reached the point of attack, and that Edson's command would be on the ridge waiting to stop them.

All day on 12 September, while scouts reported the approach of the enemy, the Raiders and the parachutists dug in along the ridge. That night at

CARLSON'S MAKIN RAID

While Vandegrift's Marines fought and died in the jungles of Guadalcanal, 222 men from the 2nd Raider Battalion under Lieutenant Colonel Evans F. Carlson disembarked on 17 August 1943 from two submarines and went ashore on Japanese-held Makin Island. Carlson, an unconventional Marine, had resigned from the Corps in 1930 to study the tactics of Chinese Communist forces fighting in North China. There he picked up the term "Gung Ho," which meant "Pull Together," a doctrine he passed along to his specially trained Raiders.

While the purpose behind the Makin assault remains obscure, Major General Holland Smith described it as "a piece of folly" intended to distract the Japanese from the struggle in the Solomons. Carlson's surprise attack disrupted the enemy force on Makin, and despite many tactical errors the Raiders overwhelmed the small Japanese garrison on the island. In heavy surf, Carlson hastily withdrew. He left thirty Raiders behind, presumably killed in action. At least nine of them survived the fighting, only to be eventually captured and beheaded by the enemy.

The attack produced two outcomes, one good and the other not so good. On the minus side, the attack spurred the Japanese to reinforce and fortify their islands in the Pacific, making it much more costly for the Marines who assaulted the Gilberts and Marshalls in 1944. On the positive side, moviemakers produced two stirring war movies, "Gung Ho" and "Marine Raiders," both flagrant fictionalizations of what actually happened. "Marine Raiders," starring Pat O'Brien, Robert Ryan, and Ruth Hussey, was advertised as "So stirring, so thrilling you'll want to shout with

Left: *Lt. Col. Evans F. Carlson, commanding the 2nd Raider Battalion, used the Chinese phrase "Gung Ho" (Pull Together), and created another theme for a wartime movie.*

Below: *After Carlson's poorly executed raid on Makin Island in August 1942, the USS* Nautilus *returns the survivors to Pearl Harbor.*

pride and excitement. The drama of the men who are bashing their way to Tokyo...and the girls they're fighting for!" Nobody kept count, but several thousand young men probably enlisted in the Marine Corps to share the glory of Carlson's Raiders.

▶ **16 SEPTEMBER:**
Major Gregory
"Pappy" Boyington
shoots down five
planes of the twenty-
eight claimed for him
during the war, the
most of any Marine.

28 OCTOBER: The
2nd Marine Paratroop
Battalion attacks
Choiseul.

*Right: On 11 November
1943, a squadron of
B-25 bombers flown by
Marines and Army Air
Force pilots slip
between the flak and
sweep into Rabaul
harbor. Flying at low
level, they turn the
docks and shipping
into a holocaust of fire
and smoke.*

*Below: On 30 June
1943, three Army
divisions, augmented
by Colonel H. B.
Liversedge's 1st
Marine Raider
Regiment, go ashore at
Rice Anchorage, New
Georgia.*

As the year 1943 came into focus, American planners were not altogether certain what to do next. General MacArthur, Supreme Commander Southwest Pacific, planned to outflank the Japanese base at Rabaul and approach the Philippines from the south. Halsey's force composed of Marines planned to isolate Rabaul by driving up through the Solomons chain. Admiral Nimitz, using other carrier groups and more Marines, put the wheels in motion to drive through the Marshalls, Carolines, Palaus, and Marianas in the Central Pacific. The final assault would run from three staging areas to the Japanese mainland, one through the Philippines and Okinawa, another through the Marianas and Iwo Jima, and a third through the Aleutians, where the Japanese had established a strong but temporary presence.

In the southwest Pacific area – from New Guinea to the Philippines – the U.S. Army under MacArthur shouldered the task of defeating the enemy. The Marine Corps, to carry the proposed landings in the Solomons and the Central Pacific, needed to have 300,000 men under arms by mid-1943. Demands for such unprecedented expansion induced the Corps to reluctantly abandon a long-standing policy of segregation and admit blacks into the ranks. The first blacks entering the Corps served in segregated units commanded by white officers and NCOs, but by the end of the war 15,000 blacks honorably served in combat.

On 23 February 1943, twelve days after securing Guadalcanal, the island-hopping campaign began. The Marine 3rd Raider Battalion with elements from the 10th and 11th Defense Battalions seized and occupied the Russell Islands. Marine Air Group 21 followed as soon as an airstrip could be carved into the landscape.

DEATH OF YAMAMOTO

In mid-April American code-breakers intercepted a Japanese transmission containing the itinerary of Admiral Yamamoto's inspection tour. One of the admiral's flights took him to Buin on Bougainville, a point within range of U.S. aircraft. Admiral Nimitz passed the information to Rear Admiral Marc A. Mitscher, commanding Air Solomons, who on 18 April dispatched sixteen long-range P-38 Lightnings from Henderson Field. The squadron spotted two Mitsubishi G4M

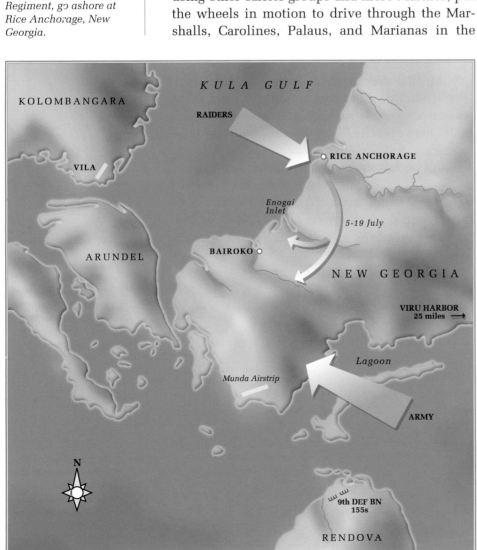

"Betty" bombers coming into Kahili, near Buin, and shot them down, ending the life of Japan's foremost strategist.

On 24 June, working up the Solomons, Army units reinforced by the 1st Marine Raider Regiment (1st and 4th Raider Battalions) attacked the New Georgia group (Operation Toenails), and after a bitter struggle through jungle and swamp, captured the island and the strategically important airfield at Munda. The 4th Raider Battalion crossed the island to secure Viru harbor. "Every time you'd take a step, they'd get caught on some kind of vine," one Raider recalled. The platoon had started into the jungle with a full complement of weapons. Two miles and four hours later they began throwing away the heavier weapons, leaving them as souvenirs for a future generation. One platoon sergeant grumbled, "The only souvenir I wanted to get home was my own ass." The capture of New Georgia on 30 August brought the Marines 350 miles closer to Rabaul.

With New Georgia, Kolombangara, Rendova, and Vella Lavella secured, General Vandegrift formulated plans for attacking Bougainville (Operation Cherryblossom), a large island with five airstrips located 200 miles from Rabaul. On 28 October he sent the 2nd Marine Parachute Battalion, commanded by Lieutenant Colonel Victor H. "Brute" Krulak, on a diversionary attack to the island of Choiseul. Krulak's force tore up Japanese dispositions, ambushed the approaches to Voza, and drew reinforcements from Bougainville before withdrawing six days later.

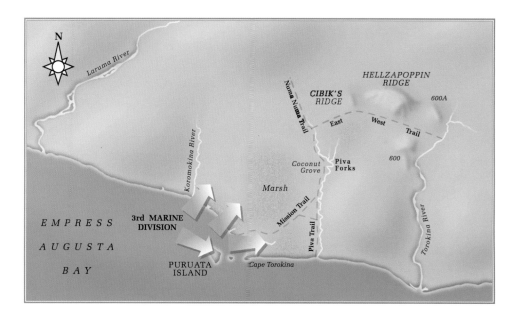

On 1 November Major General Allen H. Turnage, operating as part of the I Marine Amphibious Corps, landed the 3rd Marine Division against heavy opposition at Empress Augusta Bay on Bougainville's west coast. Lessons learned from the landings on Guadalcanal and New Georgia, especially in the functions of combat loading and logistics, added immeasurably to the success of the assault. The Marines also learned that it was faster and easier to build an airstrip than to waste time and take casualties capturing one built by the enemy. The strategy also coincided with an axiom of amphibious warfare – never hit a defended beach when the objective can be reached over an undefended one.

Above: On 1 November 1943 the 3rd Marine Division lands against heavy opposition on Bougainville's west coast and by nightfall establishes a strategic beachhead. Getting through the jungle proves to be no easier.

Left: Moving inland on Bougainville, Marines capture the Torokina airfield and take up defensive positions using 75mm pack howitzer crews. A badly battered Japanese battle flag hangs limp behind the gun-pit. The Marine on the right with earphones is getting firing direction coordinates from spotters.

▶ **1 NOVEMBER:** The 3rd Marine Division lands on Bougainville.

20 NOVEMBER: The 2nd Marine Division of the V Amphibious Corps assaults Betio Island on Tarawa Atoll.

17 DECEMBER: The neutralizing of Rabaul begins.

26 DECEMBER: The 1st Marine Division lands at Cape Gloucester, New Ireland.

Right: At Bougainville, Marine Raiders and their dogs leave on patrol. Though dogs are used for scouting and running messages, they can also sniff out Japs burrowed in holes.

Below: This Bougainville field hospital on 5 January 1944 can provide little more than stretchers and emergency first aid.

Right: Three pilots from the Marine Torpedo Bombing Squadron 232 gather for a chat by the squadron's scoreboard.

Admiral Mineichi Koga, Yamamoto's successor, mustered all the ships available at Rabaul to crush the Marines on the Bougainville beachhead. Two U.S. Navy task groups, one under Rear Admiral A. Stanton Merrill and the other under Rear Admiral Frederick C. Sherman, met the Japanese ships in Empress Augusta Bay and shattered the enemy's two squadrons.

For three weeks the Marines plunged through some of the worst battle conditions of the war, fighting side-by-side with the Army to push from the beachhead to a perimeter 5,000 yards inland. Marines had been involved in bloody battles with Japanese defenders before but none so nightmarish as Bougainville. Swamps gave way to dense jungles, jungles gave way to sharp ridges, and every few hundred yards the terrain repeated itself, revealing more coconut fortifications and more pillboxes. In the Bougainville jungle a patrol could pass within a few yards of a Japanese outpost and never see it or be seen.

Every afternoon it rained, making it impossible to stay dry. The sun never penetrated the jungle, adding humidity to the heat of the day. When night came, Marines hunkered into a wet hole in their damp poncho and "got so goddamn cold you thought you were going to die." During the first days on Bougainville, nobody slept. Every sound emanating from the jungle sounded like Japanese infiltrating the lines. Insects made life unbearable, choking the nostrils and feasting on Marine blood. "Compared with Bougainville," one Marine lieutenant recalled, "everything I ever heard about Hell sounded like a picnic."

The Marines never intended to capture the entire island, just enough space to build airstrips. This they did, leaving thousands of Japanese soldiers to die of disease in the jungle.

From airstrips laid down by Seabees on Bougainville, Marine air evolved an important new tactic – close air support, a technique conceived by Lieutenant Colonel John Gabbert, air officer for the 3rd Marine Division. There had been prearranged air strikes on Guadalcanal,

some even involving depth charges used as bombs, but never one joined by radio communication and controlled from the front lines. The system received its first of ten trials on Bougainviile when twelve TBFs from VMTB-143 and VMTB-223 dropped 144 100-pound bombs 120 yards in front of the 2nd Battalion, 9th Marines, and blew the Japanese out of fortified positions in the village of Piva. Marine close air support, born a decade before in the jungle of Nicaragua, sprang anew in the jungles of Bougainville.

By the end of 1943 it became clear that American lives would never be lost by a ground assault on Rabaul. On 26 December the 1st Marine Division landed on the western side of New Britain, secured enough terrain to build airstrips, and never bothered to cross the island to Rabaul. Land-based aircraft of the Army Navy, and Marines flying from nearby fields destroyed the usefulness of Rabaul to the enemy, and the Solomons campaign, except for mopping up expeditions, came to an end.

Above: *On 26 December, the 1st Marine Division landed on Cape Gloucester and four days later captured the airfield.*

Above left: *Marines wade ashore at Cape Gloucester, holding their rifles high above their heads.*

THE WOMEN MARINES

World War II changed the social character of the Marine Corps, especially with regard to women. On 13 February 1943 the secretary of the navy announced the Women's Reserve Program, and much to the chagrin of Commandant General Thomas Holcomb, thousands of women swelled the ranks of the Corps. Instead of calling their ladies WACS or WAVES, as the Army and Navy did, respectively, the Marine Corps referred to their unwelcome women reservists as "WRs," despite the fact that females joined the Corps with far more enthusiasm than many of their male counterparts. By December 1943, women serving in the Marine Corps numbered 13,201.

With the ranks filling with women, Commandant Holcomb faced new problems. Activist groups badgered him to make the Marine Corps a sexless organization, and Eleanor Roosevelt urged him to put the so-called "WRs" through basic training, including field and weapon training. Holcomb resisted the pressure and assigned his women reservists to administrative, clerical, and a limited number of technical jobs. The women never moved very close to ground or air combat, but they met the Marine Corps' standards in appearance and discipline and replaced men in rear-area jobs, freeing them for assignments in the Pacific.

Holcomb soon discovered that his women

were serving as aviation mechanics, truck drivers, and performing other tasks normally accomplished by males. Before he retired as commandant on 3 December 1943 he said, "There's hardly any work at our Marine stations that women can't do as well as men. They do some work far better than men. . . . What is more, they're real Marines. They don't have a nickname and they don't need one. They get their basic training in a Marine atmosphere, at a Marine Post. They inherit the traditions of the Marines. They are Marines."

By the end of World War II, 23,000 had women joined the Marine Corps Reserve. Unlike the WACS and WAVES, they were never an acronym. They were Marines.

Above: *Two members of the Marine Corps Women's Reserve satisfy their urge to fight by engaging in a spirited display of fisticuffs. A member of the Coast Guard enjoys the fight from above ringside as Pfc. Natalie Black (left) jabs a left at Cpl. Dean Stidham.*

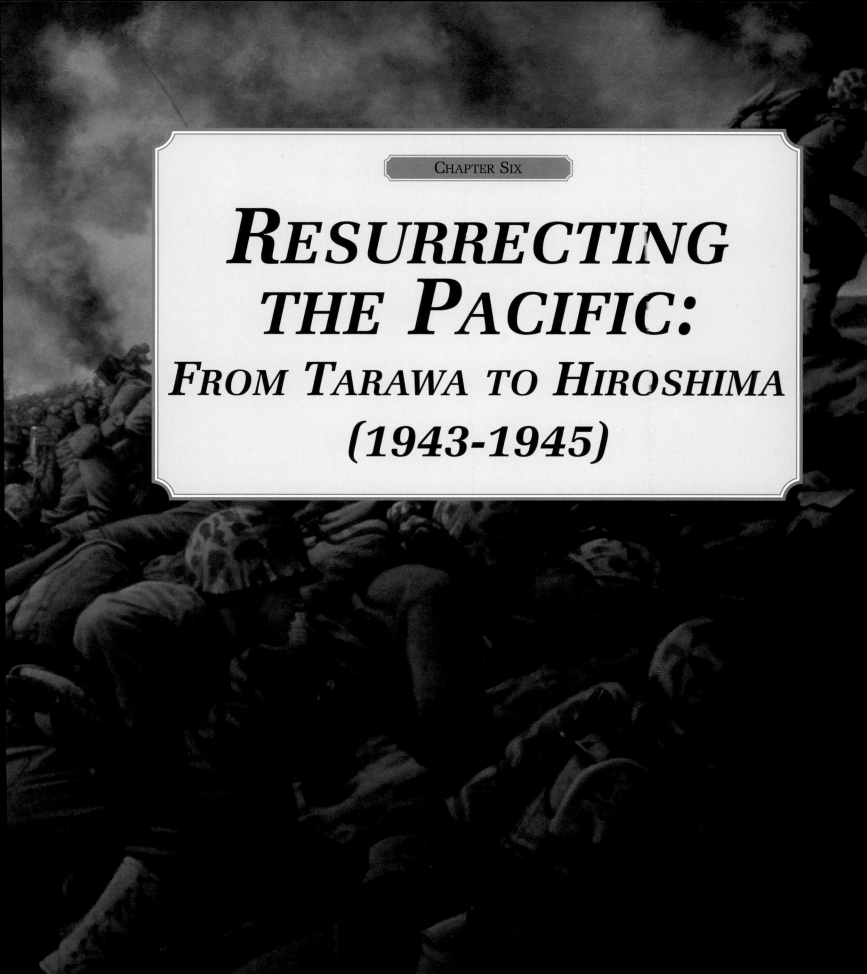

CHAPTER SIX

RESURRECTING THE PACIFIC:
FROM TARAWA TO HIROSHIMA
(1943-1945)

TIMELINE

1943

20 NOVEMBER:
Marines land on
Tarawa Atoll.

17 DECEMBER:
Marine air units begin
daily attacks on
Rabaul.

Previous page: *It was a
long way by water
from the Solomon
Islands to Hiroshima;
the great epic-making
island-hopping
campaign began at
Tarawa and Makin in
the Gilbert Islands,
taking Marines from
the jungles of the
South Pacific to the
burning black sands
of Iwo Jima, where
Mount Siribachi looms
here in the distance.*

In 1943 the Joint Chiefs of Staff decided that the effort directed at the Japanese homeland should be divided, one force under General MacArthur to work through New Guinea to the Philippines, and the other force under Admiral Nimitz to leapfrog through the Gilberts, Marshalls, and Marianas in the Central Pacific. In each island group the JCS wanted strategic airfields large enough to accommodate B-29 Superfortresses for raids up the island chains to the Japanese homelands, and they wanted fighter-bomber fields for aggressive offensive operations against Japanese ground and naval forces threatening the flanks.

Thirteen hundred miles to the northeast of the Solomons lay the equatorial Gilbert Islands, an outpost of Japanese strength concentrated on the atolls of Tarawa and Makin. Nimitz considered these specks in the Pacific strategic stepping-stones to the Marshalls and Marianas. The atolls of the Pacific presented problems markedly different from conditions on the islands of the Solomons. Tarawa and Makin were not typical islands, but tips of submerged mountains sur-

rounded by rings of razor-sharp reefs and tiny atolls bridged by coral. Natural landing sites were few, and the low contour of the islands offered little or no cover for American amphibious vehicles bringing assault troops ashore. Japanese defenders, sheltered in bunkers and fortified emplacements, could withstand with little loss the heaviest air and naval bombardment.

Major General Holland M. "Howling Mad" Smith drew the assignment for Operation Galvanic, the capture of Tarawa Atoll. The chain resembled a triangular necklace of flat coral islands 18 miles long on its hypotenuse with Betio, a two-mile-long sand and coral island shaped like a sawed-off shotgun, its strategic center. The widest section of Betio, a 300-acre island, contained an important airfield that Nimitz wanted for land-based aircraft.

Holland Smith formed the V Amphibious Corps around the 2nd Marine Division, commanded by Major General Julian C. Smith, and the Army's 165th Infantry Regiment, which he assigned to assault Makin. The Marines were in good fighting trim, having recuperated and trained for seven

months in New Zealand. The only question in Julian Smith's mind was whether he could count on using the 6th Marines, which Holland Smith and Admiral Turner had placed in reserve.

To augment the attack, Vice Admiral Raymond Spruance assembled the mightiest task force ever formed in the Pacific. His role – to reduce Betio to a mound of rubble. He fretted that the Japanese fleet might interrupt the operation, and the admiral's distraction annoyed both Marine generals.

The Japanese fortified Betio so well that Rear Admiral Meichi Shibasaki, commanding the 4,836-man garrison, bragged that it would take a million Americans one hundred years to conquer the island. His defenses were formidable. Shibasaki had sited mines, barbed wire, and anti-boat obstacles offshore to canalize assault vehicles into fire-lanes for weapons emplaced ashore.

> '*Even though you Navy officers do come in to about a thousand yards, I remind you that you have a little armor. I want you to know that Marines are crossing the beach with bayonets, and the only armor they'll have is a khaki shirt.*'
>
> GENERAL JULIAN SMITH TO REAR ADMIRAL
> H. F. KINGMAN IN BETIO BEACHHEAD.

A coconut-log seawall five feet high surrounded the island. Along its length were 103 steel-reinforced concrete pillboxes equipped with .13mm machine guns. For static defense the Japanese had also located 14 coast defense guns, 25 field guns, and 14 tanks around Betio.

At approximately 5:00 a.m., 20 November 1943, the Pacific campaign opened when Spruance's battleships and cruisers opened fire on Betio. After pounding the island for an hour, naval gunners paused while aircraft bombed the island. While three waves of boats filled with Marines formed for the assault, destroyers and control vessels moved cautiously into the lagoon. Clouds of smoke and dust reddened by fires hung like a pall over Betio. Marines approaching in amphibious tractors doubted if anything could still be alive, but they were wrong. As soon as the shelling stopped, thousands of

Below: *On November 20, 1943, when the 2nd Marine Division assaulted Betio Island, Tarawa Atoll, they found unforgiving coral reefs that prevented landing craft from getting ashore, and immense fortifications so well constructed that the naval bombardment barely made a dimple in the enemy's defenses, leaving hard work for the Marines.*

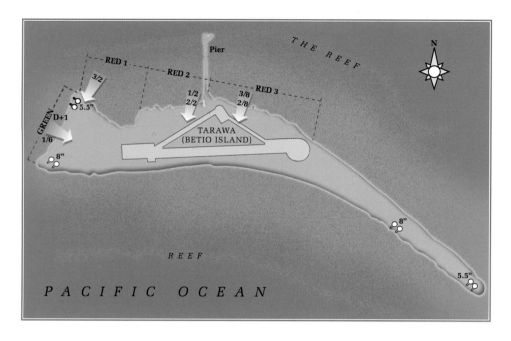

Above: The battle plan looked good on paper, but when the first wave of Marines hit the beaches, enemy fire scattered the assault force.

Below: Marines take out a pillbox on Betio and then hover behind it for protection as they regroup to plan their next assault.

'*No sooner had we hit the water than the Japanese machine guns really opened up. There must have been five or six of these machine guns concentrating their fire on us… I don't believe there was one of 15 men who wouldn't have sold his chances for an additional twenty-five dollars added to his life insurance policy. It was painfully slow, wading in such deep water. And we had 700 yards to walk slowly into this machine gun fire, looming into larger targets as we rose onto higher ground.* '

ROBERT SHERROD IN *TARAWA*.

Japanese emerged from underground blockhouses and began delivering a murderous fire against the assault force off Red Beach 1, 2, and 3.

When the exhausted Marines reached shore, they hunkered down behind the coconut seawall. Many paused in the water, taking cover under a long pier jutting into the lagoon off Red Beach 2. Half of the LVTs were destroyed in the water, and many of those making it to shore landed on the wrong beach. None of the vehicles could mount the seawall, so there they sat, unable to move forward or return through the bloodstained water of the lagoon. To compound the problem, an unexpectedly low tide stranded LCVPs (Landing Craft Vehicle Personnel) on reefs hundreds of yards from shore. Marines toppled into chest-high water bobbing with the corpses of their comrades. Smaller men, weighted down by equipment, drowned in water over their heads.

At headquarters on board the battleship *Maryland* (BB-46), Julian Smith received grim news from the battalion commanders on the beach. The 3rd Battalion, 2nd Marines — decimated while attempting to land on Red Beach 1 — reorganized on the western end of the island. On Red Beach 2 the 2nd Battalion took heavy casualties coming ashore but received reinforcements when part of the 1st Battalion landed on the wrong beach. On Red Beach 3 the 2nd Battalion, 8th Marines, supported by fire from the destroyer *Ringgold*, landed in better shape and closed with the severely thinned forces of Colonel David Shoup's 2nd Battalion, 2nd Marines. The two battalions mounted an attack supported by medium tanks, crossed the airstrip taxiway, and established a 300-yard perimeter. The battalion commanders anticipated a Japanese counterattack after dark and radioed for reinforcements.

The expected counterattack did not materialize, mainly because the enemy's island communications had been destroyed during the bombardment. Julian Smith released the 1st Battalion, 8th Marines, which came ashore in the morning but lost 350 of their 800 men before linking up with Colonel Shoup's 2nd Marines on Red Beach 2. In the meantime, scattered elements from Red Beaches 1 and 2 joined forces on the western end of the island and in the morning moved inland with tanks and flamethrowers.

Julian Smith now fought his second battle, this one with Admiral Turner, who had detained the 6th Marine Regiment as division reserves. Smith won the argument and by late afternoon reserve battalions came ashore to keep the Japanese from fleeing Betio.

By nightfall on the second day, Shoup had pushed across the airfield to the southern shore of the island, cutting Betio in two. On 23 November the last Japanese survivors — a small enemy force of 175 men — put up a final stand on the eastern end of the island, and the grueling battle for Tarawa ended. Only 146 Japanese surrendered. The Marines lost 985 killed and 2,193 wounded

while annihilating an enemy force of nearly 5,000. The butcher's bill on Tarawa raised some eyebrows. The Marines had lost half as many men in seven days on Tarawa as they had lost in six months on Guadalcanal – a worrisome omen of things to come.

During the fight for Tarawa, a force consisting of the 165th Regimental Combat Team of the 27th Army Division captured Makin, and a Marine Reconnaissance Company from the submarine *Nautilus* bested an enemy platoon on Apamama. With the Gilberts secured, Admiral Nimitz began final preparations for Operation Flintlock, the invasion of the Marshalls.

The battle of Tarawa marked the first time a seaborne assault had been launched against a strongly defended coral atoll and the first time amphibian tractors had participated in the landing. The operation validated the soundness of Marine amphibious doctrine while accenting areas for improvement. The lessons learned at Tarawa proved to be of great importance, perhaps even greater than the future operations for which they paved the way.

AMPHIBIOUS TACTICS

On Tarawa, Admiral Spruance's "softening up" tactics fell short of expectations. In future, rockets and high-angle armor-piercing shells would be used on steel-reinforced concrete bunkers and strongly barricaded defenses. To remove obstacles from the shallows, Underwater Demolition Teams (UDTs) would be employed to blast openings for LVTs. For the next round of assaults, the Marines would have "go-anywhere" amphibian vehicles armed with bunker-busting weapons. The Marine Corps had become the amphibian guinea pigs of the Allied powers, and the planners of Marine tactics believed that with a few improvements the Corps could get ashore no matter what the obstacles. The invasion of the Marshalls (Operation Flintlock) had been in the planning stage since mid-1943. Tarawa paved the way for developing the tactics.

▶ **26 DECEMBER:** 1st Marine Division lands at Cape Gloucester, New Britain.

1944

1 JANUARY: Major General Alexander A. Vandegrift becomes 18th Commandant of the Marine Corps.

Left: *The big enemy bombproof on Betio between Red Beach One and Two held out for four days before Marines captured it by frontal assault.*

Below: *The capture of Betio drew a number of curious high-ranking officers. In the foreground right is Marine Major General Julian Smith, commanding the assault. Behind him and climbing over the pillbox is Army Lt. Gen. Robert C. Richardson. Walking behind and dressed in khakis is Admiral Chester A. Nimitz.*

▶ **31 JANUARY:** 4th Marine Division assaults Roi-Namur on Kwajalein Atoll, Marshall Islands.

Right: *On 1 February 1944 the 24th Marine Regiment landed on Namur Island, Kwajalein Atoll, in a flanking operation designed to capture the airfield on Roi. The devastation on the beaches gives testimony to the effectiveness of the heaviest air-sea bombardment since the beginning of the war in the Pacific.*

Below right: *On 1 February 1944 a light tank provides cover on Namur while communications men set up equipment to keep in touch with the command post.*

Below: *The Marines assaulted Roi and Namur from the lagoon to keep the landing craft away from the treacherous reefs on the other side of the island.*

After Tarawa, Howland Smith turned his attention to beefing up the V Amphibious Corps for Operation Flintlock. Kwajalein lay 750 miles northwest of Tarawa. Eniwetok, a second atoll and an important enemy naval base, lay another 325 miles up the Pacific. Smith assigned the capture of Kwajalein, on the southern tip of Kwajalein Atoll, to the Army 7th Infantry Division, which was commanded by Major General Charles H. Corlett. Simultaneously, Major General Harry Schmidt's newly organized 4th Marine Division would strike the twin islands of Roi-Namur, located on the northern tip of the atoll and defended by 3,600 Japanese navy and naval air troops. Namur contained a major Japanese airfield that Nimitz wanted secured for operations against the Marianas.

On 30 January 1944 the naval guns of Admiral Spruance's Fifth Fleet opened on targeted positions on Kwajalein Atoll with a devastating and drastically improved effect compared with Tarawa. Carrier- and shore-based aircraft wiped out Roi's once powerful 24th Air Flotilla. UDTs cleared the lagoon of obstructions, enabling LCI-gunboats to get inside the lagoon.

AMPHIBIOUS TRACTORS

On the morning of 1 February Smith put 240 LVTs and 75 armored amphibians to work transporting the 23rd Marines ashore near Roi and landing the

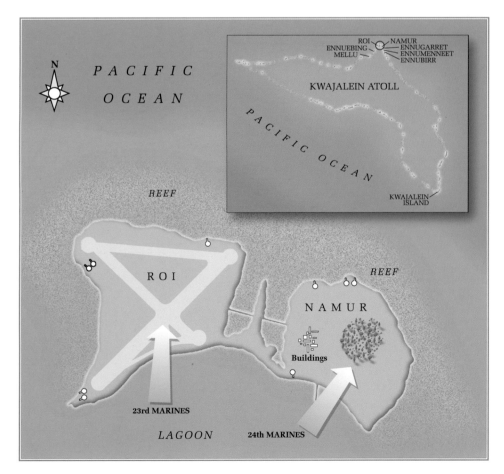

24th Marines on the islets flanking Namur. All the assaults originated from inside the lagoon using amphibious tractors, which, as a result of Tarawa, were now being run off stateside assembly lines at the rate of 500 a month.

Little went according to plan. The Marines blamed the Navy for failing to get the tractors to the line of departure on time, missing an opportunity for the 24th Marines to have overrun Namur in the first hour or two. The Navy retorted that since the plans ultimately worked, nobody should complain. But the Japanese defenses of Roi-Namur could not compare in strength to those on Tarawa. After four days of erratic fighting, nothing remained but to mop-up small pockets of resistance scattered around the long, thin, triangular atoll. Only 91 members of the Japanese garrison surrendered. The 4th Marine Division lost 195 killed and 545 wounded, reflecting improvements in amphibious techniques made since the bloody experience on Tarawa.

On 17 February the V Amphibious Corps moved up to Eniwetok. A fire-support squadron of old battleships and cruisers, commanded by Rear Admiral Henry W. Hill, opened on the atoll's three principal islands. Reserves had never been needed at Kwajalein. That force, composed of the 22nd Marines and the 106th Infantry Regiment under Brigadier General Thomas E. Watson, USMC, led the assault. Already pummeled by

carrier air strikes, the three strategic islands on the atoll – Engebi, Eniwetok, and Parry – were divided up among the strike force. The assignment of capturing Engebi, thought to be the strongest because of its airfield, fell to Colonel John T. Walker of the 22nd Marines. Once Walker secured Engebi, the 106th Infantry Regiment would assault Eniwetok.

After nightfall, the V Amphibious Corps Reconnaissance Company moved ashore on two unoccupied islets next to Engebi. Next came Marine and Army light artillery battalions, which hammered the 1,200 defenders of Engebi throughout the night. In the morning the 22nd Marines landed from the lagoon with medium tanks, and attacked straight across the island. Late in the

> 'There had to be a Tarawa. This was the inevitable point at which untried doctrine was at length tried in a crucible battle. The lessons learned at Tarawa had to be learned somewhere in the course of the war, and it now seems providential that they were learned as early and at no greater cost than was involved.'
>
> CAPTAIN J. R. STOCKMAN IN
> *THE BATTLE OF TARAWA.*

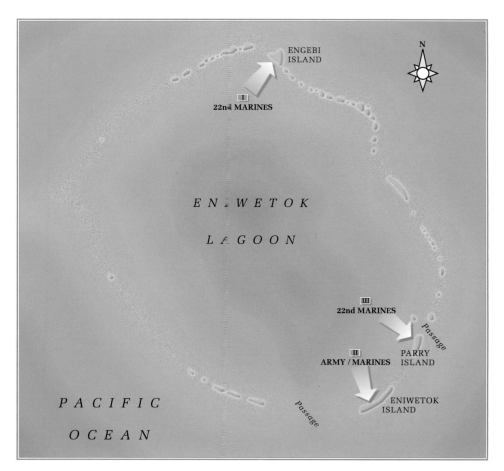

▶ **18 FEBRUARY:**
Marines attack and
capture Engebi and
Parry Islands during
Eniwetok campaign.

Below: *On 22 February
1944 the 3rd Battalion,
22nd Marines, began
mopping up Parry
Island, where air
attacks and a naval
bombardment had
turned the island into
a clutter of battered
and severed cocoanut
trees.*

afternoon the leathernecks secured Engebi,
except for a few pockets of the enemy hidden in
"spider-hole" emplacements.

The capture of Eniwetok Island took a little
longer because the 106th Infantry ran into unexpected resistance. Watson sent in the 3rd Battalion, 22nd Marines, as reinforcements and later
learned that the battalion became involved in
heavy fighting and bore the brunt of the battle.
Disenchanted by the performance of the 106th
Infantry at Eniwetok, Watson pulled them from
the attack on Parry and on 22 February sent in the
22nd Marines. By evening, after spurts of stubborn enemy resistance, the Marines pushed the
last defenders into a 400-yard tip of the island
and declared Parry secure.

On 17-18 February, after getting the V
Amphibious Corps ashore on Kwajalein and Eniwetok, Admiral Spruance sent task groups from
the Fifth Fleet to neutralize the Japanese base at
Truk, the cornerstone of enemy naval strength in

the southwest Pacific. Flying more than 1,200
sorties, carrier planes sank a cruiser and three
destroyers and damaged or destroyed 265 aircraft.
The battleships *Iowa* (BB-61) and *New Jersey* (BB-
62) caught an enemy cruiser and destroyer fleeing
from the harbor and sent both of them to the bottom, thus eliminating Truk as a threat to operations in the Marianas.

NEW TACTICS

Every campaign became a new test of Marine
Corps amphibious assault doctrine, and the Marshalls added another chapter. Naval gunfire support drastically improved when coordinated by
specialized communication teams who controlled targeting from key observation points. The
new armored LCI-gunboats, when employed in
mass, laid down covering fire as Marines went
ashore. For the first time naval star shells turned
darkness into a panorama of light and illumi-
nated enemy counterattacks. New rocket-carrying
aircraft were able to pinpoint and demolish targets near the beach. The 4th Marine Division used
the first highly effective system of tactical air
observation, targeting on enemy positions not
readily seen from the air. Specially designed command ships provided mobile headquarters and
communication centers for control and coordination of attacks. In addition to armored amphibian
tractors, amphibian trucks (DUKWs) provided
logistics support. Of equal importance, after the
Marshalls campaign ended the Marine Corps had
another veteran unit in the Pacific, the 4th Marine
Division.

During every campaign from Guadalcanal to
the Marshalls an ongoing internal battle ensued
over who would be responsible for amphibious
operations, Admiral Turner or the Marine officer
in charge of the expedition. Despite Admiral
King's 1942 decision that the commander of the

Right: *(1) Marine
parachutist's blue
denim helmet; (2)
herringbone twill jump
smock; (3) camouflage
jump smock,
reversible; (4) ammo
bag for Johnson light
machine gun; (5)
Johnson Model 1941
light machine gun, 30
cal.; (6) Johnson Model
1941 semiautomatic
rifle; (7) spike bayonet
and frog for rifle; (8)
parachute rigger's kit;
(9) canvas rubber
jungle boots; (10) first
pattern smooth leather
jump boots; (11) non-
issue parachutist's
fleece-lined vest; (12)
parachutist's utility
knife.*

Left: *Marines' equipment included (1) .30 cal. ammo; (2) MI Garand w/M7 grenade launcher; (3) personal flotation bladder for amphibious landings; (4) M1 30 cal. carbine w/grenade launcher attachment, plus cartridges; (5) collapsible field hat; (6) amber parachute flare; (7) spigot-launched rifle grenade Type M9A1, with other models shown in (8) and (9).*

MARINE AVIATION

By 1944 Marine aviation had come a long way, but after the heroic days of Guadalcanal, flying leathernecks found little to do. The Corps had grown to five aircraft wings comprising 126 squadrons and 112,626 men, of whom 10,457 were pilots. Marine aviation evolved without a doctrine. As historian Robert Sherrod observed, "A new generation of Marine pilots matured without ever knowing the deck of a carrier."

The year following Guadalcanal became known as "the time of the aces" because more than thirty Marines (eventually there would be 120) operating from island airfields began claiming five of more "kills." Major Gregory "Pappy" Boyington of the "Black Sheep Squadron" tallied 28 kills, and had he not been shot down over Rabaul on 3 January 1944, he could well have downed 28 more. Captain Joseph J. Foss registered 26 kills and would have scored a dozen more had malaria not ended his flying days. First Lieutenant Robert M. Hanson scored 25 kills before being shot down during a strafing run. Captain Marion E. Carl joined the list because he became the first Marine ace, shooting down 18½ "Meatballs," slang for the red rising sun painted on Japanese aircraft. These men became legendary, but Marine air needed to do more than embellish the careers of a few skillful flyers.

General Vandegrift and his aviation director, Brigadier General Louis E. Woods, conceived

Above: *Major Gregory Boyington commanded the most unorthodox Marine aviation squadron in the Corps, and tallied 28 kills.*

Below left: *Boyington's Black Sheep Squadron favored the speed and maneuverability of the durable F4U Corsairs.*

Below right: *The Grumman F6F Hellcat fighter-bombers became one of the Marine Corps' most reliable night fighters.*

the idea of putting Marine air groups on eight escort carriers for amphibious operations. Holland Smith approved the idea because the aircraft would be responsible to him. Even the Navy agreed. Major General Roy Geiger, the most respected aviator in the Corps and director of Marine aviation, also liked the idea, and tactics began to change.

Four new aircraft revolutionized Marine tactics in the skies. The immensely powerful Vought 4FU Corsair became the finest carrier-borne fighter-bomber in the Pacific. Because of early problems with the Corsair's carrier-landing ability, all the early deliveries went to the Marines, most notably to Boyington's land-based VMF-214 "Black Sheep" flyers. In 1944 the new Grumman F6FN "Hellcat" night fighters came off the line and introduced an entirely new concept in air reconnaissance and night combat. In 1944 the Marine Corps also received the naval version of the twin-engine North American B-25 "Mitchell" medium bomber. Before the war ended, Marines were flying four-engine Consolidated Vultee PB4Y-2 Privateers, which had been derived from the design of the B-24 Liberator.

The new doctrine, combined with a full range of carrier-based aircraft, vaulted Marine Aviation from a unit disconnected from the Navy to a versatile force that became an integral part of future amphibious operations, a relationship that would establish enduring precedents for years to come.

▶ **6 JUNE:** D-Day in France, the Allies land on Normandy.

15 JUNE: The 2nd and 4th Marine Divisions assault Saipan.

Right: *Wake Island was one of the first islands, along with Guam, to be captured by the Japanese. Though the island never became a strategic target for capture during the 1944-45 campaigns, Liberators returned from time to time to give the Japanese defenders a taste of their own medicine.*

landing force should be co-equal with the naval commander, and Nimitz's directive that when time for the assault came the landing force commander would take full control of the fighting ashore, Turner still tried to muscle Holland Smith, the Marine commander, aside. Admiral King thought he could upstage the Marine Corps by giving Turner and Spruance another star but not Smith or any other Marine in the Pacific. The secretary of the navy scuttled the subterfuge, overruled King, and the V Amphibious Corps now had a lieutenant general. General Smith's advancement did not change his attitude toward, or his squabbles with, Admiral Turner.

Since the beginning of the war, Admiral King had maintained an unwavering conviction that the Marianas held the key to the Central Pacific. Located 1,000 miles west of Eniwetok, the island group's airfields offered strategic bases for attacking the enemy's sea-air communications. From the Marianas, American forces could strike the Palaus, the Philippines, Formosa, and China. Enemy fortresses at Rabaul, Kavieng, and Truk would be isolated and left to die on the vine. General Henry H. "Hap" Arnold, commanding the Army Air Forces, tendered his support because from the Marianas his Boeing B-29 Super-

fortresses could reach the Japanese mainland. Admiral King had been looking for a way to draw out the Japanese Navy, and he believed attacking the Marianas would do it.

On 12 March 1944 Holland Smith and Vice Admiral Turner went to work designing Operation Forager, an assault on the greater islands of the Marianas — Saipan, Tinian, and Guam. After mastering the problem of attacking small islands on coral atolls, they now had to shift their attention to a more difficult objective — advancing into rugged, mountainous terrain carpeted with deep forests and defended by 60,000 enemy troops. Half of that number defended Saipan, a 72-square-mile island surrounded by reefs and containing a large civilian population.

> '*We are through with the flat atolls now. We learned how to pulverize atolls, but now we are up against mountains and caves where Japs can dig in. A week from today there will be a lot of dead Marines.*'
>
> GENERAL HOLLAND SMITH, QUOTED IN *ON TO WESTWARD*, BY ROBERT SHERROD.

Right: *From left to right, the 1st Marine Division patch contains the word Guadalcanal, where the first American assault of the war began; the 2nd Marine Division led the attack on Tarawa: the 4th Marine Division at Iwo Jima; Marine Raider units struck at Tulagi during the Guadalcanal assault and became the first commando units in the Marine Corps.*

Left: *The 2nd and 4th Marine Divisions assault Saipan on 15 June 1944. During the final stages of the conquest of the island, reinforcements coming ashore are struck by Japanese sniper fire, which hits two Marines as they work toward the brush at edge of the beach.*

On 23 February 1944, as Forager entered the final planning stage, Vice Admiral Marc A. Mitscher's Task Force 58, comprising four fast carrier groups, launched the first air attack on the Marianas. Mitscher returned often to gain and maintain air superiority.

For the amphibious assault, Admiral Spruance's Fifth Fleet pulled together more than 800 ships to land and support three Marine divisions, two Army divisions, and a reinforced Marine brigade — a total of 127,000 men. Admiral Turner headed the Joint Expeditionary Force while Smith, charged with the capture of Saipan and Tinian, led the V Amphibious Corps. General Geiger, commanding the III Amphibious Corps, drew the Guam assignment.

On the morning of 15 June, after a prolonged

ATTACK ON SAIPAN

bombardment, the 2nd and 4th Marine Divisions of Smith's V Amphibious Corps fought their way ashore near the town of Charan Kanoa on Saipan's southwest coast. Four battleships, eight cruisers, and seven destroyers arced a rolling bombardment over the first wave of leathernecks. Twenty-four LCI-gunboats armed with 44mm machine guns covered the landing. As veterans of the Marshall's campaign hit the beach, 700 amphibian tractors pressed inland, some armored and carrying a new 77mm gun. Overhead, strafing aircraft flew close support. In thirty minutes Marines landed 8,000 men over a six-mile front. Holland Smith trusted the heavy work to his Marines, holding the 27th and 77th Army Infantry Regiments in reserve.

Major General Thomas E. Watson, commanding the 2nd Marine Division, swung north and attacked Mount Tapotchau, a 1,554-foot fortified crag located in the center of the island. Major General Harry Schmidt, commanding the 4th Marine Division, advanced on Mount Fina Susu, a fortified ridge blocking the way to Aslito Airfield. Behind these terrain features Japanese Lieutenant General Yoshitsugu Saito waited with massed field artillery, tank regiments, and reserve infantry. Saito's plan had been to demolish the enemy on the beach, which he failed to do, and by nightfall the Marines had landed 20,000 men, seven pack-howitzer battalions, and two armored units.

Below: *During American air attacks on Saipan, damaged and Japanese patrol boats, freighters, and tugs lay smoldering or disabled all along the island harbor in Magicienne Bay.*

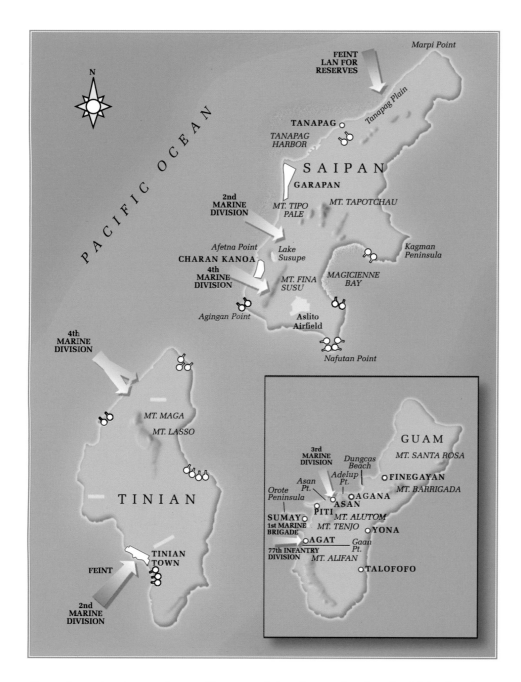

Above: Operations in the Marianas involved three Marine divisions: the 2nd and 4th Divisions at Saipan and Tinian, and the 3rd Marine Division at Guam.

Top right: Men of 6th Marines watch as Naval bombardment softens up Japanese positions on Saipan.

Bottom right: In July 1944, trucks mounted with rocket launchers take positions on Saipan's heights to pummel the front lines of the enemy.

Progress inland remained painstakingly slow. By sunset, only the 25th Marines, 4th Division, had secured their first day's objective on the far right flank. Enemy troops clung to ridges overlooking the beaches and pinned down the 2nd Marine Division. After dark, the enemy came out of their holes and launched a counterattack using a reinforced armored battalion against the 6th Marines. Saito missed his best opportunity to inflict damage by not adequately contesting the landing. With the aid of naval gunfire, the 6th Marines threw the enemy back with heavy losses but suffered serious casualties themselves. When General Holland Smith learned that his Marines had lost more than 2,000 men and half of the 68 armored amphibians, he pointed a blunt finger at the Navy and said, "We did not soften up the enemy sufficiently before we landed."

While the Marines struggled to expand their beachhead against counterattacks, another important event developed at sea. As Admiral King predicted, the Japanese Imperial Fleet came to the rescue of General Saito, bringing nine carriers, 5 battleships, 13 cruisers, and 28 destroyers. Vice Admiral Jisaburo Ozawa, commanding the Japan-

ese fleet, intended to exploit the greater range of his aircraft and remain beyond the reach of Spruance's strong naval force. He made one serious mistake. Ozawa planned to use Saipan's Aslito Airfield to refuel and rearm, thus enabling his aircraft to shuttle-bomb the American fleet. This miscalculation cost Ozawa 346 of his 473 planes because Mitscher had already disabled the airfield and Marines on the ground had bracketed it with the field artillery.

SUCCESS AT SEA

Navy and Marine flyers mirthfully referred to the air battle as the "Marianas Turkey Shoot," but the action did not end off Saipan. American submarines and Mitscher's carriers went after Ozawa's fleet and in the Battle of the Philippine Sea sank three carriers, two oilers, and knocked down 65 more planes, leaving the fleeing Ozawa without his flagship and only 35 aircraft.

On 17 June, to accelerate progress on Saipan, General Holland Smith came ashore, set up a command post at Charan Kanoa, and landed the 27th Infantry Division on the southern flank. Five days later the Marines declared the southern section of Saipan secure, including Aslito airfield. As the Marines pressed northward, the pace began to slow. Army and Marine commanders quibbled over doctrinal differences. Major General Ralph Smith of the 27th Army Division advocated a cautious advance. Holland Smith, aware of the vulnerability of the offshore fleet and anxious to get onto Guam and Tinian, urged utmost speed. Ralph

Smith lost the argument, and on 24 June Holland Smith relieved him, setting in motion another skirmish between the Army and the Marine Corps having nothing to do with fighting the Japanese.

On 6 July, Marines pinned the remainder of the Japanese army in the northern sector of Saipan. Humiliated by defeat and worn by fatigue, General Saito gathered his staff together for a farewell feast of canned crabmeat and sake. Then he cleaned off a spot on a rock, faced east, shouted "*Banzai!*" and carved out his bowels with his ceremonial sword.

▶ **19-20 JUNE:** Marine flyers participate in the "Marianas Turkey Shoot."

HOLLAND "HOWLING MAD" SMITH

Sixty-two-year-old Holland Smith earned his nickname "Howling Mad" in 1916 while serving as a lieutenant in the Dominican Republic. In June 1917 he went to France as a captain with the famous 5th Marine Regiment and, as the post-war Marine Corps grew, so did Holland Smith.

"Howling Mad," being a combative sort, was also one of the fathers of modern amphibious warfare, a superb strategist, and probably the most competent commander in the Corps on amphibious doctrine and assault tactics. Marines who served under him during World War II described him as a vigorous and demanding commander, irascible and quarrelsome, and, like Douglas MacArthur, one of America's colorful field commanders. When on 24 June 1944 he relieved Major General Ralph C. Smith from command of the 27th Infantry Division, the incident underscored the difference between the aggressive operational style of the Marines and the Army's more conservative approach to warfare. The removal of Ralph Smith sparked an embarrassing controversy for Admirals Turner and Spruance because they approved the dismissal, and for Admiral Nimitz, because he tried to ignore it.

During the war in the Pacific, five Army generals were relieved, but only one by a Marine Corps officer. Whether Ralph Smith lacked "aggressive spirit," as Holland Smith claimed, can be argued, but for various reasons the 27th Division stalled progress being made by two Marine divisions slogging north through Saipan. The 2nd Marine Division on the left pushed into the outskirts of Garapan, Saipan's principal city, and the 4th Marine Division stormed through stiff opposition on the right and crossed the Kagman Penisula. Both wings overlapped the 27th Infantry Division, which had bogged down in the center. After one Smith relieved the other Smith, news correspondents fueled the incident into a bitter inter-service rivalry.

On 12 July, before the fighting stopped on Saipan, Lieutenant General Robert C. Richardson, USA, arrived to square accounts. Without consulting Admiral Nimitz, for whom he worked, Richardson convened a board to investigate "the summary relief and displacement" of his friend, Ralph Smith. By his action, Richardson cast himself into the position of passing judgment on Marine and

Navy officers neither under his command nor answerable to him. Richardson then went directly to the 27th Infantry Division and passed out decorations without the concurrence of Holland Smith. Spruance pleaded with Holland Smith to not explode when he met with Richardson, no easy task for "Howling Mad." Despite one of the greatest victories of American arms, due mainly to Marines, Richardson cornered General Harry Schmidt of the 4th Marine Division and declared:

> '*You and your commanders aren't as well qualified to lead large bodies of troops as general officers in the Army. We've had more experience in handling troops than you've had, and yet you dare to remove one of my generals! You Marines are nothing but a bunch of beach runners anyway. What do you know about land warfare?*'
>
> RICHARDSON STATEMENT QUOTED IN *CORAL AND BRASS*, BY HOLLAND M. SMITH.

Holland Smith constrained his temper, but Admirals Turner and Spruance kept the controversy going until 1948, and historians picked it up from there. Holland Smith's death on 12 January 1967 gave veterans an opportunity to rekindle the almost forgotten feud, and it continued to simmer.

Above: Lieutenant General Holland "Howling Mad" Smith (left) congratulates Major General Clifton B. Cates following the victories on Saipan and Tinian. Smith planned the operation with Vice Admiral Richmond Kelly Turner, seated center. Cates delivered the assault using the 2nd and 4th Marine Divisions.

▶ **15 SEPTEMBER:** The 1st Marine Division lands on Peleliu.

20 OCTOBER: MacArthur's forces return to the Philippines and land on Leyte.

Above right: Wet weather on Guam persists as Marines in July 1944 move inland. Hearing gunfire ahead, they advance cautiously, taking shelter along the roadside as tanks lead the way up the hills and along muddy roadways.

On Guam, Marines developed tactics that enhanced future amphibious operations in the Pacific. Admiral Conolly, working with Navy and Marine pilots, perfected a system that allowed naval gunfire and air support to be delivered against the same target area at the same time. By limiting pullout levels of supporting aircraft, Navy vessels could continue to deliver flat trajectory fire while aircraft delivered plunging fire. The tactic gave birth to the idea of placing Marine aircraft on escort carriers for the sole purpose of supporting Marine infantry units on the ground. This led to the development and implementation of the Marine air-ground team.

While Marines mopped-up Guam, General Geiger went to work on his next campaign – the capture of the Peleliu in the Palaus, an island lying 500 miles east of the Philippines. The code-name, Operation Stalemate, proved fittingly conceived, along with the question of whether the island really held any strategic value. On July 31 General MacArthur's forces secured New Guinea, opening his way to the Philippines, and the 12 square miles of Peleliu, like Truk, now seemed of little significance. Nimitz, however, wanted the island neutralized to keep the enemy off MacArthur's flank. One reason no one seriously questioned the worthiness of the operation

emanated from Major General William H. Rupertus's optimism: "We're going to have some casualties, but let me assure you that this is going to be a short one, a quickie. Rough but fast. We'll be through in three days. It might take only two." (Quoted from George McMillan, *The Old Breed.*)

The Rupertus "quickie" cost the Marine Corps 1,252 killed and 6,526 wounded, and the Army 208 killed and 1,185 wounded, the highest ratio to date of American to Japanese casualties in any campaign. Of 10,700 Japanese defenders, only 302 surrendered. Eight Marines won the Medal of Honor. The capture of Peleliu eliminated any Japanese threat from the western Pacific against America's planned recapture of the Philippines, but was it worth the cost? At least one admiral thought not.

> *'If military leaders were gifted with the same accuracy of foresight that they are with hindsight, undoubtedly the assault and capture of the Palaus would never have been attempted.'*
>
> REAR ADMIRAL JESSE B. OLDENDORF, 25 MARCH 1950.

Right: The 1st Marine Division prepares to go ashore on Peleliu on 15 September 1944. As landing craft make way toward the shore, naval gunfire pummels the beaches and rockets burst in the air.

PELELIU – A PLACE CALLED HELL

Major General William H. Rupertus believed so thoroughly in the ability of the 1st Marine Division to conquer Peleliu in two or three days that he refused to accept, against the advice of General Geiger, an Army regiment from the 81st Infantry Division. Marine planners warned that 10,700 Japanese on the island came from one of the Imperial Army's best infantry divisions, but Rupertus waved off the advice. Aerial reconnaissance showed that the island contained hundreds of honeycombed caves embedded in the Umurbrogol ridge, and that the small island contained an ominous mixture of defenses like those on Tarawa and Saipan. Other photographs showed a thick, impenetrable mangrove swamp that encircled the island inside the reef. But Rupertus adamantly rejected any help from the Army.

On the morning of 15 September 1944, Rupertus landed three regiments 500 yards from the Japanese airfield on the southwestern tip of the island. After five days of heavy fighting the 5th and 7th Marines captured the airfield and secured the surrounding area, but the 1st Marines under Colonel Lewis B. "Chesty" Puller ran into heavy resistance at Umurbrogal Ridge and could not advance. Puller realized – if Rupertus did not – that the 1,406 tons of Navy projectiles expended on the island had not touched the enemy defenses tunneled into the ridge. Puller's battalion commanders reported that forward positions were being wiped-out faster than replacements could arrive from the rear. Puller called Rupertus for reinforcements just as Colonel Kunio Nakagawa launched a coordinated tank-infantry counterattack across the northern end of the airfield, cutting between the flanks of the 1st and 5th Marines. Puller's line held, and his leathernecks wiped out the tanks with bazookas, antitank weapons, and pack howitzers.

Instead of attacking the ridge, Rupertus decided to go around it. Encirclement choked Umurbrogal Ridge but did not eliminate thousands of Japanese still hiding in caves. Much to Rupertus's dismay, Geiger threw in

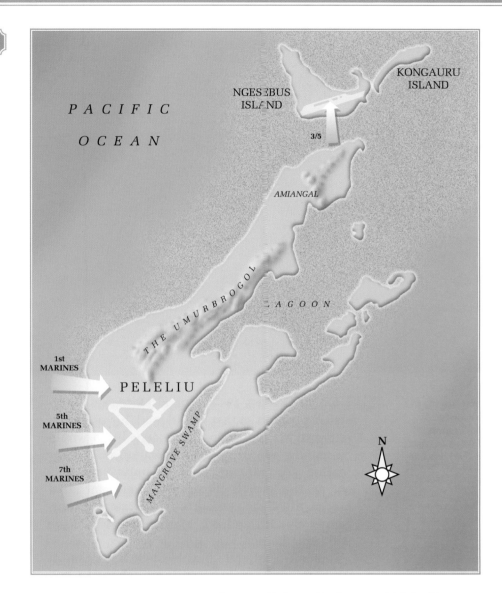

the 321st Infantry Regiment, which had just captured the nearby island of Angaur.

Rupertus discovered that Umurbrogal was not a single ridge but a series of five ridges pocked with caves interlocked by tunnels, all of which had to be blown one by one. What Rupertus envisioned as a three-day "quickie" took one day more than a month and delayed operations elsewhere. After the 18th Infantry Division relieved the Marines on 16 October, six weeks elapsed before the Army declared the island secure.

Above: *Major General William H. Rupertus thought the 1st Marine Division would capture Peleliu in two or three days. His division found the island ringed by a morass of mangrove swamps and covered by a dense jungle with a strongly defended ridge called the Umurbrogol. The "two or three day" affair would take six weeks.*

Left: *An American F4U Corsair drops bombs on enemy positions concealed on one of the many hills making up the Umurbrogal ridges.*

Right: *A distressed General Rupertus, flanked by Colonel Lewis Puller (left), who commanded the 1st Marine Brigade, attends a burial ceremony after the battle ended.*

On the map: PACIFIC OCEAN; KONGAURU ISLAND; NGESEBUS ISLAND; 3/5; AMIANGAL; THE UMURBROGOL; LAGOON; 1st MARINES; PELELIU; 5th MARINES; 7th MARINES; MANGROVE SWAMP; N

Above: *The objective of the 4th and 5th Marine Divisions was to silence the guns of Mount Suribachi and quickly capture the two large cirfields, but it would take four Marine divisions to do it.*

Right: *Marines of the 5th Division struggle through black volcanic sands on Red Beach No. 1, slowly ascending the rise beyond the beach. Part of the division will assault Mount Suribachi while the other units begin working up the island toward Airfield No. 1.*

more guns emplaced than anyone anticipated. For three days Marine aircraft on carriers dropped napalm and fired rockets into the lunar landscape of Iwo Jima. Unable to extend the days of bombardment, General Holland Smith predicted 15,000 casualties, but nobody believed him. On the evening before the assault, James Forrestal, secretary of the navy, sat beside Smith during the final conference and said, "My hat is off to the Marines," adding, "I can never again see a United States Marine without experiencing a feeling of reverence."

SUCCESS ON SURIBACHI

On 19 February, dawn broke bright over a calm sea dotted by 450 vessels of the Fifth Fleet. Holland Smith and Blandy watched as landing craft maneuvered into position off the southeast coast of Iwo Jima. Marine battalions, grouped among 482 chugging LVT(A)s, waited while Blandy's squadron laid down a creeping barrage. Sixty-eight LVT(A)s carrying the first seven battalions of Marines peeled off for the 4,000-yard dash to shore. Forty-five minutes later amtracs hit the black-sand beaches with Rockey's 5th Division on the left and Cates's 4th Division on the right. Meeting only light resistance, Marines pushed 300 yards inland. General Kuribayashi made a fatal mistake by letting the Marines reach the beach. The Japanese suddenly opened fire from concealed positions, and a hail of fire raked the flanks of the assault force, but the Marines weathered the storm and fought back. By nightfall, no fewer than 30,000 Marines supported by tanks, artillery, and bulldozers crowded onto the beachhead and secured the neck of the island, cutting off Mount Suribachi and gaining a foothold on

and even during periods of clear weather enemy AA kept Navy air spotters too high to locate targets. A number of LCI-gun and rocket boats came too close to shore while covering UDT teams and received heavy fire from concealed positions on shore that nobody knew existed. On the final day of bombardment, Blandy tried to clear the landing beaches of shore batteries, only to discover far

▶ **1945**

19 FEBRUARY: The 4th and 5th Marine Divisions land on east coast of Iwo Jima.

24 FEBRUARY: The 3rd Marine Division enters battle for Iwo Jima.

Left: *A Marine with a flamethrower breaks from his squad to incinerate Japanese holed up in a pillbox.*

Below left: *Lt. Gen. Holland Smith (left) and Maj. Gen. Harry Schmidt confer in front of the Fifth Amphibious Corps Command Post on Iwo Jima.*

Below: *On 23 February 1945, Associated Press photographer Joe Rosenthal captured on film the historic moment when Marines raised the flag on Mount Suribachi.*

Airstrip No. 1. The cost came high, 2,400 casualties with 600 dead.

On the right flank the 28th Marines, commanded by Colonel Harry B. Liversedge, spent three days capturing Mount Suribachi. The bulging crater resembled an enormous anthill perforated with hundreds of cavities. Marines climbed the slope step by step, using grenades, flamethrowers, and satchel charges to blow the enemy out of their holes. On the morning of 23 February the 2nd Battalion reached the crest and amid an eerie silence planted a small American flag. The appearance of the Stars and Stripes brought a sudden outburst of enemy fire. Sergeant Louis B. Lowery, who had photographed the flag raising, lost his camera but not his film. Two hours later Joseph Rosenthal of the Associated Press came to the summit accompanied by Marines carrying a larger flag. He snapped eighteen shots; one of them was to become the most famous symbol of the war.

On 24 February the 3rd Marine Division came ashore to break through the center of General Kuribayashi's iron belt of cross-island defenses protecting Airfield No. 2. The Marines now had 82,000 men ashore, the 4th Division on the right and the 5th Division on the left. Artillery units could barely move through the stinking sulfur pits, the lunar-like jagged crags, and the sunken pockets afflicting the landscape. Tanks sank in

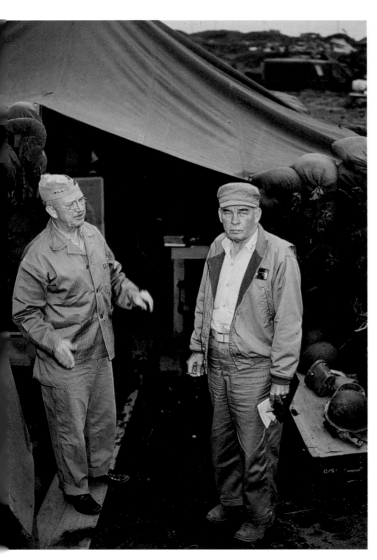

137

1 APRIL: The III Amphibious Corps under General Roy Geiger lands on Okinawa.

6 APRIL: *Kamikaze* attacks begin off Okinawa.

Right: *In March 1945 the battleship USS Idaho opens on the beaches of Okinawa in a pre-invasion effort to break up enemy defenses on the airfield at Yontan.*

Below: *Long and slender, Okinawa presented a combination of problems unlike other Japanese-controlled islands. The main enemy resistance would occur at the airfield and along the Naha-Shuri line.*

Tenth Army, consisting of the III Amphibious Corps under General Roy Geiger and the XXIV Army Corps under Major General John S. Hodge. The choice of Lieutenant General Simon Bolivar Buckner, USA, to command the assault force marked the first major landing under Admiral Nimitz where a Marine did not hold the top command. Marine elements included the 1st, 2nd, and 6th Divisions and a number of air groups attached to the Tactical Air force.

On 1 April, after a furious week-long bombardment, Americans went ashore on the southwest coast of the island. Marines landed near the Yon-tan Airfield, and the Army came ashore farther south and closer to the city of Naha. The 2nd Marine Division demonstrated along the southern tip of the island but did not go ashore. For three days the 6th Marine Division pushed north against light resistance, splitting the island in two by occupying the Ishikawa isthmus, while the Army units advanced south. Resistance stiffened as the Marines reached the Motobu Peninsula, but on 20 April they secured the position.

Working south, General Hodge's 24th Army Corps ran into a hornet's nest. General Ushijima had delayed his counterattack, waiting for

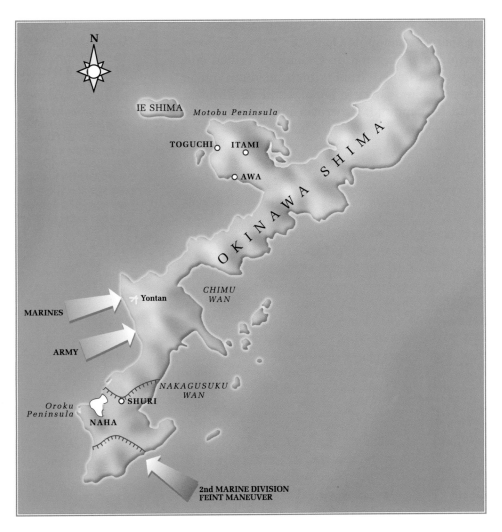

> *'It is going to be really tough. I see no way to get the Japanese out except blast them out yard by yard.'*
>
> GENERAL HODGE TO GENERAL RICHARDSON,
> 17 APRIL 1945.

kamikazes to destroy or drive away the American support ships. The enemy emplacements dug into the southern third of the island began at Naha on the west coast, ran through the dominating high point of Shuri Castle, and ended on the eastern shore at Yonabaru on Nakagusuku Bay. The Japanese burrowed into caves that interlocked and connected with more caves on the reverse slope. The defenses resembled everything the Marines had experienced on Iwo Jima and Peleliu, but nobody in Hodge's 24th Army Corps had been there.

While the Navy fought *kamikazes*, Geiger considered an amphibious end-run along the southern shore, but Buckner thought another landing too risky. Instead, he brought the 6th Marine Division down from the Motobu Peninsula and sent ashore the 1st Marine Division, which had been held in reserve. While the Army held its gains, the 6th Marine Division, already reduced in number, took heavy casualties securing a trio of mutually supporting hills named Sugar Loaf, Horseshoe, and Half Moon Hill, which anchored the western flank of the Shuri line. The 1st Division, one of the toughest units in World War II, took severe casualties attacking Dakeshi Ridge, the key terrain feature in the Corps sector, and Wana Ridge, the most formidable eminence and worst deathtrap in Ushijima's line of defenses. As the attack slowly progressed, spring rains began to fall and turned the island into a sea of mud.

After the 10th Army struck a stalemate against Ushijima's defenses on the Oroku Peninsula, General Geiger finally convinced General Buckner that the easiest way to break the bottleneck without excessive losses was to launch an

Above: *The landscape of Okinawa resembled areas in the southeastern United States, with farmlands, hills, and scattered brush. Marine tanks, followed by riflemen, moved against Japanese positions lodged in the ridge ahead and made good targets as they crossed miles of open fields.*

Left: *On 11 May 1945, a mortar team from L Company, 3rd Battalion, 7th Marines, begin bracketing their weapons on Japanese positions along one of the many ridges where the enemy refuse to budge from their concealed positions.*

Far left: *Lt. Gen. Simon Bolivar Buckner (left), commanding the Tenth Army, and Marine Maj. Gen. Roy S. Geiger (right), commanding the Third Amphibious Corps, discuss matters on Okinawa. With victory in sight, General Buckner would be killed by enemy artillery fire, and General Geiger would temporarily take his place.*

141

12 APRIL: President Franklin D. Roosevelt dies of a cerebral hemorrhage. Harry Truman becomes president.

1 MAY: III Amphibious Corps secures northern sector of Okinawa.

8 MAY: V-E Day: The war in Europe ends.

21 JUNE: Okinawa is secured.

6 AUGUST: The first atomic bomb is dropped on Hiroshima.

15 AUGUST: V-J Day: the Japanese surrender.

2 SEPTEMBER: Japanese sign official surrender on USS *Missouri.*

30 SEPTEMBER: Marines of III Amphibious Corps land in North China and begin disarming 630,000 Japanese.

6 OCTOBER: Near Tientsin, Marines exchange the first fire with Chinese Communists.

Above right: *At Yontan Airfield, Brig. Gen. William Wallace (left) and Maj. Gen Francis Mulcahy confer on plans to deal with the latest* kamikazi *attacks on naval vessels off Okinawa.*

Right: *On 6 May 1945, the dusk patrol of the 2nd Marine Air Wing Corsairs land at Yontan Airfield, giving way to the forthcoming patrol of the night fighters.*

amphibious assault in the rear of the enemy. Lieutenant Colonel Victor H. Krulak put the plan together in five days, and on 4 June the 4th and 29th Marine Regiments landed from LVTs and LCTs and pushed rapidly inland. After ten days of fighting the 6th Marine Division, working with the 4th and 29th Marines, squeezed the Japanese into a corner. Ushijima wired the mainland, "Enemy tanks are attacking our headquarters cave. The Naval Base Force is dying gloriously." To add to the number of those "dying gloriously," Ushijima committed suicide.

Others who died gloriously during the final assault included General Buckner. Three days before the battle ended an enemy artillery shell took his life. General Geiger took command of the U.S. 10th Army, the only Marine to command a field army during the war. The Army did not want a Marine in charge of their bailiwick and

pulled General Joseph W. Stilwell out of retirement to replace Geiger.

During the 82-day battle for Okinawa, the Marines lost 3,400 killed and 15,500 wounded. The total count of casualties in the 10th Army stood at 65,000 killed and wounded against 110,000 dead Japanese. Only 7,000 Japanese surrendered.

WAR'S END

The war in Europe ended during the Okinawa campaign, and the United States began moving more divisions into the Pacific. More than 300,000 men trained on Okinawa for the assault against Japan. However, President Harry Truman shortened the war by authorizing the use of the

---

KAMIKAZES AND CORSAIRS

General Buckner's command contained the Tactical Air Force, Tenth Army, which was not an Army unit at all but mainly composed of the 2nd Marine Air Wing, commanded by Major General Francis P. Mulcahy, whose biggest job was air defense. Mulcahy, the first commanding general of AirFMFPac, brought more than 12,000 men to Okinawa. Before the battle ended, he had twenty-two shore-based squadrons operating from the island, ten from the carriers *Bennington, Bunker Hill, Block Island,* and *Gilbert Islands*, an air-warning group, four Grasshopper observation units, and several Army squadrons under his command. The nerve centers that controlled his aviation were two: Air Defense Command under Brigadier General William J. Wallace, whose job was to defend against *kamikazes*, and Landing Force Air Support Control Units under Colonel Vernon E. Megee, who had perfected close-air support on Iwo Jima.

Because of General Ushijima's unorthodox tactics, Mulcahy obtained possession of Okinawa's two airfields – Yontan and Kadena – early in the action. Within a week after the landings, Corsairs from Colonel John C. Munn's MAG-31 began flying out of Yontan. Their first kill occurred the day they flew off the deck of escort carriers for Yontan and intercepted a

kamikaze making straight for the USS *Sitkoh Bay*. Two days later Colonel Ward E. Dickey landed MAG-33 at Kadena, bringing the number of Marine aircraft on Okinawa to more than 200.

The first great *kamikaze* blitz – a wave of 355 planes – occurred on 6 April while Marine aircraft were still on carriers. Marine squadrons took off from *Bennington* and *Bunker Hill* and shot down seventeen, but *kamikazes* got through the screen and struck twenty-two ships. On 12 April *kamikazes* came again – 185 strong – but mud grounded Marine flyers on Okinawa. Four Marine carrier squadrons took to the air and knocked down fifty-one *kamikazes*. On 16 April *kamikazes* tried to sink the outlying radar picket ships that warned the fleet of incoming attacks. Twelve Corsairs came to the rescue of the USS *Laffey* (DD-724), which had been hit by five suicide attacks. The captain of the USS *Hugh W. Hadley* (DD-774), hit four times by an earlier attack and then screened by Corsairs said, "I am willing to take my ship to the shore of Japan if I could have these Marines with me."

The air battle over the Ryukyus continued until the war ended. Flying from carriers and airfields on Okinawa, Marine flyers accounted for 506 kills.

atomic bomb. When the first bomb exploded over Hiroshima on 6 August, 80,000 inhabitants died. On 9 August a second bomb devastated Nagasaki. Six days later the Japanese surrendered unconditionally. On 2 September Imperial Japan signed the official surrender on the USS *Missouri* in Tokyo Bay. General Geiger represented the Marine Corps during the ceremony. He also represented 86,940 leathernecks who had died during an unbroken series of victories, eighty Marines who were awarded Medals of Honor, and all those who served in the Corps on every front. General MacArthur, supreme commander of U.S. forces in the Pacific, affixed his signature to the surrender documents and said, "These proceedings are closed."

During World War II, the Marines never became a major factor in the European theater. Those in Europe served almost exclusively on ships. There were exceptions. Fifty-one Marines served with the U.S. Office of Strategic Service (OSS) and engaged in behind-the-lines covert missions in North Africa and Europe. They worked with partisan and resistance groups in France, Germany, Yugoslavia, Italy, and other countries occupied by the Nazis. One Marine, Colonel Peter J. Ortiz, received two Navy Crosses for heroism while serving with the French Resistance.

More than 98 percent of the Corps fought in the steaming jungles of the Solomons, on the fire-swept beaches of Tarawa, and against the caves on Iwo Jima and Okinawa. Unique among Marines were the 400 Navajo Code Talkers. They served in all six Marine divisions, in Marine Raider battalions, and with Marine airborne units, transmitting messages by telephone and radio in their native language – a code the Japanese never broke. The Japanese, who were skilled code-breakers, remained baffled by the Navajo language. Lieutenant General Seizo Arisue admitted that while they learned to decipher the codes used by the U.S. Army and Army Air Corps, they never cracked the code used by the Marines.

> '*Were it not for the Navajos, the Marines would never have taken Iwo Jima.*'
>
> MAJOR HOWARD CONNOR,
> 5TH MARINE DIVISION.

The Corps' six divisions made fifteen major amphibious landings, and its air arm destroyed 2,355 enemy aircraft. Growing from a force of 70,000 in December 1941, 670,000 men and women passed through the Corps during World War II. On V-J Day, 15 August 1941, the Corps still numbered 458,000 officers and enlisted personnel. The war had been a great experience for the Marines, but once again, the future of the Corps remained in doubt.

Above left: *The 1st Marine Division joins with the 7th Army Division to cheer the flag-raising on Hill No. 89 on 27 June 1945.*

Above: *On 30 August 1945 the 4th Regiment, 6th Marine Division, are among the first to land in the Tokyo area.*

Below: *Throughout the war in the Pacific, the Japanese were never able to understand the language of the Navaho code-talkers.*

CHAPTER SEVEN

KOREA:
THE BEGINNING OF THE COLD WAR (1946-1959)

TIMELINE

1946

6 MAY: Commandant Vandegrift informs the Senate Naval Affairs Committee, "the bended knee is not a tradition of our Corps."

The end of World War II found the Marine Corps and Commandant General Vandegrift with a multitude of daunting tasks. Demobilizing 500,000 officers and men topped the list, but the Marines still had work to do.

General Schmidt's V Amphibious Corps (2nd and 5th Marine Divisions) had been making preparations for the invasion of Kyushu, southwest Japan. After V-J Day, Vandegrift sent the two divisions to occupy southern Japan, but their stay was short. In December 1945 the 5th Division went home for disbandment. Seven months later the 2nd Division followed but remained active, becoming the first division assigned to the newly created Fleet Marine Force Atlantic.

In September 1945, General Rockey's III Amphibious Corps (1st and 6th Marine Division), instead of invading the Tokyo Plain, went to North China to repatriate the Japanese forces there. The Corps had a dual mission: to stabilize the country and prevent it from falling under the influence of Soviet Russia or Chinese Communists. Marines tutored the locals in warfare, unaware that Communists would steal the Chinaman's frail fidelity and make him the enemy. In April 1946 the Corps disbanded the 6th Division but retained the 3rd Brigade in China.

Finding no more work for the 3rd, 4th, and 6th Divisions, Vandegrift disbanded them and converted the bulk of the 1st Division into the Fleet Marine Force Pacific. By mid-1946 he had cut the Corps to 100,000 officers and enlisted men.

In August 1946, a month after two atomic bombs thundered over Bikini Atoll, Vandegrift received a challenging letter from General Geiger, who had witnessed the tests:

"Under the assumption that Atomic bombs can be produced in large quantities, that they can be used in mass attacks against an enemy objective, and that our probable future enemy will be in possession of this weapon, it is my opinion that a complete review and study of our concept of amphibious operations will have to be made. It is quite evident that a small number of atomic bombs could destroy an expeditionary force as now organized, embarked, and landed." (General Geiger to General Vandegrift, 21 August 1946.)

Although Geiger died six months later, Vandegrift put a team of senior officers together under the chairmanship of Major General Lemuel C. Shepherd to restudy the mission of the Marine

Previous page: When the 3rd Battalion, 5th Marines assaulted Wolmi-do off the coast of Inchon, they became wary. So unlike the determined and suicidal Japanese fighters, the North Koreans seemed willing to surrender without much of a fight. Such unexpected behavior naturally made the Marines extra cautious.

Right: Immediately after the war with Japan ended, Marines of the 1st Regiment landed in China to free American POWs and repatriate the Japanese. They marched through the crowded streets of Tangku to board trains to Tientsin, where they intended to join forces with the 7th Regiment, which had come ashore earlier during the initial landings.

Corps. While Shepherd's task force worked on one assignment, a second group comprised of war-tested colonels such as Robert E. Hogaboom, Merrill B. Twining, and Victor H. Krulak submitted a landmark compilation of amphibious doctrine for the postwar Marine Corps.

The atomic bomb made an indelible mark upon the thinking of every strategist and tactician. Shepherd's team concluded: "Under atomic attack, the World War II amphibious assault was finished. Normandy and Okinawa would never be repeated."

One of the views expressed by the junior board came from Colonel Krulak, who said, "[A new military philosophy] consists of thinking in terms of the next war instead of the last. This means starting with ideas, when you have nothing more tangible, and developing them into the concepts, procedures, and weapons of the future."

For future operations the board looked for new tools such as transport seaplanes and helicopters. The maximum carrying capacity for a helicopter at the time was one pilot and two Marines, but Vandegrift understood the potential of wingless aircraft and in December 1947 established the Marine Helicopter Experimental Squadron at Quantico. As Colonel Robert D. Heinl observed, "It was 1933 all over again."

The Marine Corps had reason to hurry. Roosevelt, during his four terms as president, had always championed the cause of the Navy and the Fleet Marine Force. Truman's long association with the Army included an inexplicable enmity toward admirals. "When Roosevelt was here," Truman said of the White House, "this place was like a damned wardroom. As long as I am here, the admirals will never get in again." Nor did they.

COLLINS PLAN

When Secretary of the Navy James Forrestal presented the role of the postwar Marine Corps to Truman, he discovered that Army Chief of Staff General Eisenhower and General Carl W. Spaatz, who had succeeded in separating the Air Force from the Army, had already bent the president's ear on the so-called "Collins Plan." Lieutenant General J. Lawton Collins, working on behalf of General George C. Marshall, had produced a proposal so radical that it meant the end of the Navy establishment and especially the Marine Corps. Behind the proposal was General Spaatz's assertion that all future wars would be mainly atomic and dependent upon air power.

The "Collins Plan" concluded that Marines would never again be required except "in minor shore combat operations in which the Navy alone is interested." The plan proposed that the Marine Corps should be limited to no more than 60,000 men, with no expansion during war, and that the Marine Corps Reserve should be immediately abolished. As for Marine aviation, the aircraft and pilots should be assimilated into the Air Force or the Navy. As for amphibious operations, the Marines would no longer be fighters and act only as landing craft crews and beach labor parties.

Collins also advocated the establishment of a new secretary of defense who would be empowered to determine the roles and missions of the armed services without congressional oversight. Such an arrangement would remove the Marine Corps from the protection of Congress and enable Collins, a staff officer to Marshall, to elevate the whims of the War Department over all other branches of the service and, in particular, the Navy.

Forrestal, who had stood on the bloody sands of Iwo Jima in 1945 and said that the Marine Corps had earned its future for the next 500 years, now had a dilemma. On 6 May 1946, while the secretary searched for answers, Commandant Vandegrift took hold of the issue and addressed the Senate Naval Affairs Committee. The blue-eyed, physically fit, fifty-nine-year-old veteran spoke softly and firmly. Members of the committee fixed their eyes on the general's Medal of Honor ribbon as he spoke, listening as he convinced each of them, one by one, that "the War Department is determined to reduce the Marine

▶ **1947**

26 JULY: President Harry Truman signs the National Security Act organizing the armed forces under the secretary of defense and creating a separate Air force.

23 SEPTEMBER: James V. Forrestal becomes the first secretary of defense.

1948

1 JANUARY: Major General Clifton B. Cates becomes the 19th Commandant of the Marine Corps.

23 MAY: During exercises at New River, N.C., Marines come ashore by helicopter for the first time.

10 NOVEMBER: The first eight enlisted women are sworn in as Marines.

1949

18 NOVEMBER: The commandant orders that all male Marines, regardless of race, be assigned to vacancies in any unit.

Above right: *On 3 October 1950, Lt. Col. Ray Murray, commanding the 5th Marines, shows a captured Korean "duck gun" to General Clifford B. Cates, the Marine Corps commandant. Koreans used the ancient nine-foot shotgun to illegally bag large numbers of wildfowl.*

Corps to a position of studied military ineffectiveness – and the passage of the unification legislation as now framed will in all probability spell extinction for the Marine Corps." He did not ask any concessions, nor did he come "on bended knee," but he convinced the committee that the Marine Corps had "earned the right to have its future decided by the legislative body that created it" in 1798.

The Senate tabled the legislation and temporarily preserved the Marine Corps, but Truman intended to continue the fight. When General Merritt "Red Mike" Edson, another Medal of Honor winner, got wind of the plot, he resigned from the Corps. As a civilian now free from military shackles, he headed straight for Capitol Hill. With the same tenacity that he had held "Bloody Ridge" on Guadalcanal, Edson shattered Tru-

GENERAL CLIFTON BLEDSOE CATES

Fifty-four-year-old Clifton Cates fought in both world wars, distinguishing himself at Belleau Wood, Saint-Miheil, and Meuse-Argonne (where he was gassed and wounded) in 1918, and at Guadalcanal, Saipan-Tinian, and Iwo Jima in World War II. Before becoming 19th Commandant of the Marine Corps on 1 January 1948, he fought another battle, this one before the House Armed Services Committee during the writing of the National Security Act of 1947. His testimony contributed to the defeat of the "Collins" clique and led to a number of amendments that enabled the Marine Corps to remain a force-in-readiness.

In 1948 the Marine Corps still had the same old enemies – the Army, Air Force, and President Truman. Perhaps speaking out of context, Army Brigadier General Frank Armstrong best voiced the adversarial attitude with a laconic comment:

"As for the Marines, you know what Marines are. They are a small, fouled-up Army talking Navy lingo. We are going to put those Marines in the regular Army and make efficient soldiers out of them." (General Armstrong to the *Saturday Evening Post,* 5 February 1949.)

General Cates replied to the attack with more dignity than it deserved.

"My biggest worry is to keep the Marine Corps alive. ...There are lots of people here in Washington who want to prevent that, who want to reduce us to the status of Navy policemen or get rid of us entirely." (General Cates to the *Saturday Evening Post*, 20 February 1949.)

By 1949 the National Security Act had reached its second year of life, but enemies of the Marine Corps persisted in tearing at the establishment. Cates continued to lobby friends in Congress on one hand while simultaneously crafting a new concept for the Marine Corps on the other – amphibious assault landings using helicopters as landing craft and aircraft carriers as transports. The landing-from-the-air concept envisaged an assault without concern for reefs, beaches, beach defenses, tides, or surf; one free of the tactical problems associated with airborne landings and shore defenses against landing craft. At the time, Cates had only five two-passenger helicopters, no aircraft carriers with which to

experiment, and many doubters in the Navy.

Ignoring the opposition, Cates formed squadron HMX-1 from his five helicopters, added "Employment of Helicopters" to the Marine Corps Schools' curriculum, and borrowed an old jeep carrier (the USS *Palau)* from the Navy as a practice vessel.

Encouraged by Cates, manufacturers of helicopters took interest in the Marine program. In late 1948 new machines began to appear, among them the Piasecki HRP-1 "Flying Banana," the world's largest wingless aircraft.

While Cates moved with speed to change the complexion of the Marine Corps, the new secretary of defense, Louis A. Johnson, attempted to undo everything Forrestal accomplished while serving as the first secretary of defense. Johnson did not have the authority to eliminate the Corps, but he did have the authority to reduce its size, so he did. Cates fought back, and was still warring with Johnson when the Korean War began.

Cates and Truman never got along. Just before the Inchon landing Congress thought that a Marine should be given a seat on the Joint Chiefs of Staff. Truman retorted, "For your information the Marine Corps is the Navy's police force and as long as I am President that is what it will remain." After being thrashed by the press, Truman apologized to Cates for the outburst. Cates accepted the apology with grace, but turned the picture of Truman in his office to the wall and left it that way.

man's proposed legislation piece by piece, taking his arguments to the public and rallying Congress. Instead of ushering the Marine Corps to an ignominious end, Congress passed the National Security Act of 1947, reaffirming a Fleet Marine Force of ground, air, and a Marine Reserve. The act also preserved the Corps' mission of seizure and defense of advanced bases and made the Corps the primary agency for developing amphibious warfare doctrine.

Edson, who could very well have been the next commandant, sacrificed a brilliant career to save the Corps. In doing so he paved the way for Lieutenant General Clifton B. Cates to become commandant after Vandegrift retired on 31 December 1947.

While Truman and his secretary of defense conspired to merge the Corps into other services or eliminate it altogether, Cates kept the Fleet Marine Force busy around the world. Every five months he rotated a new reinforced infantry battalion and one or two fighter squadrons with the U.S. Sixth Fleet in the Mediterranean. The five-month regimen included vigorous training with amphibious landings on friendly shores supported by air cover. Training also included behavior ashore, where Marines earned respect as ambassadors of good will in North Africa, Spain, Italy, and France. When a sniper killed the U.S. Counsel General in Jerusalem, Marines from the Sixth Fleet landed immediately to protect the life of his successor and to maintain an armed presence.

In 1949 the 1st Marine Division began cold weather training in Alaska and on the snow-capped mountains of California's Sierras Fighting in the tropics had ended, and Cates believed that Marines needed to be hardened to the harsher climes. In light of Soviet Russia's attempt to dominate the world, the training seemed to be well timed.

Cates spread the training around the Corps, which by mid-1950 had diminished to 78,000 men. He still had 90,000 reservists, the majority being combat veterans from World War II. Every year they received two weeks of training in the field.

MARINE REDUCTIONS

On the eve of the Korean War, the Marine Corps consisted of one combat division and one aircraft wing on each coast. Both were under-strength. General Omar Bradley, the new Chairman of the JCS, persisted in Truman's efforts to emasculate the Marine Corps. On 24 June 1950, when Secretary of State Dean Acheson informed Truman that the North Korean People's Army (NKPA) were poised to invade South Korea, the average Marine regiment had been shrunk to battalion-size, and the average company consisted of barely enough men to fill two platoons.

On the morning of 25 June 1950 six NKPA divisions and three Border Constabulary brigades, supported by 100 Russian-made T-34 tanks and flocks of Yak fighters, advanced across the 38th Parallel and streamed southward. After waiting

Left: *Korean War era Marine clothing included (far left) M1944 pattern utility coat (shirt), with rank stenciled in black, as was common practice then; (center) 1950 fur cap; (left) 1947 Navy deck parka. By winter in Korea the Corps, without cold weather gear, had to fill this void; this parka, originally designed for standing watch aboard ship, was quickly adapted for use by the 1st Marine Division around the Chosin Reservoir.*

▶ **1950**

25 JUNE: The Korean War begins when six North Korean infantry divisions invade the Republic of Korea.

27 JUNE: President Truman authorizes General Douglas MacArthur to use American air and naval forces to support South Korea.

30 JUNE: President Truman authorizes the use of ground forces in Korea.

2 AUGUST: The 1st Provisional Marine Brigade, under Brigadier General Edward A. Craig, lands at Pusan.

7 AUGUST: Marines go into action, attacking Chinju from the southwestern corner of Pusan's perimeter.

Below: On 3 September 1950 the 5th Marines, 1st Marine Division, came to the rescue and closed in on Yongsan, a key point across the Naktong River. The North Koreans attacked the area in an attempt to break through the perimeter and assault the flanks of the joint forces defending Pusan.

two days to study the "Korean Incident," Truman authorized General MacArthur, Commander-in-Chief, Far East, to use American air and naval forces to support South Korea, but he waited until the NKPA had captured Seoul before authorizing MacArthur to use ground forces. On 30 June the so-called "incident" became the Korean War and MacArthur began airlifting to Pusan the only force in Japan, flabby occupation soldiers of the 24th Army Division. A day later the main body began embarking on transports. By then the NKPA blitzkrieg had gathered headway, rolling over ineffectual South Korean resistance. The only encumbrances blocking the NKPA's rapid advance were thousands of refugees clogging roads to the south.

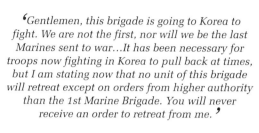

> '*Gentlemen, this brigade is going to Korea to fight. We are not the first, nor will we be the last Marines sent to war…It has been necessary for troops now fighting in Korea to pull back at times, but I am stating now that no unit of this brigade will retreat except on orders from higher authority than the 1st Marine Brigade. You will never receive an order to retreat from me.*'
>
> GENERAL CRAIG QUOTED IN *THE NEW BREED*, BY ANDREW GEER.

During the six days that Truman temporized over the Korean incident, General Cates, on his own responsibility, ordered the 1st Marine Division to get ready for war. Behind the scenes the JCS thought of the Korean conflict as a "police action," something that could be settled without Marines. While the JCS plotted, Cates went to Admiral Forrest Sherman, Chief of Naval Operations, and offered a full brigade on short notice. Sherman asked, "How soon?" Cates replied, "Two weeks." Sherman sent a private message to MacArthur asking if the general wanted a Marine brigade complete with air. In addition to the 24th Army Division, MacArthur still had the 7th and 25th Infantry Divisions in Japan, but they were under-strength, poorly equipped, and indolent from lack of training. On 2 July he radioed the JCS

asking that the Marines be sent with haste. When the JCS convened to consider MacArthur's request, Cates showed up uninvited. Trapped by their own ill-conceived policies, the JCS approved Cates's offer because the Marines represented, as they had for 171 years, the only force in America ready to fight.

Five days later Brigadier General Edward A. Craig's 1st Provisional Brigade, with major elements built around the 5th Marines (Lieutenant Colonel Raymond L. Murray) and Marine Aircraft Group 33 (Brigadier General Thomas J. Cushman), began forming at Camp Pendleton, California. On 12 July the 6,534-man brigade sailed from San Diego. General Cates gave them a send-off, saying, "You boys clean this up in a couple of months, or I'll be over to see you."

While the 1st Provisional Brigade headed for Pusan, General Shepherd flew to Tokyo and met privately with MacArthur. During the conversation MacArthur rose, walked to a large map of Korea, and poked the stem of his pipe at the city of Inchon. "If I only had the 1st Marine Division under my command," he said, "I would land them here and cut the North Korean armies attacking the Pusan perimeter from their logistic support and cause their withdrawal and elimination." Shepherd agreed to have the 1st Division ready by 1 September if MacArthur would ask for it from the JCS. Sherman drew up the request on behalf of MacArthur and the general forwarded it to the JCS. With guarded reluctance, the JCS

approved the request, and Cates went to work mobilizing the 1st Marine Division.

Meanwhile, on 3 August, the 1st Provisional Brigade arrived at Pusan. General Craig found the perimeter around the city in shambles and backstopped by Army and ROK (Republic of Korea) units. Pressure from NKPA divisions stretched in an arc from the port of Chindong-ni in the south to the port of Pohang in the east. Within hours after the brigade landed, Marine F4U Corsairs from VMF-214 (the old "Black Sheep Squadron") flew off the USS *Sicily* and scored the first Yak kills over Inchon Craig looked at the situation on the ground, found many gaps along the Pusan perimeter, and sent his leathernecks to fill them.

PUSAN

Marines defending the Pusan perimeter found more than holes to plug. On 7 August the first major engagement occurred at Chindong-ni, fifty miles west of Pusan. After Marines relieved the 27th Army Regiment, the North Koreans launched a pre-dawn assault against positions held by a battalion of the 5th Marines. After stopping the enemy attack in its tracks, Marines launched a counterattack and in temperatures exceeding 110 degrees captured the NKPA hill position. Two days later the entire brigade engaged in a counteroffensive. Supported by Corsairs from the jeep carrier *Badoeng Strait*, Marines drove through the 6th North Korean Division and advanced on the enemy's headquarters thirty miles beyond the perimeter at Chinju.

On 12 August, as the brigade pushed toward Sachon, the 3rd Battalion, 5th Marines, received an urgent call to plug a gap twenty-five miles away where 2,000 North Koreans had infiltrated through the perimeter and overrun two Army artillery battalions. Helicopters delivered the 3rd Battalion to the site, and the infiltration ended in disaster for the Communists. During six days of fighting, two Marine fighter bomber squadrons, night fighter squadron VMF(N)-513 from Japan, and observation squadron VMO-6, using helicopters and light planes, joined ground elements and provided direct support. Before Marines could rid the area of the enemy, the 4th NKPA Division crossed the Naktong River thirty miles to the north, pushed back the 24th Army Division, and compelled Craig to plug another hole.

During a series of fiercely fought engagements, Marines blasted T-34 tanks with rockets, fought off repeated infiltrations, recovered the dominating terrain of "No Name Ridge," and on 18 August began smashing one NKPA position after the other. The enemy, completely routed, streamed back across the river to regroup. Every plane in MAG-33 and VFM(N)-513 hammered the river crossings. The rapid destruction of T-34 tanks so impressed General Collins, the Army Chief of Staff and author of the infamous "Collins Plan," that he sought and obtained a letter from General Craig explaining how the Marines did it.

MacArthur wanted Craig's brigade for the Inchon invasion, and on 5 September the 2nd Army Division relieved the Marines. The 1st Provisional Brigade filed back to Pusan, their heads held high. At a cost of 902 casualties, including 172 killed, they had marched 380 miles in 38 days and fought three major engagements without one Leatherneck becoming a prisoner. Marine Air Group-33 flew 1,500 sorties, 1,000 of them in close-air support over ground units, and for the first time in war, Marine pilots flew helicopters in combat.

'The Marines on our left were a sight to behold. Not only was their equipment superior to ours, but they had squadrons of air in direct support. They used it like artillery. . . . General, we just have to have air support like that or we might as well disband and join the Marines.'

COLONEL PAUL FREEMAN TO GENERAL RIDGEWAY, QUOTED IN *THE NEW BREED*, BY ANDREW GEER.

Above: *Tanks of the 5th Marines, after aiding in operations to push the NKPA back across the Naktong River, roll into the forward supply base to refuel and rearm, 3 September 1950. Asked about conditions on the front line, tank crews reported "good hunting" and that they were eager to resume the attack.*

Left: *Helicopters from VMO-6 made their first appearance during the Korean War. First used as observation aircraft, they quickly demonstrated their versatility by removing the wounded or inserting and extracting observation and combat troops into key areas behind enemy lines. As the war progressed larger helicopters began replacing the original "Grasshoppers."*

15 August: Marines counterattack and banish the 4th NKPA Division on the Naktong River.

15 September: The 1st Marine Division under Major General Oliver P. Smith spearheads the attack on Inchon.

On 12 September, after returning to the Pusan staging area, the 1st Provisional Brigade folded into the recently arrived 1st Marine Division. Craig's tactics added a new chapter to modern warfare. His brigade marked the first time that air and ground elements, task-organized under a single commander, had engaged in combat.

Mobilizing the 1st Marine Division for an immediate assault on Inchon became a critical priority for General Cates. Slashed to the bone by the president and his secretary of defense, what little remained were reservists still ready to fight the moment called. The JCS exacerbated the problem. MacArthur made three requests to the JCS before they released the 1st Marine Division because, among other reasons, they did not believe the division could be deployed before November or December. Cates put them straight when he guaranteed that the division would be ready for the Inchon assault.

Cates could not make good on his promise without mobilizing the entire Marine Reserve, which he promptly did with Truman's unenthusiastic blessing. To assemble men needed to build the 1st Division, Cates borrowed 6,800 troops from the 2nd Division on the east coast and moved them to Pendleton. He pulled the 3rd Battalion, 6th Marines, from the Mediterranean 6th Fleet and sent them through the Suez to Japan. He drew the balance of his force – some 4,500 men – from posts around the world. By adding Craig's brigade, already in Korea, Cates assembled in fifty-three days some 24,000 Marines for a reinforced war-strength division and 4,000 more to fill the air wing. As an unexpected augmentation, the 1st Marine Division picked up a South Korean infantry regiment. Guided by Marine advisers, this rugged unit eventually became the 1st Korean Marine Corps Regiment.

On 22 August Major General Oliver P. Smith, commanding the division, arrived in Tokyo with his planning staff. Neither he nor his planners knew that MacArthur had already established 15 September as D-Day. To float an amphibious force up to Inchon required a 33-foot tide, which occurred only on 15 September and again in mid-October. Smith did not believe he could plan the assault in the remaining twenty-four days, but MacArthur gave him no leeway. He expected Smith's Marines to form the spearhead of the X Corps' assault with the Army's 7th Infantry Division in reserve.

> '*The Pusan perimeter is like a weakened dike, and we will be used to plug holes in it as they open. It will be costly fighting against a numerically superior enemy. Marines have never lost a battle. This brigade will not be the first to establish such a precedent.*'
>
> General Craig quoted in *The New Breed*, by Andrew Geer.

MacArthur's Plan

Neither Smith nor the JCS agreed with MacArthur's Inchon-Seoul operation. Even the admirals had their doubts. But Smith had no choice in the matter, and the JCS simply voiced their objections and let MacArthur have his way.

Right: *Soon after the Korean War began, North Korean artillery struck and demolished a large military transport on the ground at Kimpo Airport, near Inchon. On 17 September 1950 the 5th Marines captured the airport and found the old transport still there and still a wreck, but at least she was back in friendly hands.*

MacArthur's plan involved four steps: an amphibious landing at Inchon; the capture of Seoul (20 miles to the east); cutting off North Korean supply lines; and then crushing the NKPA in a vise between the Eighth Army from Pusan (150 miles to the south) and the X Corps from Seoul. Opposition from the JCS came from Bradley and Collins, both of whom scorned amphibious operations. MacArthur believed in them, provided that Marines led the way.

> '*We shall land at Inchon and I shall crush them.*'
>
> GENERAL MACARTHUR TO HIS PLANNERS.

An unnecessarily complicated chain of command threatened to muddle the plan of assault. The vital working parts of the mission involved Smith's landing force (1st Marine Division), and Rear Admiral James H. Doyle's attack force (Amphibious Group One). Superimposed on this team was the X Corps commander, Major General Edward M. Almond,

> '*Make up a list of amphibious don'ts, and you have an exact description of the Inchon operation.*'
>
> VICE ADMIRAL ARTHUR D. STRUBLE QUOTED IN *THE SEA WAR IN KOREA*, BY CAGLE AND MANSON.

MacArthur's Chief of Staff and an irritating and conservative Army officer who objected to assaulting a defended city against uncertain odds and unpredictable tides. As events later proved, MacArthur would have served his cause better by leaving Almond on staff and giving the command to Smith, but putting a Marine general in charge of an Army corps would have upset Bradley's JCS.

There were better places along the Korean coast to land an amphibious force than Inchon, but none so close to the capital of Seoul and the important Kimpo airfield. Getting into Inchon presented enormous problems beyond the ticklish 8-knot tidal currents. The seaward approaches contained bottomless mud flats swept by strong currents and interposed by hazardous islets. The shores of the granite-walled city contained no beaches, adding to the difficulties of an amphibious landing. The fortified and cave-pocked island of Wolmi-do, connected by a 600-yard causeway to Inchon, defended the city and its main harbor. For the amphibious force to get up Flying Fish Channel on the evening tide, the 3rd Battalion, 5th Marines, had to go ashore and neutralize Wolmi-do on the morning tide — the window of opportunity being from 7:00 a.m. to 5:15 p.m.

More complications arose. Thirty of the 47 LSTs required for the landing had to be borrowed back from the Japanese, who used them as ferries. The 7th Marines, the division's third infantry regiment, had not arrived, nor would it until six days after D-Day. While the enemy had only 2,200 troops at Inchon, more than 21,000 more held the Seoul-Kimpo area. To succeed, the reduced 1st Marine Division had to act fast and with precision.

Despite General Almond's grousing, MacArthur maintained his timetable. Not even a typhoon that interceded on the voyage to Korea's west coast changed his mind. By a stroke of luck and

Left: *A patrol of leathernecks from the 3rd Battalion, 5th Marines, step with care through the maze of rubble as they complete mopping-up operations on the peninsula of Wolmi-do, on 15 September 1950. The capture of Wolmi-do opened the way for General MacArthur's landing at Inchon.*

17 SEPTEMBER: The 3rd Battalion, 5th Marines, capture Kimpo Airfield.

22 SEPTEMBER: Colonel Lewis B. Puller's 1st Marines capture Yongdungpo.

25 SEPTEMBER: The 1st Marine Division enters Seoul.

THE INCHON ASSAULT

At 5:45 a.m. on 15 September 1950, the morning bombardment of Wolmi-do lifted. Fifteen minutes later landing craft carrying the 3rd Battalion, 5th Marines, commanded by Lieutenant Colonel Robert D. Taplett, headed ashore. Marine squadrons from VMF-214 and VMF-323 – old reliable Corsair squadrons from Pusan – swarmed overhead and provided air cover. At 6:15 the air attacks ended, giving way to a blanket salvo of 5-inch rockets from three rocket boats. Eighteen minutes later the first wave of the battalion went ashore on Wolmi-do and eliminated the remaining enemy positions. At 7:00 a.m. Taplett broke out the colors on Radio Hill. MacArthur, watching from the deck of *McKinley*, turned to his fellow VIKs and said, "That's it. Let's get a cup of coffee." By noon the 3rd Battalion had mopped up the island and knocked out enemy positions

> '*The Navy and Marines have never shone more brightly than this morning.*'
>
> GENERAL MACARTHUR, 15 SEPTEMBER 1950.

flanking the main landing area at Inchon.

Throughout the day naval fire and air strikes continued to pound Inchon. At 5:30 p.m. elements of the 1st and 2nd Battalions, 5th Marines, dragged ladders through the mud, reached shore, and began scaling the high seawall surrounding Inchon. Once inside the city the regiment advanced against light resistance, moving to the south and southeast. On the far right flank and covered by another naval bombardment, Colonel Lewis B. Puller's 1st Marines landed south of Inchon, swinging north to the highway and rail line to cut off enemy reinforcements coming from Seoul.

By the afternoon of 16 September, the assault phase of the operation had ended in a smashing success. The Marines got off cheaply with 22 killed and 174 wounded.

General Smith left the Korean Marines behind to mop up the city and pushed on to Seoul. On 17 September the 3rd Battalion of Colonel Murray's 5th Marines captured Kimpo Airfield, midway between Inchon and Seoul. By nightfall the first Marine helicopter landed with General Sherman and Colonel Krulak. Two days later MAG-33 landed at Kimpo and began flying shore-based air support for the X Corps.

Puller's 1st Marines drove towards Yongdung-po along the Inchon-Seoul highway and fought off the first of many counterattacks. On 21 September he found the enemy massed with Russian tanks for a stand on the city's outskirts. While Company A worked around the flanks of the enemy, the rest of the regiment blasted the tanks, routed the force in front, and walked into Yongdung-po in the morning.

The 1st and 5th Marines crossed the Han River and, joined by the 7th Marines and the 7th Army Division, pushed into Seoul. After a pitched house-to-house battle that lasted three days, the X Corps mopped up the last resistance in Seoul and secured the city.

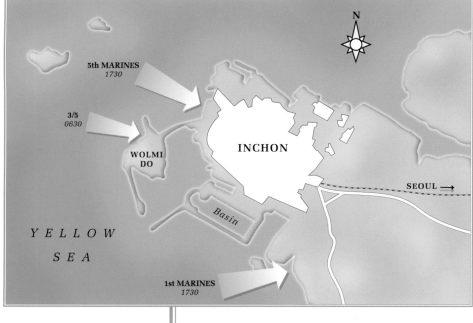

Above: *The attack on Inchon, fraught with many potential problems, was led by the 1st and 5th Marines, who accomplished every objective planned for the first day.*

Right: *Leathernecks from the 5th Marines bring up amphibian trucks and tanks to cross the Han River for the attack on Seoul, 18 September 1950.*

good sailing, all the vessels hobbled into the assembly area off Inchon. A five-day bombardment conducted by carrier-based planes and ships of the Seventh Fleet blasted the harbor and Inchon's waterfront with rockets and napalm before Amphibious Group One pulled into view. Before daylight on 15 September, MacArthur and his staff gathered on the deck of the USS *Mount McKinley* to watch the Marines assault Wolmi-do. Sailors on board the battleship soon dubbed this star-studded galaxy of admirals and generals "VIKs," short for Very Important Kibitzers.

INCHON SUCCESS

MacArthur's Inchon assault, which many military experts predicted would end in disaster, developed into a brilliant success that probably surpassed the general's own expectations. On September 29, with himself as the centerpiece, MacArthur passed out invitations to the press to photograph the return of South Korean President Syngman Rhee to his capital. To a background of artillery fire in the distance, an elaborate ceremony took place at the Government Palace. General Cates missed the affair. Four days later he arrived, just in time to watch the 7th Marines sweep north through abandoned enemy ammunition dumps and artillery to capture Uijongbu.

The Eighth Army broke through the Pusan perimeter, closed the vise on the enemy, and together with the X Corps finished the emasculation of the North Korean Army. During the campaign the Marines alone captured 4,700 prisoners, inflicted 13,700 casualties, and destroyed 44 Russian tanks without losing one of their own. While supporting ground troops, MAW-1 flew 2,500 sorties. During the campaign, Marine casualties numbered 2,774, including 457 killed. Two Marines became prisoners of war, one flyer and one rifleman. The latter won the ignominy of being the first Marine captured in the entire history of the 1st Marine Division.

Three months and four days after the NKPA invaded South Korea, the broken, beaten, and war-weary survivors fled back to North Korea. MacArthur obtained permission to conduct military operations above the 38th Parallel, and he assigned the capture of Pyongyang, the North Korean capital, to the Eighth Army. To annihilate the NKPA in another pincers, MacArthur conceived a new amphibious landing on the east coast. This time Marines would land at Wonsan, drive inland, capture NKPA troops fleeing north, and link up with the Eighth Army around Pyongyang. The poorly planned Wonsan affair marked the beginning of a series of unexpected misfortunes for the jubilant general.

On 12 October the 1st Marine Division sailed out of Inchon for Wonsan. To avoid an expertly laid Russian minefield in Wonsan's harbor, the

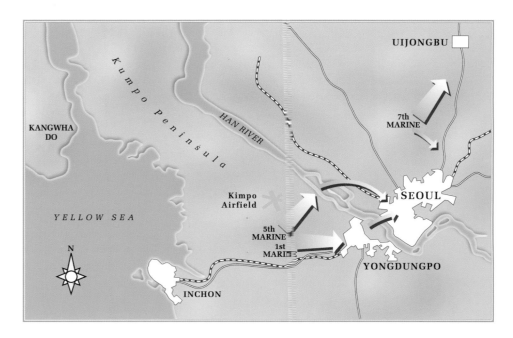

leathernecks landed instead on the Kalma-Pando Peninsula. ROK troops overran Wonsan and pushed to the north. On 20 October Pyongyang fell, producing an ebullient feeling among U.S. forces that the Yalu River – the border between North Korea and Manchuria – would be reached in a few weeks and everyone would be home for Christmas.

With the Eighth Army advancing in western Korea and ROK forces gaining ground in the east, MacArthur revamped his plans for the X Corps. He divided the Corps for a three-pronged advance to the Yalu River, placing the ROK I Corps on the right flank, the 7th U.S. Infantry Division in the center, and the 1st Marine Division on the left flank. The 3rd U.S. Infantry Division formed the reserve.

The 1st Marine Division felt a special urgency to get to the Yalu and secure the position. The first leg of their route led to Hamhung, seventy miles north of Wonsan, where they established a new base. Their sector of responsibility stretched 200 miles, doglegging to the northwest through a corridor forty miles wide, enough terrain to have taxed the resources of the entire corps. The mar-

Left: As the 1st and 5th Marines prepare to attack Seoul and Yongdungpo, they are joined by the 7th Marines, which had been held in reserve. The 7th Marines were to cut escape routes out of Seoul and attack a major North Korean supply center at Uijongbu.

Below: The 1st Marine Division's surprise attack on Inchon, followed by the assault on Seoul, so shocked the North Koreans that by 17 September Marine infantrymen could stride boldly down the main highway, passing burning Russian tanks with blown hatchways scattered here and there all along the roadway.

Above: *On 29 November 1950, after hurling back three Chinese divisions at the Chosin Reservoir, the 5th and 7th Marines were astonished when Army Major General Edward Almond ordered their retreat from Yudam-ni. When Almond then opposed a fighting withdrawal, Major General Oliver P. Smith balked and said his Marines would fight their way back. The entire 1st Marine Division became involved, fighting and defeating hordes of Chinese all the way back to the rail center at Hamhung.*

row road above Hamhung to the Chosin Reservoir and beyond wound through wild mountain passes having ridges 4,000 feet high and cliff edges toppling into deep valleys. With winter fast approaching, the first sub-zero temperatures struck the warm-weather Marines with bone-chilling winds and blowing snow.

General Smith did not like General Almond's plan of attack but failed to obtain any concessions. Smith worried about his division's scattered dispersal and the eighty-mile mountainous gap that separated the X Corps' left flank from the Eighth Army. Another annoying piece of intelligence came from a reconnaissance patrol. On 2 November the detail captured a Chinese prisoner from the 124th Division, Communist Chinese Forces (CCF). The prisoner confirmed rumors that three CCF divisions were moving into North Korean from Manchuria and that the 124th had already reached the Chosin Reservoir area. Smith hedged his concerns by stockpiling arms, ammunition, fuel, and supplies along the road to the reservoir, tucking them into gorges and gullies along the way.

On 2 November the 7th Marines, commanded by Colonel Homer L. Litzenberg, passed through ROK troops posted at Hamhung and struck out for the Yalu. Marine Corsairs covered the advance, looking for signs of the enemy. As Marines bedded down for the night, bugles suddenly wailed like coyotes, whistles blew, and green pyrotechnics rose and fell as three regiments from the 124th CCF attacked. The 7th Marines beat back the attack, and after a sleepless night continued

the march to the north. During a five-day battle and with weather continuing to worsen, Litzenberg's force reached Chinhung-ni and moved up to Koto-ri. With help from Corsairs, the 7th Marines knocked out Russian T-34 tanks and virtually destroyed the Chinese division as an organic unit.

CHINESE ATTACK

By 17 November the 7th Marines reached Hagaru, located at the lower end of the Chosin Reservoir. There they waited while General Smith attempted to close up the division. Halting for any reason was not in tune with MacArthur's efforts to get the boys home for Christmas. He had been warned not to penetrate to the Manchurian border for fear of inviting attacks from the Communist Chinese, who did not want American forces threatening their borders. MacArthur ignored the warning and bombed the Yalu bridges. On 21 November the 7th Army Infantry Division reached the Manchurian border at Hyesanjin. Four days later 300,000 CCF regulars forded the Yalu in the west and struck the Eighth Army. Another 400,000 Chinese soon followed. By then, elements of the 1st Marine Division had moved up to Yudam-ni, west of the reservoir.

On the night of 27 November, with the mercury falling to minus 20 and the wind howling, elements from three Chinese divisions under the command of General Shih-lun Sung struck the main body of the 1st Marine Division at Yudam-ni. Sung intended to isolate the main body from the 1st Marine Regiment, commanded by Brigadier General Puller, and Smith's headquarters company at Hagaru. While the Eighth Army in the west began a mass retreat back to Seoul, Marines held their positions against attacks from eight CCF divisions.

On 29 November, X Corps commander General Almond ordered the 1st Marine Division to fall back to Hamhung near the Sea of Japan. In addition to the 5th and 7th Marines on the west side of the reservoir, Smith also had units of the 1st Marine Regiment and the U.S. 7th Infantry Division under attack on the eastern side the reser-

voir. Instead of imitating the Eighth Army's panicked flight, Smith held his position at Hagaru and ordered his far-flung elements to execute a fighting retreat. While the 79th and 89th CCF Divisions furiously attacked Marine positions at Yudam-ni, the 59th CCF Division attempted to cut and hold a fourteen-mile section of road leading back to Hagaru, thereby blocking Smith's withdrawal at the treacherous Toktong Pass. With the Marine main force under siege, the 58th CCF Division attacked Hagaru, its fuel dumps and nearly completed air strip, and opened a gap in the Marine perimeter about four miles wide.

On 30 November General Almond flew into Hagaru by helicopter for a conference with Gen-

▶ **26 OCTOBER:** The 1st Marine Division lands unopposed at Wonsan.

2-7 NOVEMBER: The 7th Marines, spearheading the 1st Marine Division's advance to the Yalu, shatters the 124th CCF Division.

13 NOVEMBER: The 7th Marines reach Hagaru-ri at the Chosin Reservoir.

23 NOVEMBER: The 7th Marines capture Yudam-ni.

27-28 NOVEMBER: Eight Chinese divisions attack the 1st Marine Division at the Chosin Reservoir.

3 DECEMBER: The 1st Marine Division completes its withdrawal from Yudam-ni to Hagaru-ri.

Below: *On 1 December 1950, midway through the fighting withdrawal from the Chosin Reservoir, exhausted leathernecks from the 1st Marine Division catch a few winks wherever they can, even though the winter temperature dropped at times to 20 degrees below zero and Chinese snipers harassed the column at every bend in the road.*

"ATTACKING IN A DIFFERENT DIRECTION"

On 29 November Chinese Communist Forces completely encircled the 1st Marine Division at the Chosin Reservoir. Scattered Marine units in reserve moved up the Main Supply Line while two regiments and the three battalions at Yudam-ni began fighting their way back to Hagaru. Though General Almond disagreed with the Marines' fighting withdrawal, he nonetheless transferred the isolated 7th Army Infantry Division to Smith as the only possible means of rescuing it. Smith sent Puller's 1st Marines to open the road from Hagaru to Koto-ri, which they did with alacrity and reinforced the battalion holding the shaken perimeter. At nightfall on 3 December, after a five-day battle, the 5th and 7th Marines stumbled into Hagaru singing "The Marines Hymn." They brought all their weapons and serviceable equipment and 1,500 wounded. Smith waited at Hagaru for three days, enabling Marine R4Ds and Air Force C-47s to fly in and evacuate more than 3,100 Marines and 1,100 soldiers.

On 6 December, with his mixed force of Marines and Army troops now concentrated at Hagaru, Smith moved south toward Koto-ri. His force fought four Chinese divisions along the torturous Main Supply Line – a single narrow road that stretched for fifty-six miles back to Hamhung. To keep the enemy off the road, Marines detonated and plugged passes in the rear as they fought off attacks on their flanks. Two days later, with close-air support provided by land- and carrier-based aircraft, Smith's force of 14,000 men moved into Koto-ri having suffered only 100 dead, 500 wounded, and seven missing. With the first leg of "attacking in the opposite direction" accomplished, the Marines now faced the daunting task of fighting through Funchilin Pass to Chinhung-ni.

As expected, the Chinese reserved their main effort for the ten-mile frozen corridor through Funchilin Pass. Behind one hairpin bend at the edge of a hill the Chinese blew up a narrow concrete bridge. To save his equipment and tanks, Smith requested that a 16-ton steel bridge be airdropped in pieces. The 1st Battalion, 1st Marines, secured the hill and,

from an emergency airstrip laid down at Koto-ri, aircraft carried steel bridge sections aloft and dropped them on the road. Under constant enemy fire, engineers assembled the bridge in three hours.

Fierce fighting continued all along the road to Chunhung-ni, where Marines were joined by reinforcements that had fought their way up from Hamhung to clear the route. On 11 December Smith's exhausted but jubilant units marched into the Hamhung sector. Painted on the side of a tank rumbling by were the words, "Only Fourteen More Shooting Days Until Xmas."

On the way to Hamhung, Smith's units fought fourteen divisions from four CCF Army groups and inflicted on the enemy an estimated 38,000 casualties. Since landing at Wonsan the Marines had suffered 4,400 battle casualties, including 718 dead, 192 missing, and hundreds of cases of unattended frostbite. They left nothing behind but a battlefield strewn with Chinese corpses and useless equipment.

▶ **6-9 DECEMBER:** The 1st Marine Division breaks out from Hagaru-ri.

24 DECEMBER: The last Marines are evacuated from Hungnam.

1951

11 APRIL: President Truman relieves General MacArthur.

5 JUNE: The 1st Marine Air Wing begins operations in support of the Fifth Air Force.

Above right: *Marines probing the enemy's "Iron Triangle" hurry out of range of an enemy mortar attack and dash for cover after being surprised by the enemy, 16 April 1951.*

Below: *On 26 December 1950 a leatherneck in an F4U-5 Corsair flying close air support knocks out a Chinese Communist position on a hillside near Hagaru-ri.*

eral Smith. Almond took one look at the situation and ordered Smith to jettison or destroy all weapons and supplies and fall back immediately. Smith replied tersely that the 1st Marine Division would fights its way out as a unit and bring out its guns, its gear, and its wounded. Almond so much as said, "Impossible!" because word came that three new Chinese divisions were closing on Koto-ri and overrunning the Main Supply Line. Puller added his two cents, saying, "That simplifies our problem of finding these people and killing them." Almond departed in a state of exasperation, letting Smith have his way.

The epic battle fought by the Marines against Chinese troops on the road to Chunhung-ni was described by *Time Magazine* as "a battle unparalleled in U.S. military history" in an article that punctuated the difference between Marine Corps doctrine and that of the Army, which suffered a stunning and embarrassing reverse. On 10 December the Marines were still in fighting trim and represented the only American force north of the 38th Parallel. MacArthur ordered Smith to withdraw through Hungnam, and Rear Admiral Doyle's transports began embarking the first of 105,000 U.S. and ROK troops, 91,000 civilian refugees, and 350,000 tons of supplies and equipment saved by the Marines. The evacuation, covered by air and fire support, took two weeks. The Chinese watched but did not interfere. They were relieved to see the leathernecks go.

> '*We are not retreating. We are just attacking in a different direction.*'
>
> GENERAL SMITH, QUOTED IN *THE NEW BREED*, BY ANDREW GEER.

On 1 January 1951 Communist armies numbering 500,000 men launched a second offensive and three days later captured Seoul. By 15 January the CCF had pushed Allied forces fifty miles south of the 38th Parallel. During the retreat General Walton Walker, commanding Allied forces, lost his life in a road accident. His replacement, Lieutenant General Matthew B. Ridgeway, assumed control of all land operations under MacArthur.

After the evacuation of Hungnam, Ridgeway posted the 1st Marine Division as the Eighth Army's reserve, giving the Corps time to reorganize and replenish losses. With no more amphibious landings planned, Ridgeway incorporated Marine air units into the USAF. Like it or not, the Marines found themselves drawn into a war of attrition and shackled to the Army. On 10 January, after Chinese forces broke through the right flank of the 2nd Army Division and infiltrated the ROK III Corps, Marines rushed from their reserve position at Masan and stopped the Chinese in their tracks. Remnants from the beaten NKPA III Corps, which had flowed through the lines with the Chinese, began conducting guerilla raids. After stopping the Chinese, the Marines hunted out the guerrillas in "rice paddy patrols" and the eliminated the threat.

OPERATION RIPPER

Ridgeway vowed to get the demoralized Eighth Army back into the war and in February decided upon an offensive codenamed "Operation Killer." Public relations officials winced at the name, so Ridgeway changed it to "Operation Ripper." He chose the 1st Marine Division, now part of the IX Army Corps, for the main assault. On 21 February the division jumped off from positions in the very center of the U.N. line and into a region not unlike the French Argonne. Three days later Marines knocked the enemy off well-defended hills and rolled through the rubble of Hoensong with their tanks, driving the enemy off the high ground east of town. The division continued battling toward Chunchon, eight miles south of the 38th Parallel, and captured the important Chinese supply and communications center.

During the afternoon of 24 February the commander of IX Army Corps died of a heart attack. Ridgeway selected General Smith to command the corps until an Army general could be brought from the United States, and Brigadier General Puller became the new commander of the 1st Marine Division.

Ridgeway's U.N. counteroffensive, spearheaded by the Marines, recaptured Seoul on 14 March and by month's end had pushed the CCF back to the 38th Parallel. On 4 April the division recrossed the line and began probing the "Iron Triangle," a heavily fortified area between Chorwon, Kumhwa, and Pyongyang.

MacArthur now had a clear victory, and he wanted to fly reconnaissance missions over China and destroy the bridges across the Yalu River that the CCF used to bring in supplies and reinforcements. Restrictions placed upon him by the U.N. and Truman, who feared a full-scale war with China, made him furious. American bombers had flattened North Korea's industry. MacArthur now wanted to blockade Chinese ports and commence a strategic bombing campaign against Manchuria's industrial sites. He also saw an opportunity for returning Chiang Kai-

shek's Nationalist Government from Formosa to China, but Truman insisted that the war be limited to the Korean peninsula. Truman and his U.N. allies wanted to end the war by negotiation, and relations between MacArthur and Truman deteriorated to the point where the president removed his insubordinate commander and replaced him with General Ridgeway. On 14 April, Lieutenant General James A. Van Fleet arrived from the United States to command U.N. ground forces. One week later the Chinese launched their spring offensive.

Above: *During the spring offensive, leathernecks from the 5th Marine Regiment move through a war-torn village as they move with tanks into the enemy's Iron Triangle, 22 April 1951.*

Left: *As more of the fighting along the front degenerates into World War I style of trench warfare, leathernecks from the 1st Marine Division assault enemy positions in a landscape resembling "no man's land." Using mortars, grenades, and planted charges, they hold back the Chinese attack along their front, only to find that U.S. Army and ROK forces have fallen back, leaving the division's flanks exposed.*

▶ **20 JUNE:** The 1st Marine Division reaches the Punchbowl.

10 JULY: The first unsuccessful truce talks begin.

1952

1 JANUARY: Lieutenant General Lemuel C. Shepherd, Jr., becomes 20th Commandant of the Marine Corps.

28 JUNE: The Marine commandant is given a seat on the JCS.

12-22 JULY: Marine Major John Glenn, Jr., a future astronaut, destroys three Russian MiGs.

1953

11 JULY: Marine Major John F. Volk, flying an F-86 Sabre, shoots down his fifth and sixth MiG-15s.

Above right: On 20 October 1951 on the Korean eastern front, the Chinese shell the lines of the 1st Marine Division with white phosperous. A small piece of the substance can burn through the skin to the bone. This shell fortunately missed the Marines' machine gun position by a quarter of a mile.

Right: During the latter days of December 1951, Marine Sergeant Albert L. Ireland leads his squad back to the front lines in Korea after a patrol in frigid conditions. Following behind him along the snow-covered ridge are Pfc Linden L. Brown and Pfc Robert D. Glover, Jr.

Puller conducted his advance into the Iron Triangle with caution, buttoning-up the division for the expected counterstroke. Intelligence reported CCF forces at 700,000 with more coming. When the attack came on the night of 22 April, the Chinese caromed off the left flank of the 7th Marines, struck the adjacent 6th ROK Division, which had not buttoned-up, and shattered it. By morning the Chinese had opened a gap ten miles wide and ten miles deep, but Puller's Marines would not yield an inch. Smith ordered the Marines to pull back to the main line. Puller fought a vicious withdrawal, and by doing so, saved other elements of the IX Corps from destruction.

The CCF lost 70,000 casualties in the attack, but on 15 May they tried again, this time on the eastern side of the peninsula. The Eighth Army counterattacked and by the end of May had pushed the enemy out of South Korea. During the counterattack the 1st Marine Division and two ROK divisions advanced on the "Punchbowl," a volcanic crater east of Kumhwa and along Van Fleet's main line of defense. Marines began to work through a network of heavily wired, trenched, and mined defenses reminiscent of World War I. Puller did not know it at the time but the first ceasefire had been proposed and, from a tactical point of view, position became more important than maneuver.

Truce talks began on 10 July inside Communist lines and ended unsuccessfully in August, giving the CCF time to reform and replenish. Fighting during the negotiations never ended, especially

for the Marines hammering at the Punchbowl, where some of the fiercest fighting of the war occurred. Into this fray the Marines introduced new tactics, hit-and-run teams flying missions on the new Sikorsky HRS-1 helicopters.

TRUCE TALKS

In November 1951, as winter began, offensive action ceased except for skirmishes along the Main Line of Resistance (MLR), which had become a massive trench line that angled across the peninsula from the Sea of Japan to the Yellow Sea. Opposite the 1st Marine Division the Chi-

THE AIR WAR

During operations around the Punchbowl, the 1st Marine Division opened a new chapter in the air war. At Pusan, they used the Sikorsky HO3S-1 light helicopters for reconnaissance, rescue missions, and casualty evacuation. At Inchon the HO3S-1 did its share of direct fighting over the battlefield, but its size and lack of capacity limited its capabilities.

During August 1951 the first fifteen Sikorsky medium HRS-1 helicopters arrived in Korea with Lieutenant Colonel George W. Herring's Squadron HMR-161. The new helicopter could carry six combat-equipped Marines or airlift five casualties from the battlefield. During the hand-to-hand fighting at the Punchbowl, HMR-161 carried supplies, ammunition, and troops over terrain that could not be covered by motor transport or would take hours by foot. The HRS-1s began inserting company-sized units into the combat zone, and as more helicopters became available, Marines began to move whole battalions by air.

HRS-1s became an important new tactical weapon exploited to its fullest extent by Marines. Before the war ended, HMR-1 flew more than 18,600 sorties, carried 60,000 passengers, among them 10,000 wounded, and 7.5 million pounds of cargo.

Jet aircraft also became a factor in the war. On 1 April 1951 the Navy staged the first bombing

attack using new F9F Panther jets and destroyed a bridge at the North Korean port of Songjin. Leatherneck flyers shifted from the faithful Corsair to the Panther and the twin-jet F2H Banshee. For air-ground operations, tactics and techniques quickly changed to accommodate the higher speed and the shorter range of jets. The jet fighter-bomber proved to be a steadier platform for guns, bombs, and rockets, and the casualty rate for pilots flying close-support missions dropped by half. After the jets arrived, Marine pilots began thumbing their noses at Russian MiGs. New squadrons of Marine jet night-fighters became the escorts for Air Force B-29s, whose crews insisted upon Marine cover.

Major General Clayton C. Jerome, commanding Marine air in Korea, solved a perpetual spat between the Army and the Air Force over adequate air cover for the Eighth Army. When the dogma of separation rather than integration threatened to interfere with operations on the ground, Jerome volunteered to use Marine flyers to protect the Army's ground troops, and his flyers eventually became the tactical air force for the Eighth Army.

Above: Panther jets made their first debut during the Korean War. Because of soil conditions, once a jet landed it had to be towed to keep swirling dust from clogging the fuel lines of other jets.

Left: On 10 June 1953, a Marine pilot flying a Panther armed with four napalm bombs targets on a troop billeting and supply center in North Korea. Ninety-two planes participated in the attack, using fragmentary bombs and napalm to level the enemy installation.

nese had built echeloned belts of fieldworks ten miles deep that eclipsed Germany's colossal World War I Hindenberg Line. Marines spent their time watching and patrolling because their orders were to defend and not to attack.

Stop-and-go truce talks resumed at Panmunjon, causing occasional eruptions along the MLR. During mid-August 1952 the Chinese occupied heights designated Hill-122 from which they could pour fire into the Marine position. In an eight-day battle, the 1st Marine Division seized the hill, and at the cost of 50 dead and 300 wounded, inflicted 3,000 casualties on the Chinese.

During March 1953 heavier than usual Communist pressure began to build along the MLR as

new cease-fire talks became imminent. The CCF hit Marine outposts on Hill-122, and heavy fighting continued until July. President Eisenhower, who had replaced Truman, dropped hints that the United States would be prepared to use nuclear weapons if peace talks were not resumed. The ploy worked. Talks that began at Panmunjon on 20 July led seven days later to the signing of an armistice. After three years of war, North and South Korea remained separated, this time by a Demilitarized Zone (DMZ) that roughly split the two countries along the original 38th Parallel. Marines remained in Korea until April 1955, manning defensive positions along the DMZ.

U.S. casualties during the Korea War numbered 136,000 men killed, missing, or wounded. That

Marine Ground Operations – Korean War	
Pusan Perimeter Defense	August-September 1950
Inchon-Seoul Assault	September-October 1950
Chosin Reservoir campaign	October-December 1950
Eastern Korea and Punchbowl	January 1951-March 1952
Western Korea and Hill-122	March 1952-July 1953
Post-Armistice duty on DMZ	July 1953-April 1955

'*This Congressional action is a direct reaction to: (1) the magnificent record on the ground and in the air of the Marines in Korea; and (2) [against] the persistent attacks upon the Marine Corps by high officials inside and outside the Pentagon during and since the "unification" fight.*'

NEW YORK TIMES, 28 JUNE 1951, ON THE "MARINE CORPS BILL."

number included 28,011 Marines – 3,845 killed, 422 declared missing and presumed dead, and 23,744 wounded. Nearly half of the Marine casualties occurred while defending the Main Line of Resistance and performing "static" outpost duty reminiscent of World War I. The "rice paddy patrols" gave the Marines a glimpse of the type of fighting that ten years later would characterize the Vietnam War.

Between August 1950 and July 1953, the 1st Marine Aircraft Wing flew more than 118,000 sorties, 40,000 of which were close-support missions. During the same period, Marine helicopter squadrons evacuated nearly 10,000 wounded.

Forty-two Marines were awarded the Medal of Honor for heroism on the battlefield. All but sixteen of these awards were made posthumously. South Korean President Syngman Rhee presented another award when on 25 March 1953 he hon-

ored the 1st Marine Division with the Korean Presidential Unit Citation.

The record of the Marine Corps in Korea added another chapter to its distinguished military legacy. MacArthur used the veteran 1st Division to spearhead his most successful operations because he knew Marines were the best-trained, equipped, and disciplined fighters in the world. His demand for more Marines led to the passage of Public Law 416, the so-called Marine Corps Bill, which expanded the Corps to three divisions, enabling the Marines to become the nation's amphibious force in readiness around the world.

On 1 January 1952 – the mid-point of the Korean War – Lieutenant General Lemuel C. Shepherd, Jr., became the 20th Commandant of the Marine Corps. He succeeded General Cates, who moved to Quantico to head the Marine Corps Schools. Shepherd reorganized Marine Corps

Right: *In a solemn occasion on a rugged draw in the Korean hills, leathernecks of the 1st Marine Division gather to honor their comrades who have fallen in the fight against Chinese Communists. Small ceremonies such as this were held all over the Korean battlefields during three and a half years of war.*

Headquarters along lines similar to those of the Army's general staff. He redefined areas of responsibility, streamlined administrative procedures, and eliminated waste. With the passage of Public Law 416 he became a sitting member of the Joint Chiefs of Staff on all matters concerning the Corps. Shepherd believed in military fundamentals, and as new air and weapon technology became available he quickly incorporated them into the Marine doctrine. Such novel items as flak jackets became standard equipment for combat troops.

On 1 January 1956 General Randolph McCall Pate, who had commanded the 1st Marine Division in Korea and won the Distinguished Service Medal, became the 21st Commandant of the Marine Corps. The "Ribbon Creek Incident" marked his administration when on the night of 8 April 1956 six recruits drowned in Ribbon Creek, Parris Island, during a punishment field exercise. The unauthorized night march, which resulted in the drownings, created a stream of unfavorable publicity. Pate appeared before the House Armed Services Committee and, rather than covering up the incident, he earned the respect of its members by admitting the affair. He promised to take remedial action, made the promised changes, continued to produce efficient combat troops, and won back the confidence of the public.

The 1st Marine Division remained on Korea's DMZ while the Cold War expanded in other areas of the world. In April 1954, when Communist troops surrounded French forces fighting in Indo-China (Vietnam), the 1st Marine Air Wing flew off the carrier *Saipan* and delivered aircraft and maintenance assistance to the embattled French soldiers on the ground. In January 1955, when Chinese Communists attacked the Tachen Islands off the mainland, a battalion from the 3rd Marine Division based in Japan assisted the Navy in evacuating 26,000 Chinese to Formosa. During the latter months of 1956 the Mediterranean became the scene of another disturbance. During the war between Israel and Egypt, and the Anglo-French invasion of Egypt over the latter's nationalization of the Suez Canal, the Marines became the peacekeeping force. They evacuated Americans and foreigners while keeping a watchful eye on the canal. During 1957 the Marines stood ready to intercede when a revolt threatened Indonesia and when floods struck the island of Ceylon (now Sri Lanka).

In July 1958, dissidents supported by Syria threatened to overthrow the pro-Western government of Lebanon. President Camille Chamoun asked the United States for assistance. Thirty hours later the 2nd Provisional Marine Force from the Sixth Fleet landed at Khalde Beach, Beirut. On 15 July, after tanks came ashore, a belligerent young Muslim asked a Marine, 'What have you come here for...to start a war?' The lanky Marine recalled his briefing instructions and replied, "We are here at the invitation of the Lebanese government to protect the country's independence." Then he added, "And *not* to start a war." Four days later an Army airborne unit landed, creating among other things, command confusion. After a senior Army commander arrived, the Marines withdrew and resumed their vigil from the decks of the Mediterranean Sixth Fleet.

The Chinese Nationalist government changed the name of Formosa to Taiwan and in 1958 asked the United States for assistance in strengthening the island's air defenses. Marine Aircraft Group 11 flew into Taiwan with experienced combat units and began training Nationalist pilots. By 1959, using American aircraft, Taiwan began defending the air space over the island with remarkable efficiency.

While Marines assigned to the Fleet Marine Force circulated through the world, Marine Corps Schools continued to develop new tactics, such as vertical envelopment. The concept integrated amphibious and air assets as an assault force using "offshore bases." This required an assault vessel much like an aircraft carrier and led to the Landing Platform Helicopter Carrier (LPH) as a combat vessel. The Navy created the first LPHs from the carriers *Boxer* (CV-21), *Princeton* (CVA-37), *Valley Forge* (CV-45), and *Thetis Bay* (CVHA-1).

After much experimentation, interrupted by two wars, the Marine Corps developed the Short Airfield for Tactical Support (SATS) for their new air-amphibious warfare doctrine. The idea had originated in 1942 when MAG-12 used a land-based Navy catapult and arresting device on a Grumman F4F Wildcat. In 1956 Commandant Pate revived interest in providing tactical support airfields in areas where conventional airfields did not exist. He believed such tactics would be essential for future air operations in support of the Fleet Marine Force. In 1958 work on the program began, but not until the Vietnam War would SATS receive its baptism under fire, at Chu Lai.

▶ **27 JULY:** The Korean armistice is signed.

1954

10 NOVEMBER: Marine Corps Memorial is dedicated next to Arlington National Cemetery.

1956

1 JANUARY: General Randolph McCall Pate becomes 21st Commandant of the Marine Corps.

8 APRIL: Six recruits drown in "Ribbon Creek Incident" at Parris Island.

20 JULY: The Marines receive the first dedicated assault ship, the *Thetis Bay* (CVAH-1, later LPH-1) to carry a Marine battalion and helicopters.

26 JULY: Marine battalion from Sixth Fleet evacuates civilians from Alexandria after the Egyptian government nationalizes the Suez Canal.

1958

15 JULY: Two Marine battalions from the Sixth Fleet land on Lebanon to support the government.

1959

16 JANUARY: Fidel Castro overthrows the Cuban government.

Above left: During October 1952, 2nd Lieutenant Frank E. Petersen completed his flight training and became the Marine Corps' first black pilot. He flew more than 350 combat missions in two wars, flying F4U Corsairs in Korea and F-4D Phantoms in Vietnam. In 1979 Petersen also became the Corps' first black general. He retired in 1998 as lieutenant general in command of Quantico.

PART THREE: EVER READY TO FIGHT

CHAPTER EIGHT

VIETNAM:
AMERICA'S LONGEST WAR
(1961-1975)

Previous page: On 21 February 1968 the 3rd Marine Division, surrounded by North Vietnamese troops at the firebase at Khe Sanh, receive an airdrop of supplies from C-130 transports.

Right: Platoons of African American Marines served on the front lines in Vietnam. They fought well, often complaining in both a joking and at times a serious tone that they had come to Nam to fight a "white man's war." African Americans fighting in Nam organized their own buddy system, usually along lines of segregation.

When Commandant General Randolph McCall Pate retired on 31 December 1959, President Eisenhower searched the Marine Corps seniority list to find a man who thought like himself – someone willing to reduce the Marine Corps to units no larger than regiments. He passed up all the lieutenant generals who had sought to block his reorganization of the defense establishment and settled on Major General David Monroe Shoup, an independent and outspoken major general who had joined the Marine Corps in 1926 after passing through Army ROTC at DePauw University. Eisenhower's choice succeeded in driving several Marine lieutenant generals into retirement, but after Shoup became commandant on 1 January 1960, he proved to be a thorough Marine and a far better political tactician than Eisenhower anticipated.

Shoup never expected to become commandant, but he wasted little time growing into the job. He replaced the battle-tested M1 rifle with the new M14 7.62mm rifle and the old reliable BARs that had fought through three wars with M60 machine guns. In 1960 Shoup expanded the Marine Aviation Cadet Program to include qualification on the new Phantom jets, which were equipped with advanced weapons systems. While Marine air looked for better aircraft to advance their doctrine of readiness, other planners worked on improving the tactics of vertical assault.

Shoup demonstrated no interest in reducing the Marine Corps to regiment-size units. Instead, he sought ways to encourage and improve the quality of men joining the ranks. Before General Pate retired, the Marine Corps had experimented with the "Devil Pup" program, which enabled many young boys to spend a few weeks each summer

> *'In the vast complex of the Department of Defense, the Marine Corps plays a lonely role.'*
>
> JOHN NICHOLAS BROWN QUOTED IN
> *SOLDIERS OF THE SEA*, BY ROBDRT D. HEINL.

undergoing rigorous physical training at one of the bases. Shoup expanded the idea into the Physical Testing Program, and as a public service offered the training to high schools around the nation. The program built individual self-esteem among the young participants and enhanced the image of the Marine Corps as a civic force as well as a fighting force.

General Shoup's Marine Corps in 1961 surpassed in numbers General George C. Marshall's Army of 1939. Except during time of war, "bigness" had always been the bane of the Marine Corps, but Shoup changed Eisenhower's mind. Before the president left office in January 1961, he submitted a budget for a Marine Corps of three divisions and three air wings: a total of 175,000 personnel.

Several events, occurring in 1961, enhanced the status of the Marine Corps. John F. Kennedy, a supporter of the Corps, became president. Then, in response to the Communist invasion of Laos, Kennedy attached a strong Marine force to the Seventh Fleet and moved them into the South China Sea. A few months later he increased the number of American military advisors to the Republic of South Vietnam, where Communist insurgency sponsored by North Vietnam threatened to destabilize the country. On 12 April 1962 Marines from the Seventh Fleet landed in Thailand to support the Laotian government. During the same month Medium Helicopter Squadron 362 of MAW-1 flew into the Mekong Delta area of South Vietnam to provide support for South Vietnamese troops fighting the Viet Cong (VC).

The situation in Vietnam germinated from seeds sown during World War II when the Allies supported Communist forces led by Ho Chi Minh against the Japanese. On 2 September 1945, the day the Japanese signed the instrument of surren-

der, Ho Chi Minh issued a declaration of independence from France. Vietnamese Communists gave a clenched-fist salute as their new red flag with a single yellow star unfurled at the citadel in Hanoi. Americans watched the ceremony, and so did the French.

France did not approve of Ho Chi Minh's unauthorized declaration and attempted to reestablish control over Indochina by force. Nine years passed before the Vietnamese People's Army under General Vo Nguyen Giap surrounded and overwhelmed the French army at Dienbienphu.

U.S. BACKS DIEM

During the Geneva settlement in June 1954, France agreed to the partitioning of Vietnam at the 17th Parallel, creating a situation not unlike the two Koreas. Neighboring Cambodia and Laos became independent states. The United States accepted the terms of the agreement but reserved the right to intercede if trouble resulted. Ho Chi Minh became the leader of the new North Vietnamese government, and Ngo Dinh Diem, who soon proved to be a corrupt autocrat, became president of South Vietnam. The United States backed Diem without fully understanding the character of the man.

During the years between 1954 and 1962, Marines acted as advisors to the South Vietnamese Marine Corps. During those years Diem could not solve the country's internal problems or stop the escalating insurgency caused by Communist guerrilla activity. In 1960 guerrillas operating in South Vietnam numbered about 6,000 and were organized into a group called Viet Cong. American advisors had no authority to train the South Vietnamese Army (ARVN) in counterinsurgency tactics and continued to prepare them for conventional warfare. In 1962 Kennedy increased the number of American advisors in South Vietnam to 4,000 men, among them 600 Marines.

Meanwhile, Communist activity continued to spread around the globe. In 1962-63, beyond Vietnam, ten major or near-critical situations flared in other parts of the world, including Germany, Taiwan, Laos, Cambodia, Cuba, Panama Canal Zone, Cyprus, Haiti, South America and Zanzibar. Marines answered the call around the world, but the problems in Vietnam continued to intensify as each month passed.

On 1 November 1963 a core of South Vietnamese generals, with support from the Kennedy administration, assassinated Diem. Three weeks later in Dallas, Texas, an assassin killed President Kennedy. Lyndon Baines Johnson moved into the White House and watched as the government of South Vietnam changed nine times. On 5 August 1964, using the disputable Tonkin Gulf incident to rally American support, Johnson ordered carrier air attacks on North Vietnamese naval bases and oil depots. Two days later Congress authorized the president to "take all necessary measures to repel any armed attack against the forces of the United States..." and members of the Southeast

Above left: Anti-American demonstrations in Saigon were usually conducted by large crowds chanting protests and waving placards and banners.

Above: On 21 October 1967 Military Police hold back protesters during a sit-in conducted at the Mall Entrance to Pentagon in Washington.

Below: On 19 July 1964 South Vietnamese protest behind barriers in front of the USIS Building during a National Shame Day demonstration in Saigon.

▶ **1964**

1 JANUARY: General Wallace M. Greene, Jr., becomes the 23rd Commandant of the Marine Corps.

2 AUGUST: The Tonkin Gulf incident gives President Johnson an excuse to increase the America's military presence in South Vietnam.

7 AUGUST: Congress relinquishes its war-making powers to President Johnson.

1965

8 MARCH: The 9th Marine Expeditionary Brigade – the first Marine ground unit – arrives at Danang.

Asia Treaty Organization. Johnson now had the power to "Americanize" the war, which appeared to be exactly what he wanted to do. U.S. military strength in Vietnam increased from 4,000 in 1962 to 23,000 by the end of 1964.

On 7 February 1965 the Viet Cong attacked the barracks at Pleiku, South Vietnam, killing eight American servicemen and wounding 126 others. In response, the Navy launched Flaming Dart I and sent eighty-three planes from three aircraft carriers to bomb enemy facilities at Dong Hoi, a North Vietnamese port above the five-mile wide Demilitarized Zone (DMZ) that straddled the 17th parallel. Three days later the Viet Cong struck back, bombing the enlisted men's barracks and a

helicopter base at Qui Nhon. In reprisal, the Navy launched Flaming Dart II, and ninety-nine aircraft struck enemy facilities at Chan Hoa.

In the escalating tit-for-tat war, U.S. military planners conceived Rolling Thunder, a strategy calling for graduated air attacks. Secretary McNamara expected the incremental pressure to touch off Ho Chi Minh's "ouch level," the point where North Korea would cease supporting the Viet Cong. Minh's "ouch level" remained untouched until December 1972, when President Richard M. Nixon authorized Linebacker II in an effort to blast the North Koreans to the negotiating table. During the in-between years, Americans fought their most unpopular war.

MARINE COMMANDANTS OF THE VIETNAM WAR

American activities in war are governed through the directives of the president and the secretary of defense, whether the senior officers conducting the war agree or not. Two commandants of the Marine Corps, though they followed orders, seldom agreed with President Johnson's politically imposed military tactics.

On 1 January 1964 General Wallace Martin Greene, Jr., became the 23rd Commandant of the Marine Corps. General Shoup, his predecessor, openly opposed sending American ground troops into Vietnam. After retiring, Shoup became more vocal in his opposition to Johnson's handling of the Vietnam conflict.

Greene believed the war could be won if Johnson and Secretary of Defense Robert McNamara established the correct policy – which meant taking the war to North Vietnam by immediately blockading and mining the harbor of Hai Phong, blowing up the dams and dikes along the Red River, and conducting a surprise amphibious assault somewhere around Hanoi. Instead of being allowed to take decisive action, Greene spent most of his four years as commandant chafing over the wavering warfare policies of the administration.

On 1 January 1968 Greene relinquished the commandant's responsibilities to General Leonard Fielding Chapman, Jr., who President Johnson personally elevated over two better qualified candidates – Lewis W. Walt, hero of three wars, and Victor H. Krulak, the brilliant commanding general of the Fleet Marine Force. Johnson soon discovered that his policies pleased Chapman no more than they had Shoup or Greene.

In 1968 Chapman went to Vietnam for a first-hand look at the battle situation. He watched the Tet Offensive boil across South Vietnam. He followed the battle at Hu , and felt restrained from mopping up the North Vietnamese Army after lifting the siege of Khe Sanh. When he returned to Washington he joined the American public's disenchantment over the conduct of the war. He observed moments when the right word from Johnson or McNamara could have turned the tide and swallowed up the enemy, but those words never came. Before leaving his post on 31 December 1971, he sent an often-repeated message to the Marines in Vietnam, "Don't leave anything behind worth more than five dollars."

Right: *General William C. Westmoreland (right) confers with Marine Commandant General Wallace M. Greene (left) and Marine Lt. Gen. Robert E. Cushman (center) on tactics.*

Far right: *In August 1968, General Leonard F. Chapman, Commandant of the Marine Corps, visits a hilltop fire support base just south of the demilitarized zone.*

On 2 March 1965, with the initiation of Rolling Thunder, the role of U.S. troops switched from "advisory" to "combat." For two months Brigadier General Frederick J. Karch's 9th Marine Expeditionary Brigade (MEB) had been languishing off Vietnam waiting for orders to land. On 8 March President Johnson, using authority conferred upon him by the Tonkin Gulf Resolution, ordered the two-battalion brigade ashore to provide security for the air base at Danang. Karch's 9th MEB represented the first commitment of ground combat troops in Vietnam. Without realizing it, Johnson had committed the United States to its longest foreign war.

MARINES AT DANANG

In early March 1965 Army General William C. Westmoreland, commanding American forces in Vietnam, agreed with the administration that a battalion of Marines at Danang would not only secure the local airfield but would release ARVN units to fight the Viet Cong. General Karch's 9th MEB provided the ideal unit for the mission. The brigade had recently completed combat training in a counterinsurgency environment, which included fighting both large units and small bands of guerrillas; handling situations involving the local population; cooperating with an indigenous military; and dealing with diplomats and politicians.

The leathernecks, from colonels to privates, were mentally and physically prepared for a counterinsurgency conflict. On 8 March, led by a Marine carrying the Stars and Stripes, the 3rd Battalion plunged through the surf of Danang's sparkling crescent beach and were met by scores of garland-bearing Vietnamese schoolgirls, sightseers, smiling ARVN officers, and four American soldiers carrying a sign: "Welcome Gallant Marines." The businesslike landing came as a shock to the local mayor and his staff. What they expected to see was a light infantry force, not a battalion of commandos ready for a firefight and equipped with tanks, artillery, and a pair of nuclear-capable 8-inch guns.

Karch's next unit, the 1st Battalion, 9th Marines, landed the following day at Danang's airfield, the only airstrip north of Saigon capable of handling jets. Conveyed from Okinawa on KC-130 Hercules transports, the battalion drew fire from Viet Cong as the first aircraft approached Danang's 10,000-foot concrete runway.

Lieutenant General Krulak, who had trained his Marines for counterinsurgency service, fumed when he discovered that Westmoreland had

'It was not permitted to "engage in day-to-day actions against the Vietcong," nor were the Marines allowed to leave the air base or to be involved directly with the local population – which is what counterinsurgency is all about. This was never going to work. We were not going to win any counterinsurgency battles sitting in foxholes around a runway, separated from the very people we wanted to protect.'

LT. GEN. VICTOR H. KRULAK, *FIRST TO FIGHT*.

Below: *A Marine patrol during Operation Dagger Thrust makes contact with the enemy and hunkers down along the top of a ridge on 6 October 1965. Their task is mainly one of observation, but they maintain a watchful posture toward the enemy moving below.*

Above: McDonnell F-4B Phantom jets of Marine Fighter-Attack Squadrons VMFA-323 and VMFA-115 refuel at a Danang hardstand, January 1966. The two fighter squadrons are the Marine Corps' mainstay for providing close air support to ground troops.

Right: Amphibious assault ship USS Tripoli (LPH-10) leaves Pearl Harbor for Vietnam, May 1967, with Marine Heavy Helicopter Squadron 463 and elements of Marine Observation Squadron 6. By the end of the year Tripoli had participated in eight amphibious operations.

and 36 – two fixed-wing and two helicopter groups.

On 3 May 1965 Major General William R. Collins landed at Danang ahead of the 3rd Marine Division. He deactivated 9th MEB and merged it into the 9,000-man III Marine Amphibious Force – a reinforced division with Marine Air Group-16. But base security remained the III MAF's primary mission, mainly because the ARVN commander in the I Army Corps, General Nguyen Chanh Thi, did not want to give the Marines an expanded mission. During the doldrums of General Thi's "enclave strategy," Marines began building and expanding airstrips to accommodate Douglas A-4 Skyhawk fighter-bombers.

On 5 May, Lieutenant General Lewis W. Walt arrived to take command of the III MAF. Walt's career with the Marines had been legendary, dating back to Shanghai in 1937 and to Edson's Raiders in 1942. Already a winner of two Navy Crosses, Walt would become the most widely admired Marine general in the Vietnam War.

At the time of Walt's arrival, Westmoreland had more or less convinced President Johnson that "only American offensive operations could save Vietnam…from a VC military victory." Westmoreland divided South Vietnam into four Tactical Zones or military districts. Walt's sector became the I Corps Tactical Zone headquartered at Danang and encompassed the northernmost area – 10,000 square miles of territory flanked by the DMZ on the north and separated from the II Corps to the south by the Annamite mountain chain. The Annamites, with peaks as high as 8,500 feet, ran southward from China for 750 miles, bordering Laos on the west. As the mountains reached

restricted his leathernecks to protecting the Danang air base from VC incursion. The 9th MEB grew to 5,000 men but remained confined to an air base surrounded by a wire fence and 200,000 people, some of them hostile.

On 10 April Karch took advantage of a disturbance at the Phu Bai airfield, located 42 miles inland and six miles from the city of Hu . He dispatched two companies by helicopter, and twelve days later Marines successfully defended, without loss, the airfield in a firefight with the VC.

While leathernecks fought at Phu Bai, the first Marine fixed-wing squadron arrived at Danang – VFMA-531 flying McDonnell Douglas F-4B Phantoms. By mid-1965, four Marine Air Groups began operations in Vietnam – MAG-11, 12, 16,

the southern boundary of the I Corps, they curled to the sea and imposed a topographical barrier between the two corps.

General Thi insisted that rural and inland areas be controlled by the ARVN, but aside from scattered outposts, his forces spent most of their time at Danang and nearby Hoi Ann. Politicians in Saigon called the forty-two-year-old general the "Warlord of the North." He was a native of the region, a veteran of World War II, and a martinet in charge of 30,000 ARVN troops. Thi also controlled 23,000 men of the Popular Forces (PF), who were local part-time militia acting as a security force in their hamlets and villages.

PACIFICATION

General Thi understood the character of the 2.6 million Vietnamese who lived in the I Corps sector. They were different from the grim peasants to the north and the happy-go-lucky inhabitants of the south. Fishermen and rice farmers of true Vietnamese stock lived along the coast and in the small alluvial valleys tucked among the hills. Montagnard tribesmen were also of true Vietnamese stock who had lived for centuries in the highlands and subsisted by hunting, fishing, and slash farming. Montagnards did not like the Viet Cong and soon warmed to helping the U.S. Marines. The mix of cultures in the I Corps sector eventually led General Walt to try a new concept of warfare – pacification.

Walt could not wait for concessions from the "Warlord of the North." He needed an airfield in the province of Quang Tin and wasted no time employing the III MAF. On 7 May the 1st and 2nd Battalions, 4th Marines, and several hundred Seabees landed on a beach 55 miles south of Danang. General Krulak found no name for the site he chose for the landing and called it Chu Lai, his own name in Mandarin Chinese. The Marines landed unopposed, and Seabees went to work building their first Short Airfield for Tactical Support (SATS). On 1 June the first Marine A-4 Skyhawks flew in from the Philippines and landed on a 4,000-foot strip of aluminum matting. The new airfield resembled the deck of an aircraft carrier, complete with arrester wires. The flyers called it the "tinfoil strip" and used JATO (jet-assisted take-off) bottles to get into the air. Marines flying fixed-wing aircraft and helicopters out of Chu Lai soon became heavily involved in reconnaissance and combat operations.

By 1968 the I Corps sector operated thirteen tactical airstrips and two jet operational airfields, one at Danang and the other at Chu Lai. General Westmoreland tried to transfer Walt's F-4 Phantom and RF-8A Crusader squadrons to Major General Joseph H. Moore's Air Force command but lost the battle. Westmoreland became so impressed with Marine tactical air support that

he eventually asked for more flying leathernecks posted on carriers off Vietnam.

The ineptness of General Thi's forces became manifest on 1 July 1965 when VC raiders slipped through South Vietnamese forces around Danang, attacked the airbase, and reached the runway. Using explosives and recoilless rifles they damaged three aircraft and destroyed two C-130 Hercules transports and one F-102 strike plane. Walt confronted Thi over his policy of confining Marines to the airbase, and the general withdrew his objections.

President Johnson now had his war. In a nationally televised address on 28 July 1965 he increased the American commitment from 75,000 to 125,000 troops. The announcement expanded the Marine Corps by 55,000 men. When Johnson later upped the ante, the Corps set a target for 280,000 men and in 1966 recruited nearly 50,000 more, most of them volunteers.

During the summer of 1965 General Walt again complained to General Thi, this time about the inability of South Vietnamese forces to keep the VC under control in the rural areas around Danang. Johnson upstaged the quarrel. He abandoned his policy of restraint and secretly authorized General Westmoreland to engage in counterinsurgency combat operations. Walt responded with alacrity, sending patrols fifty miles outside the enclave to break up heavy concentrations of the enemy.

Feeling new freedom of movement the Navy authorized General Walt to strike the 1st Viet Cong Regiment, which had concentrated on the Van Tuong Peninsula south of Chu Lai. On 6 August Walt laid plans for launching Operation Satellite. A clerk erroneously transcribed Satellite

▶ **10 APRIL:** Marine Fighter Attack Squadron (VMFA) 531 – the first Marine air unit – arrives at Danang.

22 APRIL: Near Danang, Marines engage in the first ground action in Vietnam.

3 MAY: Lieutenant General Lewis W. Walt organizes the III Marine Amphibious Force in the I Corps sector.

7 MAY: The 4th Marines and Seabees land at Chu Lai to build a Marine jet-capable airfield.

Below: On 9 September 1965, Marines belonging to a recoilless rifle team dash along a rice paddy near Quinhon, South Vietnam. Two leathernecks pause momentarily to fire their weapon on Viet Cong snipers during a sweeping operation.

Below: *On 18-19 August 1865, General Lewis Walt launched Operation Starlite against the 1st VC Regiment on Van Tuong Peninsula. The battle reminded Marines of Iwo Jima. Caves and spider holes laced the countryside, as did small hamlets, and the enemy had to be driven one at a time from their cover.*

Below right: *During Operation Starlite three Marine battalions mounted the first search and destroy operation. Sikorsky CH-34D helicopters made regular supply drops to the pictured howitzer battery.*

Bottom right: *Leatherneck assault teams, ready to be inserted, rush to waiting Sikorsky CH-34s as the first helicopters prepare to take off from the stern of the USS* Iwo Jima.

into Starlite, which became the new name of preference. On 18 August, supported by Marine air and naval gunfire, Walt's Regimental Landing Team 7 engaged in the first major action between U.S. troops and the Viet Cong. Five amphibious ships of the Seventh Fleet conveyed 4,000 men of the 3rd, 4th, and 7th Marines to Chu Lai. Other elements, transported by helicopters from the carrier *Iwo Jima*, landed inland. The battle lasted six days. At a cost of 45 killed, the Marines all but annihilated the VC regiment, killing 964 of the enemy and taking 125 prisoners. The VC survivors learned a lasting lesson. They could not win a stand-up battle against Marines.

Two months passed before the Viet Cong made another appearance. On 27-28 October Communist sappers, supported by mortars, suddenly struck the Marble Mountain Marine base near Danang and destroyed or damaged forty-seven helicopters. At Chu Lai another VC raiding party damaged or destroyed eight A-4 Skyhawks. The resiliency of the VC came as a surprise to the Marines protecting the airfields. Walt launched Operation Blue Marlin to clean out the VC, but the enemy vanished into the villages and hamlets in Quang Nam province. The raid marked the beginning of VC efforts to strike Marine outposts and disappear into the society of civilians.

The Viet Cong proved to be crafty fighters. They carried modern weapons, were well trained, and superbly disciplined in their approach to guerrilla warfare. They were also well fed and clothed, deeply indoctrinated in Ho Chi Minh's Communist doctrine, and willing by the thousands to sacrifice their lives to weaken South Vietnam, capture Saigon, and unify the country as a Communist state. They infiltrated the ARVN and undermined the rank and file to the extent that the American military began to question the loyalty of some of the officers in the South Vietnamese Army. United Nations troops mingling with Marines said they had come to keep South Vietnam democratic but soon began to doubt whether the corrupt government in Saigon felt the same way.

BOMBING HALT

The war slowed to a crawl during the monsoon season. Clothing and canvas turned green and moldy; high winds at sea made unloading difficult; red earthen roads turned to muck; and low clouds pregnant with moisture obscured ground targets from air attack. President Johnson attempted to take advantage of the thick weather by calling a

SOUTH CHINA SEA

N

Phuoc Thuan Peninsula

NHO NA BAY

I M 3/3

VAN TUONG

LZ RED

I G 2/4

phase line BANANA

II 2/4

I E 2/4

LZ WHITE

3/7

Major fire fight

Major fire fight

Ambush of marine supply convoy

Operational headquarters

Green Beach

3/3

3/7

I H 2/4

LZ BLUE

Major fire fight

Major fire fight

00

▶ **18 AUGUST:** Marines launch the first large-scale amphibious assault on the Van Tuong Peninsula.

1966

31 MARCH: The 3rd Marine Division joins the 1st Marine Division in Vietnam.

Left: *A Marine gun crew, defending the airfield at Quang Ngai, fires a salvo from a 105mm howitzer at North Vietnamese troops attempting to infiltrate the hurriedly constructed base. In front of the howitzer sits a crude bombproof topped by layers of sandbags.*

bombing halt, thinking that doing so would encourage peace negotiations with North Vietnam. The effort failed, giving the VC more than a month to reorganize and re-equip. When heavy fighting resumed in January, the Marines discovered large elements of the North Vietnamese Army (NVA) concentrating along the boundary between the I and II Corps Tactical Zones.

In January 1966 General Walt combined four battalions of Marines with the Army's 1st Air Cavalry Division in an assault against the 325th(A) NVA Division in Quang Ngai Province. In the largest amphibious operation to date, the 3rd Battalion, 3rd Marines, landed near Thach Tru. On the following day, helicopters transported the 2nd Battalion, 3rd Marines, to a position five miles inland. The 2nd Battalion, 9th Marines, advanced from Quang Ngai's airstrip and moved into the mountain fringes northwest of the beach. As the Marines worked inland, the NVA trickled into the Que San Valley. During the operation, the Marines received their first unwelcome experience with the hardened NVA, who carried Russian weapons: AK-47 assault rifles, heavy machine guns and mortars, and deadly B-40 rocket-propelled grenades. The Marines punished the NVA, but casualty counts were nearly equal.

On 1 March 1966 the 1st Marine Division joined the 3rd Division in the I Corps sector, marking the first time since World War II that two Marine divisions had been committed to the same war zone. The 1st Division moved to Danang, and the 3rd Division moved north to Hu . The 5th and

THE INITIATION

'No one sleeps much before his first combat... People start getting up hours before they have to. You take extra care shaving and dressing. Steak and eggs is the traditional Marine breakfast before a landing. No one feels much like eating now. Your mouth is dry, and the food tastes like cotton...In the helicopter you keep thinking what it would be like to get shot. You have never seen combat before and you wonder if it is really like all those briefings you got back in the States... You remember the officers and men who briefed you on their experiences in Vietnam. They seemed strange – distant. You wonder if you'll become like them.'

CHARLES COE, *YOUNG MAN IN VIETNAM.*

Below: *The North Vietnamese carried excellent weapons. Here the enemy practices with a Chinese Type 69 antitank grenade launcher, copied from a Soviet RPG-7. Leathernecks reported that while captured enemy prisoners might be ragged and hungry, their weapons were always clean and in perfect working order.*

▶ **3 AUGUST:** The III Marine Amphibious Force defeats the North Vietnamese Army in the first major contact with NVA troops.

17 SEPTEMBER: Marines launch Operation Golden Fleece to protect the annual rice harvest.

7th Regiments, 1st Marine Division, remained at Chu Lai. When the 1st Division arrived, they found their sister division involved in a vigorous and novel pacification program. The Vietnam War had taken on a new dimension.

The war in Vietnam escalated into a tangled web of military, religious, and political inconsistencies. In March 1966 the Marines launched two offensives in cooperation with the AVRN to relieve a besieged South Vietnamese outpost at An Hoa. The joint force killed more than 1,000

enemy troops. At the other end of the spectrum, Buddhists overshadowed the victory by mounting a challenge to the military government in Saigon. The quarrel affected Buddhist elements in the ARVN force cooperating with the Marines. They became rebellious and wanted to join the dissidents. General Walt restored order with a minimum of bloodshed, but the action inflicted another blot on his pacification program. Viet Cong took advantage of the turmoil and wormed back into previously "sanitized" villages.

WAR BY PACIFICATION

Base security depended upon continuous patrolling. Day and night, Marine units moved through farms and villages to gather intelligence and destroy VC hideouts. During the summer months of 1965 Generals Walt and Krulak conceived a pacification program. Since Marine patrols were already circulating through the countryside, why not use them to ingratiate the villagers and stem the flow of VC infiltration? After Operation Harvest Moon killed about 400 VC infiltrators living in villages, the two generals believed that direct welfare work and civic action would "win the hearts and minds" of the inhabitants. The Marines accepted the work but changed the slogan: "Grab them by the balls, and their hearts and minds will follow."

The program began to pay dividends. Combined Action Companies, composed of a squad of Marines with local volunteers, circulated through the towns and villages clearing out VC while giving aid and food to civilians. Medical teams joined the task, set up tents, and soon had villagers standing in line for treatment. Band-aids and soap assumed more importance than bullets.

In areas occupied by Marines, volunteers turned out to build schools and orphanages, dig

Above: *While Marines concentrated on their war by pacification, the policy required implementation by force because of constant efforts by Viet Cong to interfere using raids and infiltration.*

wells, open markets, and distribute food through CARE agencies.

As "hearts and minds" were won, village councils near Danang asked the 9th Marines to provide security during the annual rice harvest. General Walt agreed and initiated Operation Golden Fleece, which became an annual event. The operation worked so well that Walt created a Joint Coordinating Council of American and Vietnamese for planning additional pacification programs.

As pacification began spreading through the villages along Highway 1, the Marines became aware that all the humanitarianism would have little lasting effect unless the villagers received permanent protection and honest government. In early 1966 Walt and Krulak initiated Operation County Fair, using mixed Marine-Vietnamese task forces combined with civic action groups to root out and eliminate VC political cadre and "sleepers" hiding in the communities. Country Fair proponents made every effort to prevent VC counteraction that might turn a village into a battleground and villagers into unintentional targets.

The strategy of pacification, though never free of problems, remained viable and continued to work with success. The Army treated the program with skepticism. In an unintended action on 16 March 1968, the Army all but destroyed the pacification effort when Lieutenant William Calley, leading an inexperienced and poorly disciplined company of the 20th Army Infantry, panicked and massacred 347 Vietnamese civilians.

'All of this has meaning only if you are going to stay. Are you going to stay?'

DISTRICT CHIEF OF LE MY TO GENERAL KRULAK, QUOTED FROM KRULAK, *FIRST TO FIGHT*.

Left: *In April 1966 Marines prepare to recover the bodies of slain South Vietnamese civilians that they discovered chained together in a field.*

THE WINGLESS ANGELS

They came from the sky, their rotors thrumming over the treetops, violently swirling the leaves and flattening the elephant grass. Though they looked like gigantic insects with a head, thorax, and tail, they were not. They were gunships, the indispensable UH-1E "Huey" of the Marine Corps. The helicopter carried a crew of four: a pilot, co-pilot, gunner, and crew-chief, all battle-hardened veterans accustomed to being in the thick of battle.

Sometimes they were in the air when a call came that a pilot was down in a rice paddy or that a patrol had been ambushed in the jungle and the wounded dragged to a clearing. As soon as the pilot received the coordinates, he flew toward the site, never certain of what trouble lay ahead. Major Stephen Pless recalled one of his rescues.

Flying low Pless spotted the clearing a few hundred yards ahead. As he passed overhead he could see Marines surrounded by VC and engaged in a firefight. The gunner began squeezing off bursts from his machine gun, sending the enemy running for cover. Seconds later enemy bullets began to rip through the thin aluminum sheathing on the Huey. Pless banked, came about, and pointed the nose of the helicopter toward the source of the firing. He pressed the button on the stick and a stream of rockets crashed into the enemy. While the gunner sprayed the woods, Pless lowered the helicopter to the ground, the rotors matting swirls in the grass. Four Marines lunged out of the foliage, carrying a man covered with blood. Another pair of riflemen aided a staggering man with a tourniquet tied to his thigh. Two men spilled out of the helicopter to lift the wounded on board. They could barely be heard above the roar of the rotors and the firing of the Huey's machine gun.

"You fellas going to be OK?" the crew-chief hollered at the squad leader.

"We'll make it out of here on our own," the sergeant shouted. "Get these men to the rear."

Pless lifted off the clearing and swung one more time over the VC position. He could only see dead bodies – no sign of life – and headed for the hospital ship lying off shore. Twenty minutes later he landed, and while corpsmen removed the wounded he began counting the fresh bullet holes in the fuselage.

Pless flew 780 missions and more than 1,000 hours of combat during the first eighteen months of war. President Johnson presented him with the Medal of Honor, and Pless became the eighteenth Marine to win the award.

Left: *Major Stephen Pless earned one of the two Medals of Honor awarded Marine pilots during the Vietnam War. He flew an armed UH-1E helicopter and made daring rescues of trapped wounded Marines while under heavy fire from the enemy. Pless and his men risked their lives on numerous occasions, and during the course of the war flew 780 missions.*

During the spring of 1966 the NVA began dictating how the war would be fought. In response, Major General Lewis J. Fields, commanding the 1st Marine Division, assigned a third of his command to each of three southern provinces – Quang Nam, Quang Tin, and Quang Ngai. The 3rd Marine Division, commanded by Major General Wood B. Kyle, scattered his troops from Danang to the DMZ. In July General Walt discovered that the North Vietnamese 324B Division had crossed the DMZ and taken up positions in Quang Tri province. Walt now had war on two fronts plus a new infiltration of Viet Cong mingling among the sea of local inhabitants who were preparing for the annual rice harvest.

On 15 July General Walt launched Operation Hastings – 8,000 men of the III MAF and 3,000 South Vietnamese troops – in a sweep through Quang Tri province to intercept the movement of the 324B NVA Division. Supported by ground-directed bombing by the Strategic Air Command, the Marines captured a 700-foot vantage point called the "Rockpile" from which they could observe enemy movement in the west-central sector of the province. After two weeks of fighting, 824 North Vietnamese lay dead among the bamboo

> '*First there was the Old Corps, then there was the New Corps. And now there's this goddamned thing*'
>
> CHARLES COE, *YOUNG MAN IN VIETNAM.*

Below: *General Creighton W. Adams (center) makes one of his rare visits to Da Nang to confer with Major General Lewis Walt (left) on strategy.*

▶ 1967

28 FEBRUARY: PFC James Anderson, Jr., becomes the first black Marine to win the Medal of Honor.

24 APRIL: The first battle for Khe Sanh begins.

31 MAY: Lieutenant General Robert E. Cushman relieves General Walt at Danang.

Right: *The Viet Cong and Cambodians were especially adept at building booby traps, using sharp bamboo stakes tipped with a variety of poisons.*

Below: *Marines in the jungle found the going especially hazardous. The enemy mined the trails and developed all sorts of ingenious explosive devices set off by trip wires.*

Below right: *When crawling through elephant grass and rice paddies, Marines never knew when they would be struck by a hidden enemy and were always prepared for a fight.*

stands and the elephant grass, but other elements dispersed and continued the fight. Walt dedicated three Marine battalions to root out the survivors, and the hunt continued for nine more months.

Rooting out the enemy, though nerve-racking, often proved to be easier than evading mines and booby traps. The simplest VC devices, some of them almost ancient in design, were often the most effective. A punji bear-trap consisted of two boards, sometimes made of steel, with spikes driven through them. When stepped upon they pivoted and drove spikes into the leg. Along jungle trails the VC laid trip wires attached to grenades. Marine rifle squads learned to walk carefully beside a trail rather than upon it. At the slightest pull on their leg, they stopped. The VC also rigged grenades fastened to a trip wire in bamboo arches above a trail. The traps could be spotted during the day, but at night they became deadly.

The VC learned that they could not win battles with Marines in a conventional fight and resorted to other tricks. They planted mines in front of their position and initiated skirmishes with patrols. As soon as the firing began, the VC withdrew, urging the Marines to attack. Marine riflemen stumbled into carefully laid minefields and suffered severe casualties. The VC also mined rice paddies. Marines advanced through the paddies behind 35-ton tracked vehicles that could detonate the mines, but amtracs grinding through a paddy churned up a muddy quagmire that clung like twenty pounds of glue to a rifleman's boots.

Marines carried enough equipment without adding an extra load of mud. Besides a backpack, canteen, steel helmet, flak jacket, and other impedimenta, each rifleman carried 150 rounds of ammunition and at least two grenades. Machine gun crews draped themselves with belts of linked cartridges numbering 1,200 rounds. In addition to a weapon of choice, a 3.5-inch rocket launcher team carried five high explosive and five white phosphorous rockets. If grenadiers joined the patrol, each carried twenty-eight 40mm shells for their stubby M79s. If a patrol expected to be met by enemy tanks, riflemen car-

ried portable antitank weapons in addition to their regular load. In the field they moved with caution. At times they found no shade and no breeze, just a sweltering 105 degree temperature and unbearable humidity.

By the autumn of 1966, Marine presence in Vietnam increased to 60,000 men. They had participated in more than 150 operations of battalion

'Back home I used to fill my own cartridges for hunting. Me and my father and my brothers used to make a hundred a year between us. I swear to God, I never saw anything like this.'

MICHAEL HERR, *DISPATCHES*

or regimental size and conducted 200,000 patrols and small-unit actions. Seventeen hundred men had been killed and 9,000 wounded, though most of the latter returned to duty. Because of the rising toll of American casualties, President Johnson demanded enemy body counts. One slightly wounded gunny sergeant returning from a patrol snarled at the company executive officer, and said, "Let the stupid son-of-a-bitch come to Nam and count his own goddamned gooks. Who the hell has time for that?"

Formalized under the code-name Sting Ray, seven-man teams that performed reconnaissance missions along the DMZ and the inland supply routes used by the enemy were developed by Marine Major Bernard Trainor (later lieutenant general). Helicopters often inserted men beyond and extracted men from behind enemy lines. The teams observed enemy movements and called in fire assaults from artillery, fighter-bombers carrying napalm, and helicopter gunships. Each team had at least two artillery pieces dedicated in direct support of their mission. They operated at will behind enemy lines, caused immeasurable damage to the enemy, and never wandered from their observation posts to take a body count.

"PRAIRIE" OPERATIONS

Some of the longest and bloodiest campaigns between Marines and the NVA occurred among the paddy fields in the vicinity of the DMZ. "Prairie I," a major search and destroy operation between the DMZ and Route 9, lasted 182 days during which the Marines lost 225 killed and 1,159 wounded. The NVA withdrew to the north, but as soon as the monsoons ended the enemy began filtering back. They used the Ho Chi Minh Trail, a network of pathways that wound through jungle and the Ammanite mountain range on the eastern border of Laos and Cambodia. The 3rd Marine Division launched "Prairie II" to clear the I Corps sector of infiltrators and to deny the enemy access to the rice-rich coastal area. Such efforts were bound to create a battle somewhere around the DMZ.

On 24 April 1967 a major engagement erupted near the Laotian border when NVA troops attacked the 3rd Marine Regiment fourteen miles south of the DMZ at Khe Sanh. In a war with many code-names, this action had none, though it became the first battle of Khe Sahn. The engagement began as an accidental encounter between a platoon-sized patrol from the 1st Battalion, 9th Marines, and an enemy force positioning itself on three hills (Hills 861, 881 North, and 881 South) northwest of the firebase. The NVA clearly intended to attack Khe Sanh and were digging-in when discovered. General Walt flew in two Marine battalions, and for the next twelve days artillery and air strikes from the 1st Marine Air

Wing pounded enemy dispositions on the hills. Marines fought their way up all three hills and secured the heights. This time President Johnson got his body count – 554 enemy killed, another 600 estimated killed and carried off. The affair cost the Marines 138 casualties.

On 31 May Lieutenant General Robert E. Cushman arrived at Danang and relieved General Walt, who had led the III MAF for two years. Cushman, another World War II veteran, had won the Navy Cross on Guam in 1944. He now had 75,000 Marines in South Vietnam. Enemy activity along the DMZ kept most of them busy throughout the summer.

Trouble began in September when NVA units struck the 4th Marine Regiment at Con Thien, located a few miles east of Khe Sanh. The enemy came in force, threatening to surround the position in an effort to inflict another disaster like the French had experienced in 1954 at Dienbienphu. Tactical aircraft strikes, naval gunfire, and ground-directed B-52s broke up the enemy concentrations as fast as they formed. By November the enemy quit, driven away by a combination of American firepower and the annual monsoons.

By the end of 1967 the I Corps sector had ballooned into 21 Marine battalions and 3,436 Navy personnel. Added to that were 31 ARVN battalions, 15 U.S. Army battalions, and 4 Korean Marine battalions – a total of 71 Free World battalions operating in the upper five provinces of South Vietnam. During 1968, most of them would be needed.

In early January U.S. intelligence sources spotted two NVA divisions gathering near the northwestern corner of Quang Tri province and warned

Above: *Densely forested banks giving the enemy perfect cover created hours of tension for Marines patrolling along the rivers and deltas. The situation became worse as Marines entered Laos and Cambodia, where the rivers narrowed and brought the banks closer to the patrols. This mortar-armed leatherneck was taking no chances and kept his eyes focused on the shores ahead.*

▶ **1968**

1 JANUARY: General Leonard F. Chapman, Jr., becomes the 24th Commandant of the Marine Corps.

21 JANUARY: The siege of Khe Sanh begins.

30 JANUARY: The Tet Offensive begins.

2 MARCH: Marines recapture the city of Hué.

Above right: The combat base at Khe Sanh became a collection of barbed wire fences, bunkers, sandbagged bombproofs, artillery revetments, trenches, foxholes, and rifle pits. The Marines built most of the base themselves and, because of its close proximity to the DMZ, kept patrols moving through forward positions in search of concentrations of the enemy.

Right: On 21 February 1968 an eruption of smoke and dust obscures part of the beleaguered Marine combat base at Khe Sanh during a North Vietnamese rocket attack. The under-siege base received continuous rocket and artillery fire for more than two months, but the Marines persevered against 20,000 enemy troops from two NVA divisions.

the Marines of a possible attack. Among several firebases that stretched from the coast to the Laotian border, Khe Sanh occupied an area close to Laos and the DMZ. The I Corps built the bases, known as the McNamara Line, to block NVA troop and supply infiltrations through Laos and along Route 9, the only good east-west road near the DMZ.

On 21 January the 2nd NVA Division cut Route 9 and isolated 3,500 leathernecks of Colonel David E. Lownds' 26th Marines at Khe Sanh. Ten days later 70,000 Communists officially launched the Tet Offensive during the most important Vietnamese holiday of the year. In the past a tacit truce had existed during the Buddhist New Year (Tet). To celebrate, half of South Vietnam's 730,000-man army went on leave. Within a

period of forty-eight hours the enemy launched attacks against Saigon, Danang, Hu , Quang Tri, and virtually every other major city in South Vietnam, including dozens of military installations. General Cushman suddenly found himself engaged on all fronts, but first he had to save the Marine battalion isolated at Khe Sanh.

> '*Westmoreland and Marine generals were astounded to learn that President Johnson so feared a defeat that he required the JCS to pledge personally that Khe Sanh would not fall.*'
>
> ALLAN R. MILLETT, *SEMPER FIDELIS.*

On 22 January the battle for Khe Sanh opened with a massive artillery, rocket, and mortar attack that blew up 1,340 tons of ammunition at the base dump. Cushman ordered the 1st Battalion, 9th Marines, a South Vietnamese Ranger battalion, and two 105mm batteries airlifted to Khe Sanh. The garrison, now 6,000 strong, kept the airfield open against 15-20,000 (some said 40,000) enemy troops from two NVA divisions.

On 6 February the 304th NVA Division opened with another artillery and mortar attack against Khe Sanh and a Special Forces camp six miles away at Lang Vei. Green Beret and Montagnard survivors fought off flamethrowers and nine Russian-made PT-76 tanks at Lang Vei until airlifted to safety by Marine helicopters.

Encouraged by their success at Lang Vei, the NVA continued to pound Khe Sanh, using artillery and mortar cover fire as they attacked hilltop positions and the Marine perimeter. Four hundred Marines held an outpost on Hill 881 (South), a critical height northwest of Khe Sanh. They suffered fifty percent casualties but held the hill, raising and lowering the Stars and Stripes to the daily call of the bugle. Three other hills – 558, 861, and 950 – all played a role in the defense of Khe Sanh, and all were held with equal valor.

The shelling reached a new peak on 23 February when 1,300 enemy missiles exploded inside the Khe Sanh perimeter. As the siege of the firebase continued, the world nervously watched their television screens, and so did President Johnson.

TWO-MONTH BOMBARDMENT

NVA artillery shelled the base, the airfield, and all the approaches to the base every day for two months. Despite the constant attacks, Khe Sanh received a daily supply of ammunition, equipment, and supplies by air. Marine C-130 Hercules, C-123 Providers, and helicopters performed miracles, flying in supplies and evacuating the wounded. The transports eventually gave up trying to land on the short airfield and devised new tactics for making successful low altitude drops. The Low Altitude Parachute Extraction System (LAPES) method for C-130s involved a low-level approach, during which a parachute filled and dragged the cargo across rollers, out the rear doors, and onto the airstrip. For the Ground Parachute Extraction System (GPES), the "Herk" came in low and snagged an arresting line that pulled the cargo to the ground. The two systems worked so well that none of the airdrops reached the enemy.

Helicopter supply and evacuation missions became especially dangerous. Marine Squadron HMM-262, flying Boeing Vertol CH-46 Sea Knight assault helicopters, lost half of their transports during February and had to be replaced by another squadron. Chopper crews made three deliveries a

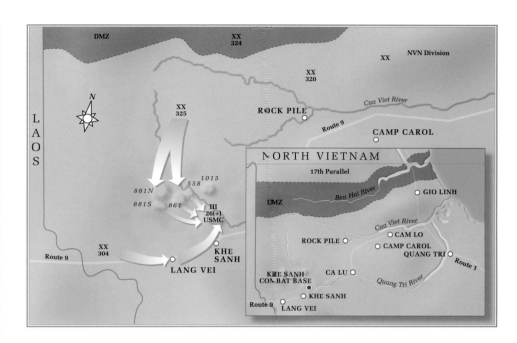

Above: The location of the Khe Sanh combat base so close to the DMZ and the Laotian border disrupted the enemy's supply lines and quite naturally invited attacks from the North Vietnamese.

Left: On 21 February 1968 C-130 cargo planes make one of their regular supply drops at Khe Sanh. The drops occurred at regular hours three times a day.

Below: Many of the C-130 Hercules and C-123 Provider airdrops to the besieged Marines occurred at low levels.

Above: Marines unload from a Sikorsky CH-53E Super Stallion in the Khe Sanh region. The CH-53s provided the Corps with rotary-wing heavy lift capability; in addition to carrying troops, CH-53Es also airlifted light trucks and supplies.

Right: On 2 December 1972 journalist Dale Hodge (left) interviews Colonel Joshua W. Dorsey III, senior United States Marine Corps advisor in Vietnam, on the progress in turning over military operations to the South Vietnamese. The process began in 1969, and by 1972 most of the combat Marine units had left South Vietnam.

day, the first at 0900, the last at 1700 hours. They came in gaggles of twelve CH-46s, each carrying 3,000 pounds of cargo, escorted by four UH-1E gunships and as many as twelve Marine A-4s.

During February and March, carrier-based aircraft flew 3,100 sorties against NVA positions around Khe Sanh. B-52s from distant Pacific bases pounded the enemy-occupied areas around the perimeter until the verdant green hillsides looked more like a wetted red-orange lunar surface swept by a monsoon. The combined and constant air attacks demoralized the enemy.

General Giap's North Vietnamese forces used siege tactics characteristic of World War I. Every night they dug trenches, zigzag approaches, and parallels, inching closer to the Marine perimeter. In the morning A-4 Skyhawks flew over the new excavations and incinerated them with napalm. Air attacks kept the enemy in their burrows around Khe Sanh. They attacked only the more vulnerable outposts. If the enemy slithered toward the perimeter, the Marines waited until their heads came in sight and then opened with 105mm batteries. Boxed in on three sides by artillery fire or by fighter-bombers, the enemy could only move forward and into the machine guns on the Marines' firebase.

BREAK-OUT

The siege continued until early April, during which American aircraft dropped 100,000 tons of bombs on enemy positions around Khe Sanh and bloodied the landscape with NVA corpses. On 1 April the Army launched Operation "Pegasus" to relieve Khe Sanh. Three days later the 1st Battalion, 9th Marines, attacked from Khe Sanh and captured Hill 471. On 6 April advance elements of the U.S. 1st Cavalry Division and a South Vietnamese airborne battalion reopened Route 9 and

established contact with the Marines on Hill 471. By 14 April the only NVA remnants south of the DMZ were corpses or prisoners.

During the course of the siege, more than 10,000 NVA died in combat against 205 dead and 800 wounded among the defenders. After the predictions of another Dienbienphu, some military experts expressed surprised that the Marines defending the firebase actually survived. They should have known better.

The Tet Offensive, which began on the morning of 31 January 1968 came as a surprise to General Westmoreland, but it also came as an opportunity. The Viet Cong and NVA had been suffering grievous punishment, their casualties running in the ratio of 10:1 against American forces. Most of the fighting had drifted away from the cities and into the fringes along the DMZ and the Laotian and Cambodian borders. Westmoreland had just reported the end of the war in sight and was planning to reduce the number of U.S. troops in South Vietnam when the Tet Offensive erupted. The Viet Cong and NVA chose to fight in the open, giving Westmoreland his best opportunity to destroy them.

Television coverage centered the attention of Americans at home on the already unpopular war and especially on Saigon, where a suicide squad of fifteen sappers penetrated the U.S. embassy and killed five servicemen before being shot to death. By concentrating news coverage on the wrong incidents, correspondents failed to report the severe losses of the enemy during the Tet Offensive. Around Saigon, some 32,000 Viet Cong and North Vietnam troops lost their lives in the assault, compared with minor losses among

American and South Vietnamese troops. The offensive's psychological impact on the American people, as transmitted by television journalists, transformed a stunning victory for American arms that might have ended the war into a political victory for the North Vietnamese. The only crisis on the battlefield occurred at the ancient city of Hu , where the North Vietnamese captured and held the former capital for a month.

During the Tet Offensive, the NVA and the Viet Cong lost 400,000 men. The horrendous losses coupled with the enemy's inability to hold any gains for more than a day or two discouraged the NVA from committing their reserves. Tet shattered the Viet Cong as a force of organized resistance, though guerrilla warfare continued on a nuisance basis. Over time, guerrilla attacks resumed and successfully disrupted the pacification program.

With the NVA recoiling and pulling back into North Vietnam, General Westmoreland recog-

nized an opportunity to win the war and stabilize the country. He asked for another 200,000 troops. President Johnson, who was now more concerned about his legacy than victory, refused the request. On 31 March he announced that he would not seek reelection and called for the beginning of peace talks. Three days later Radio Hanoi announced a willingness on the part of North Vietnam to discuss conditions for holding the proposed peace talks. On 10 April, to lay the groundwork for peace talks, Johnson removed Westmoreland and replaced him with the deputy commander, General Creighton Abrams.

Two months after Hu had been recaptured and the enemy banished during the Tet offensive, General Abrams dismantled the Khe Sanh firebase and moved everything back to Route 9. After the expenditure of immense resources to secure and maintain a virtually impregnable forward position, the withdrawal reopened a closed corri-

► **31 MARCH:** President Johnson declares he will not run for reelection and authorizes peace talks.

14 APRIL: The siege of Khe Sanh is lifted.

5 JULY: Marines are ordered to abandon the Khe Sanh base.

1969

25 JANUARY: Truce talks with the North Vietnamese begin.

26 MARCH: Lieutenant General Herman Nickerson, Jr., relieves General Cushman as commander of the III MAF.

THE BATTLE FOR HU

Located on the eastern seaboard midway between Danang and the DMZ lay the ancient, imperial capital of what was once Indochina. Out of respect for the palace and other historic buildings, a major military base had never been built at Hu . The 1st ARVN Division maintained its headquarters in a corner of the citadel, defended only by the Black Panther Company. As the clock struck midnight on the morning of 31 January, infiltrators shed their civilian clothes, rockets and mortar shells fell from the sky, and Communists took control of the Hu 's Old and New Cities.

Before dawn, the 1st Marines from nearby Phu Bai loaded into trucks and followed tanks to the Perfume River. Most of the leathernecks were short-term enlisted men accustomed to engaging Viet Cong in rural settings where superior firepower and mobility could be employed. Recapturing Hu became a point of honor for the South Vietnamese, so the Marines waited for permission from General Lam to counterattack. Lam paused four days before deciding that he needed the Marines' superior firepower, but he restricted the use of heavy weapons fearing irreparable damage to the city's historic buildings.

On 4 February the 1st Marines led the counterattack – a house-to-house affair through rubble-strewn and fire-swept streets with the odds stacked against them. Despite restrictions, Marine artillery fired 18,000 rounds on select targets. Two days later they recaptured provincial headquarters, the jail, and the hospital. North of the river, the 3rd ARVN and three airborne battalions attacked the northeastern corner of the rectangular city.

On 12 February more Marines arrived by helicopter and landing craft for the final assault across the river. Marines took the left flank, the ARVN took the center, and the South

Vietnamese Marines took the right. To placate the Vietnamese, the Marines moved in spurts, stopping to enable the ARVN to keep stride with the advance. During the street fighting, Marine M48 tanks gave way to "Ontos," a maneuverable thinly armored tracked vehicle mounting six recoilless rifles.

The enemy followed the example of the Japanese on Okinawa and gave way grudgingly. On 22 February the Marines breached the southeast wall of the citadel, backed away, and let the South Vietnamese fight for the Imperial Palace. The Black Panther Company entered the deserted palace, and on February 24 the Vietnamese flag rose above the citadel for the first time in almost a month. Only then did the Marines discover that the Communists had executed 5,000 civilians as "political enemies."

Left: *At Quang Nam in 1966, a CH-46 Sea Knight of HMM-265 accelerates out of the landing zone after dropping part of a multi-battalion of Marines into an area targeted for a search and destroy mission. The CH-46s are still used as a medium-lift assault helicopter. Young helicopter pilots of today are heard to say, "If a Sea Knight was good enough for my father to fly, its good enough for me."*

CHAPTER NINE

READINESS, TERRORISM, AND WAR

(1960-1991)

TIMELINE

1960

1 January: General David M. Shoup becomes 22nd Commandant of the Marine Corps.

Previous page: *Terrorist attacks took on a new dimension on 18 April 1983 when a truck bomb exploded outside the U.S. Embassy in Beirut, Lebanon, and killed sixty-one persons, including one U.S. Marine.*

Below: *At the Marine Corps Recruit Depot at Parris Island, conditioning comes first. Here a number of drill instructors work enlistees on a horizontal bar to do dead hang pull-ups. The number of grimacing faces suggest that some of the men will have to work extra hard to make the grade.*

On 1 January 1960 General David M. Shoup, a veteran of thirty-four years, became commandant of the Marine Corps. He believed the Corps had become too soft and determined to toughen its fiber. He started with the Officers Candidate Schools (OCS) in the woods of Quantico in northern Virginia. At the time, Shoup did not know that he would need platoon officers and company officers for the Vietnam War, but he expected to need them for something.

At Quantico, every OCS candidate endured the same arduous ten-week training regimen as enlisted men's boot camp, but Shoup made it a tougher and more grueling course. More than 30 percent of the men washed-out: some by physical incapacity, some by injury, and others by irresolute determination. At Quantico there was no secret formula for success. One bull-necked captain declared, "If a young man is physically fit and has the right mental attitude, he'll make it. That also goes for women, who do the same training as the men with modified physical test requirements."

Veteran NCOs and carefully hand-picked officers trained the aspiring young officers. The differences in training between boot camp for enlistees and OCS for officers involved leadership. Both groups went through physical fitness training, fire and maneuver exercises, an obstacle course, a three-mile run, and firing a rifle while rolling and zigzagging over terrain cluttered with hazards. OCS candidates also worked through a reaction course, taking turns to lead groups through obstacles that looked easy but were difficult to navigate. After completing the reaction course, the candidates faced the combat course, a 1,200-yard labyrinth not unlike the battlefield at Belleau Wood but with walls that had to be scaled, barbed wire to crawl under, two-plank bridges to cross, ditches, a water-filled drainage pipe, and an enemy bunker to attack. Those men and women with enough perseverance to make it through OCS entered The Basic School as second lieutenants. They spent the next twenty-three weeks learning leadership skills, battlefield tactics, firing and care of infantry weapons, marksmanship, land navigation, and physical fitness.

In the early 1960s the training of enlistees at Parris Island, North Carolina, began to change. Between the two world wars, young men joining the Marines came from farms and tended to be

> *'The Basic School's mission has at its heart a single purpose – to prepare newly commissioned officers to lead our most important asset: the enlisted Marine.'*
>
> John de St. Jorre, *The Marines.*

physically hardened. If a roughneck drill instructor (DI) greeted his new recruits with a challenge, half of the platoon stepped forward with their fists clenched. The "permissive society" of the 1960s, the Vietnam War, racial tension, and the dependence on draftees changed all that. The "Old Breed" and the "New Breed" gave way to a mixed breed of less compliant draftees. Combat training did not change, but hazing, maltreatment, corruption, and random brutality did change. Fifty push-ups, a jolt in the gut, extra duty, or the threat of being demoted to the Army once worked wonders on the derelicts. Today a DI is not allowed to touch a recruit except to adjust his uniform.

On 10 November 1975 the Marine Corps celebrated its 200th birthday. Many changes had taken place, especially in the area of training, and those changes tried to keep pace with the nation's rapidly changing culture. The Marine Corps still wanted men and women who could be shaped to meet the Corps' traditional high standards of excellence, and recruits passed through three clearly defined phases of training. The first came as a shock – a sudden transformation from the liberties of civilian life to an intensive indoctrination into the fundamentals of military life. Upon their arrival at boot camp enlistees underwent a highly ritualized psychological assault course administered by drill instructors. The DI stripped away civilian habits. He paid ruthless attention to the smallest details of dress and kit maintenance,

'Some good people might have stayed [in the Marines] if things had been tough enough to create the conditions where a guy couldn't quit. Physical fitness by itself does not mean tenacity. The thing that really disturbs me is the drill instructor being made to stand in front of his platoon and swear that he's going to be nice and not use bad language. That DI's got to be god when he walks in there. The officers aren't the problem, Congress is the problem and the American Civil Liberties Union lawyers.'

JAMES WEBB,
FORMER SECRETARY OF THE NAVY.

THE DRILL INSTRUCTOR'S CREED

These recruits are trusted to my care. I will train them to the best of my ability. I will develop them into smartly disciplined, physically fit, basically trained Marines, thoroughly indoctrinated in love of Corps and country. I will demand of them, and demonstrate by my own example, the highest standards of personal conduct, morality, and professional skill.

Below: Marine Lance Corporal Perdo Sosa, 3rd Transportation Support Battalion, 3rd Force Service Support Group, at Camp Butler, Okinawa, crosses muddy water, avoiding barbed wire only inches from his face, in the "Pit and Pond" obstacle endurance course at the Jungle Warfare Training Center in Okinawa.

Right: At Parris Island, USMC recruit Sharp waits pensively for her fellow recruits to swing across Crucible event "Gonzales' Crossing," during which they have to wear an M17 field protective gas mask to simulate chemical war conditions. As Gunnery Sergeant Chris Borghese said, "There's nothing like the challenge of taking civilians and making them into Marines."

and he administered the lessons in a loudly articulated eyeball-to-eyeball verbal assault that left the recipient sometimes humiliated, sometimes flabbergasted, occasionally amused, but mostly just madder than hell.

After long hours of drilling and a punishing routine of physical exercises, the second phase of training began on the firing range. There a recruit learned to fire and maintain his rifle. With fifty rounds, each worth five points, the rifleman had to score at least 190 out of a possible 250 points to qualify as a "marksman," 210 points as "sharpshooter," and 220 points as "expert." Competition united the platoons. Those who failed to score 190 points sometimes suffered the penalty of wearing their shooting jackets backwards, and DIs made them point the barrels of their rifles toward the ground when they marched off the firing range.

The third phase of training began when the DI announced that one platoon would be chosen as the honor platoon on graduation day. The psychological effect of more intra-platoon competition helped to unify the recruits as a cohesive unit during the final days of training. This included a day on the Confidence Course – an assault course designed to test the individual's strength, agility, and physical courage. During the final days, recruits prepared for a series of written tests, followed by one last physical fitness test and a series of drill competitions judged by senior NCOs. Family and friends received invitations to view the final graduation parade: a distinct change from the 1950s when men and women simply packed their gear in a seabag and departed for their assigned unit.

> *'There's nothing quite like the challenge of taking civilians and making them into Marines. Your focus has to be intense, and you have to be totally committed, and most importantly, you must live and breathe by the Drill Instructor's Creed.'*
>
> GUNNERY SGT. CHRIS BORGHESE,
> 10 AUGUST 2001.

Drill instructors experienced war from the inside. They had been around the world and fought in the Pacific, Korea, or Vietnam. They cared about their platoon in ways the young leathernecks would eventually learn to appreciate and respect. They taught fighting, survival, and readiness. With a Cold War escalating around the world, they trained the platoon to be ready to fight wherever called.

CUBAN MISSILE CRISIS

On 14 October 1962, with Communist insurgency on the rise in Vietnam, an American U-2 reconnaissance plane shot photographs of a Soviet missile site under construction at San Cristóbal, 100 miles west of Havana, Cuba. Two days later other photographs showed Soviet Il-28 bombers being assembled on Cuban airfields.

President John F. Kennedy spent six days evaluating the problem with his military and civilian advisors before announcing on 22 October a naval "quarantine" of Cuba – a novel term designed to avoid the war-word "blockade." Two days later the U.S. Second Fleet, carrying the II Marine Expeditionary Force (MEB), and two carrier groups moved into positions around the island. Four hundred Marine aircraft prepared to throw an aerial umbrella over Guantanamo Bay and fly cover for an amphibious assault on Cuba. In eight days the Marine Corps assembled a task force of 40,000 men, the largest amphibious gathering since Okinawa. Had the JCS ordered the invasion of the island, the II MEB would have led an assault against Cuba's well-defended beaches west of Havana. President Kennedy and Premier Nikita Khrushchev reached a mutually face-saving compromise, and the Soviets agreed to withdraw their planes and missiles.

After the crisis ended, General Shoup addressed the performance of the Fleet Marine Force. In a serious test of the Corps' readiness, the Marines had matched or surpassed the operational responsiveness of the joint forces Strike Command. Although Shoup identified areas for improvement, the very readiness of the FMF proved that the "Flexible Response" mission of the Corps could deter war as well as fight it.

When it came to protecting the interests of the United States in its traditional sphere of influence, the Marine Corps proved that it could still move swiftly and decisively. Problems with Cuban dictator Fidel Castro showed signs of escalating. The U.S. government kept amphibious forces in the Caribbean shuttling from the traditional training areas in Puerto Rico to the south coast of Hispaniola, where Castroism had begun to destabilize the governments of Haiti and the Dominican Republic. A prolonged period of political turmoil followed the 30 May 1961 assas-

sination of pro-U.S. dictator Rafael Trujillo. Unlike in Haiti, where François "Papa Doc" Duvalier passed without war his power to his son, the Dominican Republic dissolved in political chaos with the death of Trujillo. The United States remained watchful for four years while the Dominican Republic tried to create a stable government, but every passing year brought the Communists closer to power.

In the meantime President Johnson, on 7 August 1964, received approval from Congress to expand America's role in Vietnam and Marines began spilling into Danang. With America's attention reverted to the growing conflict in Southeast Asia, street fighting engulfed Santo Domingo and sparked a civil war between the new military junta and leftist insurgents. Obsessed with a Castroite plot to control the Dominican Republic, Johnson responded to an appeal for help from the Dominican Republic's junta. On 28 April 1965 he ordered the 6th Marine Expeditionary Unit (MEU), which consisted of the 3rd Battalion, 6th Marines, and the Marine Medium Helicopter Squadron-264 (HMM-264) into Santo Domingo. Both units were attached to the U.S. Navy's six-ship squadron of the Caribbean Ready Group.

> *'The Marine Corps is in the best condition of readiness that I have seen in my thirty-seven years of naval service.'*
>
> COMMANDANT GENERAL WALLACE GREENE TO HOUSE OF REPRESENTATIVES, NOVEMBER 1965.

▶ **1962**

14 OCTOBER: The Cuban Missile Crisis begins.

22 OCTOBER: President Kennedy announces the "quarantine" of Cuba. Marines at Guantanamo Bay go on alert.

28 OCTOBER: The Cuban Missile Crisis is resolved.

1964

1 JANUARY: General Wallace M. Greene, Jr., becomes the 23rd Commandant of the Marine Corps.

1965

28 APRIL: The 3rd Battalion, 6th Marines, intervene in the Dominican Republic, followed by the 4th Marine Expeditionary Brigade.

6 JUNE: Troops from the Organization of American States relieve Marines in the Dominican Republic.

1968

1 JANUARY: General Leonard J. Chapman, Jr., becomes the 24th Commandant of the Marine Corps.

1972

1 JANUARY: General Robert E. Cushman, Jr., becomes 25thCommandant of the Marine Corps.

Left: *During the Cuba missile crisis in 1962, Pfc Robert E. Bealls, stationed with a special detachment at Guantanamo Bay, scans the Cuban hills on Fidel Castro's side of the cactus fence enclosing the U. S. Naval base. At the time, the Marines at Guantanamo were all on a twenty-four hour alert.*

▶ **21 NOVEMBER:** A Marine guard is killed when a mob storms the U.S. Embassy at Islamabad, Pakistan.

5 DECEMBER: The Corps announces the formation of a joint-services Rapid Deployment Force (RDF).

1980

1 MARCH: Lieutenant General Paul X. Kelly takes command of the first Rapid Development Joint Task Force.

24 APRIL: The joint rescue attempt to free American hostages held in Teheran ends in disaster.

1981

20 JANUARY: After 444 days, Iran releases more than 65 hostages, among them 14 Marines.

Top right: *Sea Stallions making it back to the* Nimitz *after the crippling sandstorm at Desert One all required major repairs to the mechanism driving their rotors.*

Above right: *A C-130, with its tail nipped off by a Sea Stallion, sits in the sands of Desert One. The troops that were inside escape and stand nearby in a state of shock.*

Right: *The unexpected collision of the Sea Stallion with the C-130 set off Redeye missiles, which set the aircraft on fire and literally blew the props off the wings, adding tragedy and more embarrassment to President Carter's debacle.*

Beckwith intended that his 118-man Delta force and their equipment be loaded onto Sea Stallions and flown to Desert One, a staging area hide-site in a desolate area 200 miles from Teheran. From there, Beckwith planned to free the hostages by launching a complicated operation supported by massive firepower from C-130 gunships. While the gunships smothered the embassy compound with fire, Marine-piloted helicopters would fly into designated areas to extract the Delta assault teams and the hostages and ferry them to Manzariyeh Airfield, thirty-five miles to the south. There a force of U.S. Rangers would be waiting with a flight of Lockheed C-114 StarLifter transports to take everyone out of Iran. Beckwith's intricate game plan read more like a script for the next Chuck Norris movie, and had it worked, may have become one.

DISASTER IN THE SAND

Desert One, as the operation has come to be called, began unraveling soon after it began. Two of the crucial Marine helicopters experienced mechanical trouble in a dust storm and returned to the *Nimitz*, leaving six to finish the mission. At a desert refueling site, a third chopper conked out, leaving too few aircraft to complete the rescue. Colonel Beckwith cancelled the operation. He ordered everyone off the helicopters and into the transports, leaving the Marines to fly the

'*I tell my Marines if you want to have a few drinks and hire a hotel room or go to your girlfriend's place, that's fine. But not in the Marine house. A moral code is important; if not, there's chaos.*'

MASTER GUNNERY SERGEANT RICHARD W. CARLISLE, QUOTED IN *THE MARINES*, BY JOHN DE ST. JORRE.

empty Sea Stallions back to the *Nimitz*. During the withdrawal a fourth helicopter collided with a troop-laden transport on the ground. The Hercules burst into flames, setting off Redeye missiles that exploded in all directions. The troops inside the transport made a miraculous escape, but the five-man crew of the C-130 and three Marines lost their lives. Beckwith abandoned the remaining Sea Stallions and the eight charred bodies of the flyers and hastily departed on the remaining air-craft. President Carter remained distressed over the incident for the remainder of his term. After 444 days Iran made an undignified gesture toward the Carter administration, which had suffered a terminal blow in the recent elections. On 20 January 1981 the Iranians released the hostages, the day of President Ronald Reagan's inauguration.

During the 1980s the Marine Corps experi-enced an unprecedented malaise, attributable in part to what the Corps perceived as a disgraceful end to the Vietnam War. Terrorists wore no uni-forms and could not be distinguished from local inhabitants on the street. Their actions could not be predicted, leaving Marines on station around the world somewhat baffled over designing effec-tive countermeasures in the face of recent politi-cal restraints. Three Marines suffered wounds in Costa Rica when a mine exploded under their vehicle. In San Salvador four Marines were among thirteen persons killed at a sidewalk caf . Such incidents, once considered anomalies, had now become commonplace.

In 1986 the Corps experienced a new embar-rassment having nothing to do with terrorism. A few leathernecks began to sneak charming Soviet espionage agents into classified areas inside the embassy. A sex-for-secrets court-martial trial con-victed one Marine sergeant of aiding and abetting espionage.

LEBANON EVACUATION

Since the 1950s problems between rival Christian and Islamic factions in the Middle East had become more intractable as each year passed. The Israeli wars made the situation worse. Nowhere were the problems more manifest than in Lebanon, where the insurgency of the Palestinian Libera-tion Organization (PLO) threatened to increase the country's chronic instability. Since the sum-

mer of 1975 Lebanon had been engaged in a civil war spurred by religious differences. In mid-1976 Syria intervened and secured a temporary truce, but the warring factions could not reach agreement among themselves and the conflict continued.

In June 1982 Israelis invaded Lebanon in an effort to drive out the Syrians and stabilize Beirut by putting an end to the PLO. In advance of the Israeli invasion, Marines landed to evacuate any Americans wishing to leave. Two months later U.S. envoy Philip Habib negotiated an Israeli withdrawal, but the Lebanese government feared more trouble and asked for an international peacekeeping force. During America's military involvement in the Lebanon, Marines suffered severe losses at the hands of fanatical terrorists.

On 1 July 1983 General Paul Xavier Kelley became the 28th Commandant of the Marine Corps.

Below: *In August 1982 a Marine from the 32nd MAU stands guard next to a shot-up Lebanese passenger liner at the Beirut airport. The American intervention came at the invitation of the Lebanese government during a time when Israelis were warring with the PLO lodged in Beirut.*

Above right: Marines stand guard outside the U.S. Embassy after terrorists exploded a truck bomb near the entrance. Sixty-one persons lost their lives in the explosion. The strike marked the beginning of a new form of suicidal terrorism.

LEBANON – THE NEW TERRORISM

On 25 August 1982, Colonel James M. Mead led 800 Marines from the 32nd Marine Amphibious Unit (MAU) ashore at Beirut to shepherd the evacuation of PLO fighters trapped in Beirut by Israelis. On 10 September, after evacuating more than 12,000 Palestinians on vessels of the U.S. Sixth Fleet, the 32nd MAU withdrew from Beirut. Three days later Syrian sponsored assassins murdered Lebanon's newly elected the Maronite Christian president, Bashir Gemayel.

Israeli forces moved back into Beirut on the pretext of being the only stabilizing force in the area. On 16 September they made the mistake of standing idly by while Maronite Christian militia massacred Palestinian refugees in Beirut's suburban camps. President Ronald Reagan believed Israel's inaction would lead to further trouble and recommitted American forces to the area. On 29 September Colonel Mead returned to Beirut with 1,200 men from the 32nd MAU to join a Multinational Peacekeeping Force consisting of 2,200 French and Italian troops.

Marines moved onto the Beirut International Airport for what would become a long and anguished stay. Marines ashore patrolled the streets, though against what or who they were never sure. Every few months one Marine amphibious unit relieved the other. Sometimes the units took casualties without ever knowing the source. The situation appeared stabilized until 18 April 1983 when a truck bomb exploded outside the U.S. embassy in Beirut, killing sixty-one persons. Among the seventeen American dead, one Marine lost his life. Eight others received wounds.

On 17 May Israel agreed to withdraw from Lebanon, but Syria, which had moved sizeable forces into the country, refused to join the accord. The peacekeeping force kept the two rivals at bay until the summer of 1983 when they began drawing fire from Syrian-supported Druze militia. On 29 August two Marines died from enemy fire during a rocket, artillery, and mortar attack on their positions around Beirut's airport. The Sixth Fleet frigate *Bowen* (FF-1079) moved into position and with her 5-inch guns became the first American vessel to fire upon Syrian batteries in the hills above the city.

The presence of a Christian peacekeeping force in Lebanon only made matters worse. At

0625 on Sunday, 23 October, a Muslim suicide bomber driving a yellow Mercedes truck packed with at least 2,000 pounds of high explosives crashed through wire barricades outside the four-story concrete Marine headquarters building. After penetrating the lobby, the suicide-driver detonated the equivalent of six tons of TNT, killing 241 Americans, 220 of them Marines, and wounding 70 others. Minutes later and two miles away, 58 members of the French force died when a second truck rammed into their quarters. The Iranian-backed Shiite Hezbollah faction, representing themselves as enemies of "The Great Satan" (meaning the United States), took credit for the bombing.

The fighting between the peacekeeping force and the Syrian-backed and Iranian-backed militias continued to escalate, drawing America and the Sixth Fleet closer to war in the troubled Middle East. By 7 February 1984 President Reagan had seen enough of the incomprehensible convolutions of Lebanese politics and ordered the Marines out of the country. Having lost 260 men in Lebanon, the withdrawal marked one of the blackest days in the Marine Corps' history.

Because of his first and middle name, everybody referred to him as "P.X.," a common abridgement for the Post Exchange that served as a general store on every large American military base. Kelley had run the gamut from commanding the 1st Marines in Vietnam to becoming the first commander of the Rapid Deployment Joint Task Force. When he took over the reins from Commandant General Barrow, the situation in Lebanon had not yet become a crisis. The Marines liked their new, gregarious commandant whose winsome personality contrasted so sharply with the dour demeanor of Barrow. But Kelley was not prepared for the

shock in Beirut when on 23 October a terrorist's truck-bomb snuffed out the lives of 220 Marines. At the time, he was involved in a different crisis, one in the Caribbean, but the disaster in Lebanon cast a pall over the remainder of his tenure.

On 19 October 1983, four days before the bombing of Marine headquarters in Lebanon, a Communist military coup overthrew the government of Grenada, a 133-square-mile island in the eastern Caribbean and a former British colony and Commonwealth nation. A dispute between competing factions in Grenada's Communist-tainted government led to the seizure of power by extreme left-winger Bernard Coard, who inspired the execution by firing squad of Maurice Bishop, the prime minister. This event, coupled with military construction activity financed by Russia, aroused official concern in the United States over the safety of a thousand or so Americans on the island who were mostly students at St. George's University Medical School. From all appearances, the Soviets were converting Grenada into a springboard for the spread of communism among the independent eastern islands of the Caribbean.

Left: *In 1983 the 133-square-mile Caribbean island of Grenada became involved in a Soviet-sponsored attempt by Cubans to convert the former British colony into a haven for Castroite communism. When intelligence units informed President Ronald Reagan of communist intentions, he sent in the Marines.*

OUSTING MARXISTS

President Reagan considered the military buildup on Grenada a direct threat to American security and in many respects as dangerous as the Cuban crisis of 1962. He used the safety of American lives as a pretext for intervention, but his real objective was to oust the Marxists and restore a pro-American government. He diverted to Grenada a task force of twelve ships en route to Lebanon with 1,900 men of the 22nd Marine Amphibious Unit. The JCS augmented the strike force with the 75th Infantry (Ranger) Regiment, U.S. Army paratroopers from the 82nd Airborne Division, Navy SEALs, Army Special Forces, and a Delta anti-terrorist unit. In addition to the U.S. force, Grenada's Caribbean neighbors agreed to provide 400 police and military personnel who act as a stabilizing garrison after U.S. forces had secured the island.

On 22 October the Organization of Eastern Caribbean States, fearful that Grenada would become a Cuban-Soviet base, officially asked the United States to intervene. Two days after the amphibious force, led by the carrier *Independence* (CV-62), arrived off Grenada, President Reagan ordered the units to occupy the island.

Above: *Four hundred Marines borne by CH-53 Sea Stallion helicopters based on the amphibious assault ship* Guam *land on Pearls Airport and seize the only operational airfield on the island.*

Left: *On 27-28 October 1983, CH-46 Sea Knight helicopters brought heavy equipment into the landing zone on Grenada; what the helicopters could not carry was supplemented by LVTs from the MAU's amphibious attack force.*

▶ **27 OCTOBER:**
Grenada is secured.

1984

7 FEBRUARY:
President Reagan orders Marines removed from Lebanon.

1987

1 JULY: General Alfred Mason Gray, Jr., becomes the 29th Commandant of the Marine Corps.

The intervention at Grenada almost passed from three days of distorted television coverage into the oblivion of a brief sentence in history books. However, film actor/director Clint Eastwood revived the incident in 1986 with the movie "Heartbreak Ridge." Anybody looking at the title might associate the movie with the Korean War, but the film actually recreated the 1983 Grenada intervention. Right down to the profuse use of four-letter words, the movie offered a more realistic rendering of the operation than the many television crews posted at the airfield or on the campus of the medical school.

After Grenada, the United States put a tenuous latch on the spread of Communism in the Caribbean, but a crisis of a different nature threatened America – the flow of Colombian narcotics through Panama and into the streets of America. President Reagan attempted to disrupt Panama's involvement in the drug traffic by deposing the drug-dealing dictator, General Manuel Antonio Noriega. As relations with Noriega's government deteriorated, Reagan increased the company-sized Marine Corps Security Force in Panama City to a full battalion. The drug cartels skirmished with Marines and killed one Leatherneck. A few days later the assassination of a Marine lieutenant at a Panamanian checkpoint infuriated George H. W. Bush, who in 1989 succeeded Reagan as president. Bush ordered a massive intervention by a predominantly Army joint task force. On 20 December 1989 the strike force landed in Panama City and engaged in a week-long conflict that took the life of another Marine

OPERATIONS ON GRENADA

Before dawn on 25 October 1983, Vice Admiral Joseph Metcalf III sent a SEAL team ashore to infiltrate St. George's, the island's capital, and secure the Government House, where Governor General Sir Paul Scoon had been detained since the coup. As SEALs reached shore, 400 heli-borne Marines from the amphibious assault ship *Guam* (LPH-9) landed on Pearls Airport and seized the only operational airfield on the island. At 0600 USAF C-5A and C-130 transports from Barbados airdropped Army Rangers over a nearly complete 9,000-foot jet airfield being built by Cubans at Point Salinas on the southern end of the island. Cuban troops on the island, numbering about 800, staged a stiff resistance, but by mid-morning the Marines had moved across seven-eighths of the island, secured the airfield, and taken possession of the medical school's campus.

During the evening another detachment of 250 Marines with five tanks made an amphibious landing at Grand Mal Bay, just north of St. George's. On the morning of 26 October they reached Fort Frederick and its Richmond Hill prison where they found the SEALS, who had landed the day before, besieged by Cubans. The Marines raised the siege, and at the governor's request airlifted him and thirty-two government officials to the *Guam*. Marines at the Grande

Above: *On their way to St. George's, Marines pass through Grenville, keeping watch for signs of the enemy hidden in homes and behind fences.*

Below: *American medical students wave to U. S. troops as they move to board aircraft bound for the United States.*

Anse medical school campus, having given American students at the school time to pack some of their personal belongings, began evacuating them to the Point Salinas airfield. Cubans and a small number of troops from the Grenadan People's Revolutionary Army outside the campus sniped at the Marines but hit none of the students.

On 27 October American forces secured all the military objectives on the island and captured more than 600 Cubans. Although a few pockets of resistance remained, Marines and Rangers mopped them up before nightfall. Of eighteen Americans killed and 116 wounded, the Marines lost three killed and fifteen wounded. Cuban and Grenadan casualties ran about the same.

Discoveries made later justified the attack on Grenada. During the roundup of prisoners American forces found 49 Russian, 24 North Korean, and 13 Eastern European diplomats and advisors busily engaged in converting the island into a fortified base for Cuban communism. Marines discovered warehouses crammed with Russian weapons and documents revealing plans for providing a garrison of nearly 7,000 Cuban troops. Though some of the Grenadans had cast their lot with the communists, the majority of the inhabitants greeted the Americans as liberators.

and wounded three more. The operation led to the capture of General Noriega but did not end the drug traffic.

PROTECTING U.S. INTERESTS

Throughout the 1980s the situation in the Persian Gulf remained unsettled. Muslim nations situated around the area, coupled with the spread of the Iranian Ayatollah's anti-American propaganda, threatened to disrupt the supply of oil to the United States. Soviet Russia's invasion of Afghanistan in 1979 added more destabilization to the region and threatened pro-Western states in the area. President Carter made it clear that Amer-

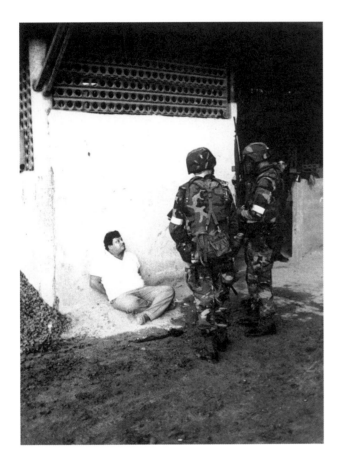

ica stood ready to support with military force any intrusion into its interests by hostile forces. The bungled attempt by Delta forces to rescue hostages from Teheran made the warning ring hollow.

Six weeks after Ronald Reagan became president the Marine Corps created the Rapid Deployment Joint Task Force with headquarters at McDill Air Base at Tampa, Florida. In October 1981 the unit became a separate task force having joint control of all forces assigned to it. Future Marine Commandant Lieutenant General Paul "P.X." Kelley took command of the force and put it on standing readiness for operations anywhere in the world, including the Persian Gulf. The Marine Corps now had a highly mechanized Marine Amphibious Brigade with three Maritime Prepositioning Ships ready to move at a moment's notice.

In 1984, during the eight-year Iran-Iraq conflict, a "tanker war" erupted in the Persian Gulf. Iraq struck Iranian tankers and the Iranians retaliated by going after the tankers of Iraq's Persian Gulf supporters. Three years later the Kuwaiti tanker *Bridgetown*, operating under the registry of the United States, struck an Iranian mine. General George B. Crist, USMC, part of the Navy's Middle East Force, dispatched anti-mine helicopters from amphibious assault ships to locate and destroy the Russian-made mines planted by Iran. Crist also used attack helicopters against Iranian oil platforms, and before the war ended in 1989, rendered a number of them inoperable.

IRAQ'S MONEY-GRABBING SCHEME

Saddam Hussein, who had seized power in 1979 and made himself the new Iraqi president, spent $500 billion on the war with Iran. By 1989 he had generated an $80 billion national debt while becoming the world's largest arms importer. With one million troops, he also operated the world's fourth largest military force. He intended to use

Left: On 20 December 1989 Marines from the Second Light Armored Infantry Battalion and the First Anti-terrorism Security Team round up troublemakers in the town of Arrijan on the west side of Panama. Dressed in civilian clothes, terrorists and insurgents cannot be distinguished from the average man, woman, or youngster on the street.

Left: Marines take a little cover outside a suspected haunt occupied by insurgents near Arrijan, Panama. Warned to be wary of booby traps, two Marines work ahead of the squad and call out in Spanish for the people inside to surrender.

I need $30 billion and if they don't give it to me, I'm going to take it from them.

Saddam Hussein.

Top: *A few days prior to Desert Storm, the 1st Battalion, 2nd Marines, from Camp Lejuene, form in the Saudi Arabian desert for their last exercise before going into battle.*

Above right: *U. S. Marine AH-1W Sea Cobra helicopters of Utility/Attack Squadron 369 (HMLA-369) are refueled during exercise Imminent Thunder during the final phases of Operation Desert Shield.*

the army to free his nation from debt. At a 1990 conference of Arab nations, he demanded funds from his rich Persian Gulf neighbors.

At 2:00 a.m. on 2 August 1990, on the pretext of reprisals against Kuwait for pumping oil from fields lying under southern Iraqi soil, 100,000 troops from eight Iraqi Republican Guard divisions began crossing into Kuwait. Columns of Iraqi tanks led the assault along the six-lane super-highway leading to Kuwait City. Jet fighters and armed helicopters flew air cover over the advancing army. As the morning sun rose in the sky, Iraqi forces smashed into Kuwait City as the emir of Kuwait and other members of the ruling family fled in limousines from the opposite side of the city and disappeared into Saudi Arabia. Six days later Saddam Hussein announced the annexation of Kuwait to Iraq. President Bush promptly replied, "This will not stand! This will not stand! This aggression against Kuwait." On 7 August

In the life of a nation, we're called upon to define who we are and what we believe. Sometimes the choices are not easy.

President George H. W. Bush, 8 August 1990.

1990 he announced Operation Desert Shield, and American troops began heading for the Gulf.

Before JCS Chairman General Colin Powell perfected plans to implement Desert Shield/Storm, he extracted from President Bush a promise not to micro-manage the war as President Johnson had done during Vietnam. Powell asked the president to "set a clear political objective, provide sufficient forces to do the job, then keep out of the way." Bush agreed, giving birth to one of the most remarkable campaigns in modern warfare.

Desert Shield triggered the expedited movement of the 7th Marine Expeditionary Brigade (MEB) from California to the Persian Gulf. On 15 August more than 15,000 Marines began landing at Al Jubayl on giant C-5A Galaxy transports. A few days later the brigade's combat supplies and combat equipment arrived by ship: 123 tanks, 425 artillery pieces, and 124 tactical aircraft. Ten days later the brigade commander informed General H. Norman Schwarzkopf, Central Command's commander-in-chief, that the men and women of the 7th MEB were prepared to hold a line forty miles north of Al Jubayl. Across the Kuwaiti-Saudi bor-

der 7th MEB faced tens of thousands of Iraq's finest troops. Despite a woeful weakness in numbers, the Marines arrived just in time to discourage Hussein from assaulting Saudi Arabia's economic centers along the eastern Gulf coast.

BUILDUP IN SAUDI

On 21 August the 1st MEB arrived by air from Hawaii. Lieutenant General Walter A. Boomer consolidated the 7th MEB with the 1st MEB and formed the powerful I Marine Expeditionary Force (MEF), which included Major General Mike Myatt's 1st Marine Division and the 1st Marine Aircraft Wing. By the beginning of November, Boomer had 42,000 Marines – a quarter of the Corps' active strength – in Saudi Arabia.

General Alfred Mason Gray, Jr., who on 1 July 1987 had become the 29th commandant of the Marine Corps, saw a magnificent opportunity to get his forces into a real battle again. He called up 23,000 Marine reservists, moved many of them into the 2nd Marine Division commanded by Major General William Keys, added the 2nd Marine Aircraft Wing, and formed the II MEF. He shipped it to the Gulf at the end of the year and a

> *'Camp Lejeune looked like it must have during World War II, with Marines reporting at all hours of the night, then starting out first thing the next morning to train for combat.'*
>
> FROM *THE GENERAL'S WAR*, BY MICHAEL R. GORDON AND BERNARD C. TRAINOR.

few weeks later added the 5th MEB. With preparations in their final stages, Gray packed his bags and departed for Saudi Arabia to share in the planned attack.

Gray and Boomer fully endorsed Central Command's tactical plans. General Schwarzkopf assigned Boomer's I MEF to spearhead a frontal assault against the Saddam Hussein line while the bulk of the U.S. and Coalition forces swung wide around the Iraqi right flank. Schwarzkopf called it his "Hail Mary" attack – a term more familiar to football fans. He might better have called the scheme an "end run," as he planned to get his main force around the Iraqi flank and into the rear of the Republican Guard, taking hold of the enemy's supply routes. He also planned to have a Marine amphibious force lying offshore to feint a landing near Kuwait City but not to come ashore unless needed.

Before dawn on 16 January 1991, the entire world watched as the offensive operation Desert Storm's aerial campaign blossomed bright over Baghdad. Tracer bullets from Iraqi antiaircraft guns streaked through the air at unseen attackers as Navy Tomahawk cruise missiles struck strategic targets in the city. In the early action F/A-18 Hornets of the 1st Marine Aircraft Wing, flying about one-quarter of the fixed-wing tactical aircraft in the Gulf, hit enemy communications and military targets on the ground. In the days that followed, Marine pilots from the 3rd MAW flew most of their sorties to soften-up the enemy's positions along the I MEF's designated sector of attack. Desert Storm marked the debut of the Marines Corps' new F/A-18D two-seat, all weather, night attack version of the Hornet fighter-bomber that would eventually replace the venerable A6-E Intruder.

Left: Lt. Gen. Walter Boomer, commanding the 1st Marine Expeditionary Force in the Persian Gulf, takes the podium on the hospital ship USNS Mercy (T-AH-19), which is in the region to support Operation Desert Shield. General Boomer lays out requirements for handling the wounded in the forthcoming battle with Iraq during Desert Storm.

Below: General Alfred M. Gray, commandant of the Marine Corps, holds a conference on the amphibious assault ship USS Nassau (LHA-4), anchored near Morehead City off the coast of North Carolina. While he speaks, Marine units embark for a trip to the Persian Gulf to participate in Operation Desert Shield.

Above: *A plane captain directs movement of an F/A-18 Hornet from Marine Fighter-Attack Squadron 333 (VMFA-333) onto the taxiway during Operation Desert Shield. More Hornets wait in the background.*

Above right: *In Saudi Arabia, an M60A1 main battle tank equipped with reactive armor, mine-clearing rollers and plows, stands by at the head of a column of AAVP-7A1 amphibious assault vehicles as the 2nd Marine Expeditionary Force prepares to enter Kuwait.*

Right: *A squadron of Marine Corps AV-8B Harrier II attack aircraft from Marine Attack Squadron 513 (VMA-513), originally from Yuma Marine Air Base, Arizona, fly in formation during Operation Desert Shield. The unique Harrier, having short takeoff and landing platform capability, provides the Marine Corps with an ideal fighter-bomber for support of amphibious operations.*

Ground fighting began on the night of 29 January when the Iraqi 5th Mechanized Division – forty-five tanks supported by infantry – drove ten miles south across the Saudi border and captured Al-Khafji, an oil-processing town on the Saudi coast. The attack made little tactical sense but nevertheless came as a surprise. The only occu-

> *'If the Iraqis are dumb enough to attack, they are going to pay a horrible price.'*
>
> GENERAL H. NORMAN SCHWARZKOPF,
> 27 AUGUST 1990.

> *'The great duel, the mother of all battles, has begun.'*
>
> SADDAM HUSSEIN TO IRAQI TROOPS.

pants of the town were small advance units of Saudi soldiers and a few U.S. Marines scouting and spotting for artillery.

The Iraqi tanks advanced into the town with their turrets turned backwards, a universal sign of surrender. Suddenly the turrets whipped around and the tanks spat fire. Baghdad radio called the attack, "a sign of the thunderous storm that would blow across the Arabian desert and destroy America."

The Iraqis held the unimportant town for thirty-six hours. Marine spotters dropped into hideouts and called in artillery. On 31 January Saudi and Qatari Coalition troops charged into the town, supported by U.S. Marine artillery, Marine Cobra helicopters, and F/A 18 and A-10 jets. The Iraqis lost twenty tanks and surrendered more than 400 prisoners. During the fight the Iraqis lost only thirty killed and another thirty-seven wounded, giving General Boomer a reason to doubt the toughness and resolution of Iraq's Republican Guard. Marines stood aside as victorious Saudis marched through the town of Al-Khafi shouting "Allah Akhbar!" – "God is great" – and waving their national banner. The Saudis had reason to cheer. They had won the first land battle in the modern history of their kingdom.

At 4:00 a.m. on 24 February General Schwarzkopf launched the ground offensive to liberate Kuwait. Boomer planned to have the 1st and 2nd Marine Divisions break through the Iraqi line at the Al-Wafrah oilfields, and eventually link up with a possible Marine amphibious landing near Kuwait City. Rain fell that morning. Overhead a low sky hung black with soot from fires set by Iraqis at Al-Wafrah.

In front of the Marines lay the Iraqi defensive line: huge rolls of barbed wire strung one on top of the other and rigged with mines and booby-traps. Behind the wire lay high barriers of sand, tank traps, trenches, and forts – the same type of obstacles the Republican Guards had used with effect against the Iranians. The Marines hunched in the cold rain, waiting for the signal, and when it came the Iraqi' bravado disappeared, along with their hold on Kuwait and its oilfields.

On 27 February President Bush announced a ceasefire. Four days passed before General Schwarzkopf began resolving the details of surrender with Iraqi generals. While the discussions continued, more than 92,000 men and women Marines in the Gulf waited for the outcome. Desert Storm became the largest single operation in Marine Corps history. General Boomer commanded more Marines in combat than did Roy Geiger at Okinawa. As a testament to the awesome efficacy of American modern military tactics, the Marines lost only twenty-four killed and ninety-two wounded, and left no MIAs. Against such losses they destroyed 1,040 Iraqi tanks, 608 armed personnel carriers, 432 artillery pieces, and 5 missile sites. They killed more than 1,500 Iraqis and captured more than 20,000 prisoners.

Not all the Marines came home upon the ceasefire. The Persian Gulf War evolved into a relief operation codenamed "Provide Comfort" for 750,000 displaced Kurds in northern Iraq. On 16 April the 24th Marine Expeditionary Unit joined an international force on the ground to protect Kurds from Hussein's attempts at ethnic cleansing, and they remained there for three months, 500 miles from their base at sea. Kurdish children called them "food soldiers," an endearing sobriquet for the recently victorious leathernecks.

In America's effort to protect Muslim nations and Muslim people from aggression by those of their faith or by those of other faiths, Desert Shield/Storm will always rank as a classic example of the willingness of the United States to bring stability to the world.

▶ **24 FEBRUARY:** The 1st and 2nd Marine Divisions breach Iraqi lines during the first day of ground fighting.

28 FEBRUARY: President Bush calls a halt to the Persian Gulf War exactly 100 hours after it began.

14 APRIL: Marines become part of a multinational force in northern Iraq to protect the Kurds.

THE 100-HOUR WAR

As the first 155mm howitzer rounds screamed overhead, signaling the Amewrican attack on Iraqi forces, Marines crawled out of sand holes and crossed into Kuwait. Cobra helicopters thrummed overhead, M60 tanks clanked forward, and armored vehicles and Humvees followed bearing thousands of Marines.

Engineers from the 2nd Marine Division cut through the barbed wire and fired Mic-Lics – rocket-propelled explosive charges – and cleared six lanes 12 feet wide and 300 feet long through the minefields. Tanks with front-fitted plows, rakes, and rollers charged through the gaps. Through these lanes poured 8,000 vehicles and 19,000 men of the 2nd Marine Division. Iraqi mortars and riflemen opened on the breach, only to attract the attention of Marine Cobras, which sprayed enemy lines with machine gun fire.

By 9:30 a.m. the 1st and 2nd Marine Divisions linked with the Army's 2nd Armored Division and achieved a breakthrough into Kuwait. As Abrams tanks smashed through the enemy's defenses, Marines witnessed Iraqis leap from their vehicles and dissolve in the smoke of battle. "We just went up the battlefield and killed everything in our path," said Marine tank Captain Roy Bierwirth. The enemy streamed out of their ditches, surrendering by the thousands. By the end of the day the 2nd Marine Division had destroyed four Iraqi brigades and captured 5,000 prisoners. The 1st Marine Division battled through the Al Burgan oil field south of Kuwait City. During the retreat the enemy set 500 oil wells on fire, making it impossible for Marines to see more than ten feet in any direction.

Along the Kuwaiti coast Marines and Saudis fought off three determined Iraqi counterattacks and destroyed dozens of enemy tanks. Despite the rain, fog, and smoke, A-10 Warthog ground-attack jets and AH-1W Sea Cobras swooped overhead, chopped the Iraqi counterattacks to pieces, and started a new wave of prisoners. Thousands of Iraqis threw down their arms,

Right: *During operations in Kuwait, two Marine M1 Abrams main battle tanks move across the desert during the early phase of the Desert Storm ground assault. The tanks swept around the Iraqi right flank and nullified the vaunted Republican Guard.*

> *'The Iraqi forces are conducting the Mother of all Retreats.'*
>
> SECRETARY OF DEFENSE RICHARD CHENEY, 27 FEBRUARY 1991.

Below: *A pair of Tiger Brigade Abrams tanks and a Bradley infantry fighting vehicle move into Kuwait to provide security.*

surrendering to anything in sight, including television camera crews and unmanned drones. Marines moved through lines of prisoners and the burning oil fields, capturing the Al Jaber air base and then the Kuwait International Airport. The Marine force afloat worked their feint so masterfully that they never needed to come ashore.

While the Iraqis concentrated their resources against attacks by the 1st and 2nd Marine Divisions, General Schwarzkopf sent the bulk of his ground and air forces around the right flank of the enemy. When the allied force hit the Republican Guard on the flank, the entire enemy line collapsed and the rout began.

On 24 February Marine ground and air forces began the 100-hour war. On 27 February they stepped aside, allowing a composite Arab battalion to liberate Kuwait City.

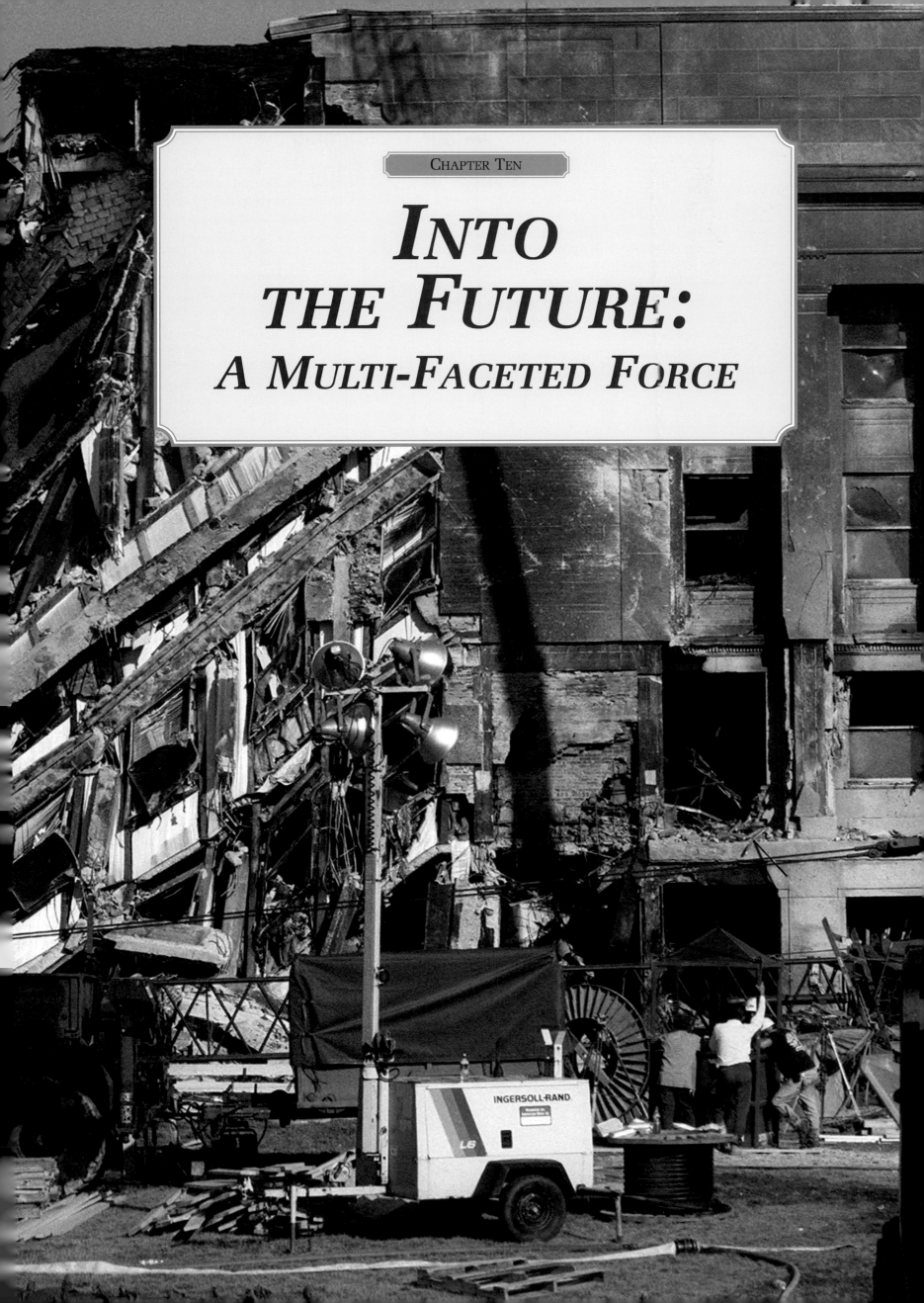

CHAPTER TEN

INTO THE FUTURE:
A MULTI-FACETED FORCE

Previous page: *On 11 September 2001, terrorists hijacked four jetliners. One struck and demolished the west wall of the Pentagon, killing 189 men and women and wounding dozens more.*

Above right: *Lt. Gen. Carol A. Mutter receives the Marine Corps System Command Organization flag. In 1996 she became the first woman of any service to achieve three-star status.*

Right: *Cpl. Robert Cutler, 5th Marines, explains the entrenching tool to Bangladeshi soldiers during Operation Sea Angel, a U.S. military effort to aid victims of cyclones.*

Not since World War II had America welcomed back her combat troops in the way that she did with those returning from the Persian Gulf. At San Diego, California, the 1st Marine Division paraded through the streets to resounding cheers from enormous crowds. At the nation's capital the 2nd Marine Division marched between a throng of merry, flag-waving enthusiasts. Commandant General Gray watched with satisfaction as his superbly trained Marines passed in review. On the eve of leaving office he had but one regret: never leading a combat mission in Desert Storm.

Some of his Marines stayed overseas. During April 1991 a devastating cyclone flooded the coastal areas of Bangladesh, on the Indian subcontinent The death toll approached 150,000. On 30 April elements of the III Marine Expeditionary Force (MEU) mounted "Operation Sea Angel," a joint rescue operation under the command of Major General Henry C. Stackpole. The mixed force, aided by U.N. workers, dispensed tons of food, potable water, and medical supplies, marking the beginning of a decade of American humanitarian missions muddled with dangerous and often ill-conceived police work.

On 1 July 1991, General Carl Epting Mundy, Jr., became the 30th commandant of the Marine Corps. He was serving as commander of the Fleet Marine Force, Atlantic, when President Bush chose him as commandant. Mundy faced the complex problems of every post-war commandant who had preceded him – scaling back the size of the Marine Corps. Nothing quite prepared him for the downsizing imposed upon the Corps by President William J. Clinton, but he did maintain a peacetime strength of 174,000 men and women, among them Carol A. Mutter, who in 1996 became the first woman of any U.S. service to wear the three stars of a lieutenant general. Because of Clinton's peacekeeping and nation-building enterprises, Mundy needed every man and woman he could muster.

> *'Events in Somalia…remind us that high technology does not always count, and that it may count much less as the world moves away from the Cold War. The Somalian disaster was perpetrated entirely by men armed with old-fashioned small arms, the largest of which can be carried on the back of a pickup truck, yet they managed to turn the country into a death camp.'*
>
> NORMAN FRIEDMAN,
> KEEPING THE PEACE IN SOMALIA.

OPERATION RESTORE HOPE, SOMALIA

Problems in East Africa began during the Persian Gulf War when on 4 January 1991 President Bush rushed Marine helicopters to Mogadishu, Somalia, to evacuate 241 people from the U.S. embassy. After the Marines departed, some fourteen clans continued to fight among themselves, inflicting death by starvation upon more than 500,000 Somalis.

On 18 August 1992 President Bush ordered 145,000 tons of food and medical supplies to be shipped to the beleaguered inhabitants. On 9 December he sent the Marines back to the war-ravaged country in an anti-terrorist campaign against warlords interfering with U.N. relief efforts and threatening the safety of American and foreign aid workers. The first Marines arrived at Mogadishu and secured the port, the airfield, and the abandoned U.S. embassy. A few days later 17,000 Marines from the I MEF under Major General Charles Wilhelm disembarked and entered the city.

What began as a food distribution and peace-keeping mission became more volatile shortly after President Clinton took office in January 1993. Marines traveling on convoys carrying food and medical supplies into central and southern Somalia became involved in firefights with bandits driving light trucks mounted with automatic weapons. In the city of Mogadishu snipers shot several Marines, killing two.

Most of the Marines departed after President Clinton relinquished the peacekeeping task to the U.N., but he remained engaged on a personal basis and endorsed the expansion of the mission from humanitarian assistance to "nation building." The change compelled the U.N. to take sides in a conflict driven by civil strife between clans. Fighting became more prevalent, more soldiers died, and in October 1993 Clinton ordered the 26th MEU back to Somalia to assist in the withdrawal of all American ground forces. The Marines performed the mission and departed, once again leaving matters in the hands of the United Nations.

In early 1995 Somali warlords besieged U.N. forces in Mogadishu, and another SOS message went out to the Marines. Lieutenant General Anthony Zinni took the call and mounted Operation United Shield. Zinni called it a "reverse amphibious landing" because the withdrawal involved a relief-in-place operation by one force of another, each from a different country speaking a different foreign language. Over the course of seven nights Marines ushered each unit, one by one, out of Mogadishu and onto ships. During the withdrawal Leathernecks fought twenty-seven firefights against snipers and Somalis armed with rocket-propelled grenades. For a brief spell, warlords stopped fighting each other to drive out the foreigners.

On the night the 26th MEU disengaged, they fought an armed mob on the beach. With gunships laying down a withering fire overhead, Marines leveled their weapons on the Somalis, keeping up the pressure as their amphibian tractors backed into the water. President Clinton's joint nation-building effort with the U.N. collapsed in defeat, but the Leathernecks got away without losing a man.

Left: On 14 March 1994 a beach master from the USS Portland (LSD-37) shields his eyes while guiding an Air Cushion Landing Craft (LCAC-45) to a landing position on Green Beach near the end of the dusty runway at the Mogadishu International Airport during preparations for the withdrawal of troops from Somalia on 25 March.

Left: Somali civilians watch as Marines walk single file down an alley in Mogadishu's Bakara Market. The Marine detail, acting in response to the Operation Nutcracker phase of Operation Restore Hope, is sweeping the market looking for arms and munitions concealed by Somali bands commanded by local warlords.

▶ **1992**

9 DECEMBER:
Marines return to
Somalia to rescue
foreigners.

1993

20 JUNE: Marines
return once more to
Mogadishu, Somalia,
to keep the peace.

*Above right: Marine
LAV air defense
vehicles depart for
cold weather exercises
in Alaska. While some
Marines train in the
tropics or in the
desert, others train in
polar regions, thereby
ensuring the Corps has
men conditioned to
fight in any climate.*

*Below: A leatherneck
from the 3rd Combat
Engineer Battalion,
3rd Marine Division,
trains with a shoulder-
launched
multipurpose assault
weapon (SMAW). All
Marines receive
weapons training,
even though their
assignments are in
different specialties.*

On 12 April 1994, as Marines from the 15th MEU were evacuating Americans and foreigners from the vicious carnage in Rwanda, East Africa, trouble erupted again in Haiti, in the West Indies. Military dictator General Raoul Cédras destabilized the country by destroying the last surviving elements of democratic rule. A joint force of Marines and the XVIII Airborne Corps under Army Lieutenant General Hugh Shelton waited offshore for the United Nations to decide whether to intervene. So that the press would not miss the point, the JCS codenamed the operation "Uphold/Support Democracy."

On 20 September a Marine air-ground task force stormed ashore at Cap Haitien on Haiti's northern coast while Army troops marched into Port-au-Prince. General Cédras did not welcome the incursion and informed his so-called military police to express their displeasure. The police, however, withheld any demonstrations until the night of 24 September when they observed a Marine patrol passing near their barracks. The Marines spotted one of the Haitians raising a rifle and shot him. When the others drew their weapons the Marines opened with a well-aimed response. In a sharp little firefight lasting no more than a few seconds, ten of General Cédras's MPs lay dead outside their barracks. Cédras accused the Marines of murder, but to no avail. The leathernecks continued their search for weapons and on 1 October 1994 returned to their amphibious ships, leaving an Army battalion at Port-au-Prince to keep the peace.

On 1 July 1995 General Charles Chandler Krulak, the youngest son of Lieutenant General Victor H. Krulak, became the 31st commandant of the Marine Corps. A daunting task lay before the new commandant, who during the brief Persian Gulf War had skyrocketed from brigadier general to lieutenant general. Like his father, Krulak believed in the importance of technology, logistics, and the

collection of intelligence. During the Gulf War he had created, virtually overnight, a huge base in the desert. He named it "Al Khanjer" (the Dagger) and used the base to successfully launch the I MEF's assault against the formidable Saddam Hussein line. From this backdrop of success he now faced the demanding changes of an approaching new century with new tactics bound together with new technology.

General Krulak stepped into a situation much different from his experiences in the Persian Gulf. Since April 1992 Marines had been participating in a wide range of air and naval operations in support of U.N. Security Council resolutions aimed at ending ethnic conflicts boiling inside the former Yugoslavia. The Balkans peacekeeping mission would eventually escalate into one of the largest U.S. military operations other than war, and the first significant military operation ever undertaken by NATO. The Marine Corps, as well as every other service, had much to learn from the experience.

SERBIAN HEGEMONY

The war in Bosnia did not fit into any established category, being neither a true civil war nor a purely ethnic or religious conflict. It became a war of aggression by Bosnian Serbs supported politically, militarily, and propagandistically by the national-socialist regime of strongman Slobodan Milosevic's Serbia. Wars to restore Serbian hegemony in Yugoslavia began in June 1991 when Slovenia and Croatia rebelled against Milosevic and declared their independence. A month later Milosevic initiated action to seize by force those parts of Croatia, Bosnia, and Herzegovina where Serbs comprised the majority of the population or were strategically or economically important to Serbia.

War in Bosnia and Herzegovina did not begin until after Serbia expanded its border into Croa-

THE RESCUE OF SCOTT O'GRADY

On 2 June 1995 Captain Scott O'Grady bailed out over a mountainous section of Bosnia. A cameraman on Bosnian Serb TV obtained a tape of the F-16 wreckage, including pictures of the pilot's parachute and g-suit, but no picture of O'Grady either dead or alive. It meant that O'Grady might have survived, but no one could be certain.

Admiral Leighton Smith, commanding NATO forces in Southern Europe, labored for a week trying to pinpoint O'Grady's signal. Colonel Martin Berndt, USMC, said he could find O'Grady and volunteered to lead a detachment of Marines and bring the pilot out. Before Admiral Smith agreed to expose any more men to possible capture, he called Commandant General Mundy for approval, warning: "We won't know whether they'll find Scott or a shepherd or a very angry bunch of Bosnian Serbs." Mundy replied, "Do it!" Before dispatching Berndt's detail, Smith sent a message to the Bosnian Serb commanders, warning, "I'm coming in to get him. Stay out of my way!" He anticipated their reply, which said the flyer had already been captured, but, said Smith, "We didn't believe it."

Soon after dark on 7 June Colonel Berndt loaded forty Marines on helicopters and took off from the deck of the USS *Kearsarge*. Berndt expected a trap and brought enough firepower to make any nosy Bosnian Serbs wish they had taken Smith's advice and stayed out of the way. The terrain below had been scouted, and Berndt felt certain that weak signals from the ground had come from O'Grady. As the helicopters lowered into a small clearing, forty Marines jumped to the ground and formed a perimeter. Rotors on the choppers kept thrumming. Weak and threadbare, O'Grady emerged from cover and grasped Berndt's extended arm. "I just reached out," Berndt said, "and hauled him into the cockpit."

Around 1:00 a.m. on 8 June Berndt's detachment deposited O'Grady safely on the deck of the *Kearsarge*. When Admiral Smith received the Marines, Berndt thanked him for letting them go after O'Grady. "These were boys," Smith recalled, "but what guts, what training."

Then he turned to O'Grady and added, "Son, I'm not the hero. I haven't the foggiest idea what it is to be a hero, but I can tell you to get ready. The next six days may be just as hard as the last six!"

As the admiral predicted, O'Grady became a national hero. Colonel Berndt and his Marines – the real heroes – lapsed back into the obscurity of Bosnian peacekeeping.

Left: *U. S. Air Force Captain Scott O'Grady was a lucky man to have Marines looking for him after he bailed out over the Bosnian mountains. Once safe aboard the USS* Kearsarge *after his dramatic rescue, O'Grady managed to work up a smile of relief.*

tia. In the spring of 1992 Milosevic detached about 70,000 Serbian regulars and transferred them to the Bosnian Serbian government for operations mainly against the Bosnian Muslims.

During the fighting in Bosnia, which ended in late 1995, the U.S. flew 109,000 sorties – slightly fewer than coalition forces flew in the Gulf War. Only four NATO aircraft were lost in combat between 1992 and 1995, and of those, only one belonged to the United States – an F-16 flown by Captain Scott O'Grady of the U.S. Air Force, who was rescued by Marines led by Colonel Martin Berndt.

The rescue of Captain O'Grady from hostile Bosnian Serb territory came close to crossing the fine line between combat and peacekeeping. The complex tactical recovery of aircraft and personnel (TRAP) mission performed by Berndt's Marines required close coordination between air and ground forces converging on the rescue site from many different locations. That it worked on an hour's notice validates the importance of countless hours of training Marines receive to be able to respond with alacrity to a signal to "Go!"

NATO peacekeeping efforts in Bosnia were still underway when fighting in nearby Kosovo

Above: *On the night of 7 June 1995, Colonel Martin Berndt, USMC, went after O'Grady with a detachment of volunteer Marines flying Sikorsky Sea Stallions. They pulled O'Grady off a small clearing on a mountain.*

Right: *During operations in the Balkans, most Marine flights originated from carriers. With sorties running day and night, ordnance men were kept busy moving an assortment of bombs and rockets to the main deck for rearming aircraft.*

Right: *On 31 March 1999, during Operation Allied Force, a Marine EA-6B Prowler takes off from the U. S. air base at Aviano, Italy, to monitor activity on the ground and to coordinate air attacks over Yugoslavia should any be required.*

Below right: *The configuration of jet aircraft has not changed much over the years, but the planes are constantly being updated with the latest technology, as was this F/A-18F Hornet fighter-bomber.*

Below: *The EA-6B Prowler provides surveillance, intelligence gathering, targeting, and a multitude of other tasks. This Prowler is firing an anti-radar missile during exercises.*

> *'The hard truth is that military personnel risk being wounded and killed in waging peace as much as in waging war.'*
>
> D. N. GRIFFITHS, "WAGING PEACE IN BOSNIA,"
> NAVAL INSTITUTE PROCEEDINGS.

between ethnic Albanians (KLA) and Serbs began to destabilize the province. Kosovo had been operating with autonomy from greater Serbia, but in 1998 Serb police and military forces began depopulating sections of the province. By 1999 the fighting had driven tens of thousands of civilians into tent cities in Macedonia and Albania. NATO members would never agree to a long war against Serbia, but on 24 March 1999 they did agree to surgical air strikes against strategic targets in Serbia. NATO aimed the air campaign against Serbia at Milosevic's aggressiveness in the Balkans. The air strikes sought to discourage him from escalating his attacks on helpless civilians; to reverse ethnic cleansing; and to damage the Serbian army's ability to wage war against Kosovo or any of Serbia's neighbors.

Once again, the Marine Corps took to the air, flying F/A-18 fighter-bombers out of Aviano Air Base, Italy. The 26th Marine Expeditionary Unit (MEU) flew AV-8B Harrier attack aircraft off the decks of the USS *Bataan*. The unit had been the first to fly Harriers in 1985 when the Department of Defense introduced the unique British jet into the American arsenal. The aircraft carried precision-guided munitions – usually laser-guided glide bombs – and HARM anti-radiation missiles for suppressing enemy air defenses. Marine F/A-18s, Harriers, and Navy carrier-based F-14s worked in conjunction with Marine EA-6B Prowlers, which helped to provide the necessary coordination of targeting and control. The twin-seat EA-6B variants also carried jamming equipment capable of disrupting enemy radar missile targeting systems on the ground.

In April 1999 the 26th MEU went ashore and provided security for thousands of Kosovar

Every man heard about the disaster in New York and Washington, and they waited for a change in orders. None came. During 15-17 September the 15th MEU performed a rapid humanitarian assistance mission, delivering medical supplies and 110 tons of food to thousands of inhabitants caught up in civil strife. Though aware of the President Bush's declaration of war Corporal Brian W. Tate said, "I'm staying focused on the mission at hand rather than thinking too much about the happenings back home. We are all just taking it one day at a time."

PENTAGON MARINES

At 9:40 a.m. on 11 September 2001, Marine Sergeant Maurice L. Bease heard the roar of jet engines and looked up, expecting to see jet fighters streaking overhead. Instead, he saw a huge white commercial airliner that seemed to be aimed directly at him. Seconds later it slammed into the side of the Pentagon, 200 yards from where he stood. A huge ball of flame blossomed from the building, followed by a carpet of black smoke filled with debris. From both sides of the burning section, people ran toward the parking lot.

Smoke enveloped the offices of Marine Aviation, located next to the crash site. Corporal Timothy J. Garofola, working security at the Pentagon, went to the office of Lieutenant General William L. Nyland, Deputy Commandant for Aviation, who had been holding a meeting when the terrorists struck. "Get us out of here!" someone said. The floor began to buckle and fire could be seen between the joints. The magnetized door would not open. "Then the 'Marine' came out in Garofola," one observer said as he watched the corporal yank on the door until it sprang free. Garofola could barely breathe in the smoke and dust, but he evacuated the floor, being among the last men out.

Lance Corporals Dustin P. Schuetz and Michael Vera worked in the administrative

section near the offices of General Nyland. When the jetliner struck, the impact sent Schuetz to the floor, and Vera's chair rolled him into the wall. The two men stepped into the corridor and realized that "Something was terribly wrong." They remembered their training back at boot camp: initiative, decisiveness, and teamwork. "It came like a breath of fresh air," Schuetz recalled. They evacuated their offices and got the staff headed away from the blinding smoke. Then they went back into the burning building, linking hands with others to get inside and respond to the feeble cries of "Help. Somebody help me!"

Sergeant Francis W. Pomrink, Jr., worked in the Department of Marine Aviation near the impact area. He heard the crash, rushed outside to investigate, and cleared the area. Concern for his fellow Marines prompted him to join a rescue party composed of military personnel from all the services. He heard screams of people shouting for help and could not turn his back on them. After liberating five injured individuals from the flames and debris, he lost count. He never found his friends – a few Marines he particularly wanted to save.

From those who returned to the holocaust to save the injured, a television correspondent asked, "Why did you go back in there?" A blackened and singed Lance Corporal Schuetz said it best, "That's what Marines are supposed to do."

Above: *Had the Pentagon not been durably built, the terrorist-hijacked jetliner that crashed into the west wall on 11 September 2001 could easily have afflicted far more damage and taken many more lives.*

Left: *In defiance against every terrorist, firemen and other rescue personnel from all services unfurl the Stars and Stripes from the roof of the Pentagon.*

THE SPECIAL OPERATIONS CAPABLE (SOC) MARINES

SOC Marines materialized from the need for a compact unit capable of planning and performing any mission on six hours' notice. MEU(SOC)s operate with an average strength of 2,200 Marines and sailors. They most commonly deploy for six-month "floats" in the Mediterranean, Persian Gulf, and in the Indian and Pacific Oceans. When at sea they operate as amphibious-ready teams from three to five amphibious assault ships and can move freely and rapidly across the seas without the usual diplomatic restraints imposed by foreign nations. Though small in size, MEU(SOC)s have become the nation's most flexible deterrent and combat-ready means of demonstrating America's influence abroad.

For many years conventional Marine units consisted of infantry battalions with support units. Battalion Landing Teams (BLTs) included a helicopter detachment. In today's Corps the battalion landing team forms only one part of the Marine Expeditionary Unit.

These highly trained, special units consist of four integrated teams. The Ground Combat Element contains an infantry battalion supported by artillery, armor, engineers, amphibious assault vehicles, and reconnaissance. The Aviation Combat Element provides an amalgamated squadron of vertical/short takeoff and landing aircraft composed of Harriers and attack and transport helicopters. The Combat Service Support Element provides a full range of logistical support from sea or shore with fifteen days of supplies and equipment ready at all times for deployment. The Command Element provides local command and control, communication with other command posts in the area, and linkage through the chain of command to the regional commander-in-chief and to authorities as far up as the Pentagon.

For a MEU to be designated "Special Operations Capable," the men undergo a

Above: *In the Adriatic Sea, the first units from the 26th MEU(SOC) load onto a CH-53D Sea Stallion on the USS* Kearsarge. *The Marines are on another peacekeeping mission, this one in Skopje, Macedonia, to support Operation Allied Force in the troubled Balkans.*

Below: *On 4 June 1998 Marines from the 26th MEU(SOC) use the flight deck of the USS* Wasp, *positioned off the coast of Albania during Exercise Determined Falcon, to perform Tactical Recovery of Aircraft and Personnel exercises.*

rigorous twenty-six week training program capped by a rigid evaluation to determine whether the unit has met the high standards of SOC. The training encompasses many actions other than combat. A MEU(SOC) must become adept at humanitarian assistance/disaster relief operations such as those in East Timor; noncombatant evacuations such as in Liberia and Zaire; amphibious withdrawals like that in Somalia; military operations in every type of terrain from city streets to snow-capped mountains; peacekeeping and peace-enforcement operations in places like Kosovo; and as an advance reconnaissance force performing intelligence gathering missions or aiding electronic warfare and target-sighting operations.

In any emergency, MEU(SOC)s may well be the first to land, secure a lightly defended port or an airfield, and clear an area for the arrival of a Marine Expeditionary Force, which at full strength consists of 46,000 men and women organized around a Marine division, an aircraft wing, and several service groups.

The JCS rushed Special Forces from all the services into Pakistan and Uzbekistan for operations inside Afghanistan. Helicopters inserted Marine units to gather intelligence and direct bombing sorties on strategic targets. Offshore, the 15th MEU(SOC), commanded by Colonel Thomas D. Waldhauser, and the 26th MEU(SOC), commanded by Colonel Andrew P. Flick, moved into position on the *Peleliu* and the *Bataan* for operational assignments in the search for Osama bin Laden, his al-Quaida operatives, and their Taliban hosts.

The war in Afghanistan, code-named Operation Enduring Freedom, brought Marine detachments through Pakistan and Uzbekistan for reconnaissance and TRAP (tactical recovery of aircraft and personnel) operations inside Taliban-controlled areas. They joined with friendly forces inside Afghanistan to fight a common enemy. Televised newsclips showed Special Forces detachments riding with the Afghani Northern Alliance through rugged mountainous terrain on horseback.

Because Afghanistan bordered no sea, MEU(SOC) commands stood offshore waiting for the moment to be called into action somewhere in southern Afghanistan. They never stopped training, but prepared each day for a call to action, and responded to that call in true Marines fashion.

> '*I'm trying not to think about the dangers of combat. I'm keeping my head up, looking forward and trying to stay focused on readying for whatever my country needs.*'
>
> CORPORAL CONOR K. DUFFY,
> IN *MARINE CORPS NEWS*.

▶ **1998**

7 AUGUST: Terrorists strike U.S. embassies in Nairobi, Kenya, and Dar es Salaam, Tanzania, killing 224 people, including twelve Americans..

1999

24 MARCH: President Clinton authorizes the bombing of Serbia, which continues until 10 June 1999.

24 JUNE: President Clinton initiates bombing attacks against Serbia and Serbian strongholds in Kosovo.

1 JULY: General James L. Jones becomes the 32nd Commandant of the Marine Corps.

Left: *On 25 November 2001, as Operation Enduring Freedom begins in Afghanistan, a patrol from the 15th MEU(SOC) near Kandahar takes to the desert to form a watchful cordon around the airfield. They carry extra ammo, bedding, observation equipment, targeting instruments, and enough supplies to last up to three days.*

▶ 2001

11 SEPTEMBER: Muslim terrorists, responding to orders from Usama bin Laden, strike the World Trade Center and the Pentagon using commercial Boeing 757 jet airliners as their bombs. President Bush declares war on terrorism.

Right: *While on board the USS* Peleliu *(LHA-5), Marines of the 15th MEU(SOC) practice close combat with an M16A2 while they await orders that will send them to an airfield near Kandahar.*

Below: *On 2 November 2001 a Marine AV-8B Harrier, attached to the 15th MEU(SOC), streaks down the deck of the USS* Peleliu *during Operation Enduring Freedom. The versatile Harrier is the Marines' favorite combat fighter.*

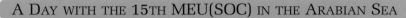

A DAY WITH THE 15TH MEU(SOC) IN THE ARABIAN SEA

On board the USS *Peleliu* (LHA-5), combat troops prepare to be called into action at a moment's notice. They work hard to be ready. Each morning they participate in the Marine Corps new martial arts program on the ship's flight deck. Most of the men have already achieved the program's first skill level, the tan belt. Later they assemble again, this time to prepare for conventional hand-to-hand combat, using the M16A2 service rifle for exercises. On board the ship's flightdeck they continue to rehearse, tactically exiting helicopters and forming a security perimeter exactly as they would in close combat conditions on the ground.

When a helicopter went down in Pakistan, Marines and sailors from the 15th MEU's Maritime Special Purpose Force (MSPF) flew into an airfield in Pakistan and retrieved the chopper under fire. The CH-53E Super Stallion and the CH-46E Sea Knight form the bulwark of Marine Medium Helicopter Squadron 163 on the *Peleliu*. Mechanics keep helicopters in constant readiness, working around the clock in a never-ending fight against corrosion from salt air.

Night sorties against strategic targets in Afghanistan keep pilots and ground crews engaged throughout the night. In eerie green nightlights aircrews clamp 500-pound Mk 82 bombs under the wings of AV-8B Harriers. From a distance the busy flightdeck looks like a deserted ship surrounded by a ghostly glow far out to sea.

Using a stick of olive drab paint, Marines scratch on bombs the names of friends lost during the 11 September terrorist attacks. For Harrier pilots, it would be their first fight against the ruling Taliban.

With pilots suited-up and ready to go, a flightdeck handler waves luminescent batons and directs a Harrier attack jet into takeoff position. He signals the runway clear, and ordnancemen remove safety devices, arming the explosives. The Harrier's powerful engines roar, reaching a deafening crescendo that eclipses every other human sense. An orange baton waves in the darkness and the first Harrier screams toward the bow and into combat. Heads turn as the plane roars by, its engines spewing a torrid, body-jarring jet blast. A few hours later the waiting crews cheer as the Harriers return, their racks empty. Somewhere in Afghanistan al-Qaida terrorists have paid a price for their fanatical violence.

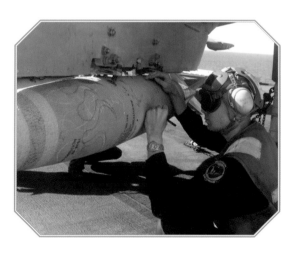

Above right: *Pilots and ordnance men take great pleasure in penning special notes to Osama bin Laden and al-Qaida on the bombs being flown by Marine pilots into target areas.*

'Everyone joined the Corps living off the legends and stories of the past. It may be our turn to do our part in keeping the traditions alive.'

CORPORAL NORMAN A. PEOPLES
IN *MARINE CORPS NEWS.*

During the war against the ruling Taliban, MEU(SOC) units on the ground at the Kandahar airfield represented the largest American force in Afghanistan. They interdicted roads, collected prisoners, performed search and destroy missions, gathered intelligence, and carved safe pathways through a country perforated by three land mines for every Afghani. When the U.S. embassy reopened in late December 2001, a detachment of

Marines entered Kabul to perform an age-old tradition – protecting the diplomatic staff. Marines were still in the field when word came that the MEU(SOC) units were to be returned to their ships and replaced by the Army's 101st Airborne Division. With the Taliban battered into submission or flight, Marines departed, leaving the clean-up work to others while they prepared for their next mission in the war against terror.

Soon after the 15th MEU(SOC) returned to the Peleliu, Operation Enduring Freedom initiated a new initiative codenamed Operation Anaconda – designed to squeeze into submission al-Qaida forces holed up in the rugged mountains around Torabora. General Tommy Franks, commanding coalition forces in Afghanistan, called in the 13th MEU(SOC) for air strikes.

One day later, AH-1W and CH-53E Marine helicopters operating from the USS Bonhomme Richard (LHD-6) began flying the first of 400 combat sorties. Harrier pilots flew 148 sorties and dropped 32 GBU-12 500-pound bombs and MK-82 bombs on specified targets. "We got shot at every night," said Sergeant Jennifer Austin, a 22-year-old crew chief from San Diego whose crew flew more than 70 of the 257 hours logged by Super Stallions. "It was all small arms fire," she said, "usually from small groups and caravans. We could see muzzle flashes."

On 15 April 2002 six Marine FA-18D Hornets landed on a new coalition airfield built in the middle of Kyrgyzstan, the first American fighter aircraft to do so. As part of the 376th Air Expeditionary Wing, they are there to attack and destroy targets remaining in Afghanistan and support ground forces operating as part of Operation Enduring Freedom. Brigadier General Wayne Lloyd, commanding the wing, said, "This is a great day for the coalition forces. The addition of

Hornets, together with other coalition aircraft, increases our capability of putting 'bombs on target' in Afghanistan." U. S. Marine Corps Captain William Gray said proudly, "The Marines have arrived." He might also have added – again.

NEW TACTICS

In preparing for the 21st Century, the Marine Corps developed a new tactical concept – Operational Maneuver From the Sea OMFTS) – directed against the enemy's center of gravity. In Afghanistan, the center of gravity was the Taliban. Throughout the world the center of gravity became Osama bin Laden and his al-Qaida network. As in the conflict in Afghanistan, OMFTS uses the sea to gain advantage, but use the air to

▶ **15 SEPTEMBER:** The 26th MEU(SOC) lands at East Timor to provide humanitarian relief.

11 OCTOBER: Marine MEU(SOC) units head for the Arabian Sea.

26 NOVEMBER: Two MEU(SOC) units land and capture an Afghani airstrip fifteen miles southwest of Kandahar.

Right: *On 17 January 2000 the pilot of an MV-22 Osprey rotates the engines to steady the aircraft precisely over the drop zone. Marine parachutists from the 2nd Reconnaissance Battalion, 2nd MEU, free-fall into the sky above Camp Lejuene, North Carolina. The controversial Osprey has many advantages over the standard Marine helicopters, being able to travel farther and faster without refueling.*

Below: *On 3 November 2001, for a night-time mission against al-Qaida and the Taliban, a flight deck handler with the 15th MEU(SOC) uses batons to direct an AV-8B Harrier into take-off position aboard the USS Peleliu.*

punish the enemy and land a combat force wherever the center of gravity exists. The sea becomes the medium for moving tactical units like the 15th MEU(SOC) and the 26th MEU(SOC) into position to launch attacks against the center of gravity. The success of OMFTS depends on superior capabilities in command and control, intelligence, mobility, logistics, weapons, and force protection – the guiding principles of MEU(SOC) training.

Into this operational milieu comes a mix of old and new weapons and equipment, beginning with a multi-mission amphibious assault ship such as the USS *Peleliu* (LHA-5), the fifth of its kind, and the upcoming San Antonio-class LPDs (amphibious transport dock), which combines an abbreviated flight deck and a well deck for landing craft. Both vessels, along with Maritime Prepositioning Shipping, are to become the key enabler for OMFTS operations.

In the future, medium-lift Bell-Boeing MV-22 Ospreys with tilt-rotor, vertical takeoff and landing capabilities will replace the Corps' aging "Sea Knight" helicopters and enable an OMFTS force to range, unlike helicopters, throughout the entire operational depth of the enemy. Ospreys operate at greater speeds and can carry, in addition to a three-man crew, twenty-four combat troops or five tons of cargo.

The new AV-8B "Harrier II" on the USS *Peleliu* will continue to be a major component with OMFTS operations and with MEU(SOC) units. The jet aircraft has been refitted with updated radar to new night attack standards, adding an important component to Marine operations in Afghanistan.

The Landing Craft Air Cushioned (LCAC) has opened the world's coastlines to the Marine Corps. The vessel moves at several times the speed of traditional landing craft and can carry everything from men and supplies to combat tanks. In the past landing craft depended upon accessible beaches, which were usually mined and well fortified by enemy defenses. LCACs can come ashore almost anywhere and do it swiftly,

Left: *A 26th Marine Expeditionary Unit Amphibious Unit prepares to drive an air-cushioned prop-driven LCAC into the well deck of the USS Wasp (LHD-1) during integrated land/sea operations off the Carolina coast. The LCAC is capable of speeds up to fifty knots.*

avoiding casualty-causing enemy defenses.

The Advanced Amphibious Assault Vehicle (AAAV) will be three times faster than the Amphibious Assault Vehicle (AAV), which is still in use. The AAAV can be launched twenty-five miles from the assault sector and arrive on the beach at three times the speed of its predecessor. It provides a unique combination of firepower, armor protection, high-speed mobility on land, and performs at speed equal to those of the modern tank during a cross-country sprint. Like the LCAC, an AAAV can be used for over-the-horizon surprise assaults, avoiding the enemy's strengths while exploiting his weaknesses.

While some of the services now depend too much on highly sophisticated 21st century weaponry, the Marine Corps still believes in the importance of the human element. For operations in the future, the Corps will continue to prepare individual Marines to meet the variables of the battlefield. They will be trained with high-technology weapons and information systems, and they will know what to do with them. They will be forged from the same traditional indoctrination and training that has produced the world's most determined fighters for more than two centuries, but they will be stronger in body and better mentally prepared for the changes coming in future warfare. Today's and tomorrow's Marines will continue to be what they have always been, warriors without peers.

Semper Fidelis!

Left: *Updated versions AAVP amphibious assault vehicle give the Marines greatly improved ground and sea tactical mobility. The AAVP might appropriately be called the great-grandson of the original LVTs that crossed the coral reefs of the South Pacific during World War II.*

Left: *Marines must be capable of fighting in all conditions. Here Chief Warrant Officer Jones and Pfc Ericson from Electronic Warfare Sqn, Marine Attack Sqn (VMA-Q4), Cherry Point, North Carolina, take part in NBC exercises.*

BIBLIOGRAPHY

Alexander, Joseph H., and Merrill L. Bartlett. *Sea Soldiers in the Cold War: Amphibious Warfare, 1945-1991.* Annapolis: Naval Institute Press, 1994.

_____. *Storm Landings: Epic Amphibious Battles in the Central Pacific.* Annapolis: Naval Institute Press, 1997.

Arthur, Robert A., and Cohlmia, Kenneth. *The Third Marine Division.* Washington: Infantry Journal Press, 1948.

Baldwin, Hanson. "The Fourth Marines at Corregidor," *Marine Corps Gazette,* November 1946-February 1947.

Bayler, Walter J. *Last Man Off Wake Island.* Indianapolis: Bobbs-Merrill Company, 1943.

Belote, James H., and William M. *Corregidor: The Saga of a Fortress.* New York: Harper & Row Publishers, 1967.

Berry, Henry. *Semper Fi, Mac: Living Memories of the U.S. Marines in World War II.* New York: Arbor House, 1982.

Butler, Smedley D. *Old Gimlet Eye: The Adventures of Smedley D. Butler.* New York: Farrar and Rinehart, 1933.

Cagle, Malcolm W., and Manson, Frank A. *The Sea War in Korea.* Annapolis: U.S. Naval Institute, 1957.

Catlin, Alburtus W. *With the Help of God and a Few Marines.* New York: Scribner's, 1918.

Chenelly, Joseph R., "Aviation Deck Operations," *Marine Corps News,* 20 June 2001.

_____. "MEU Masters Martial Arts," *Marine Corps News,* 5 September 2001.

_____. "Marines, Sailors Press On, Lend Helping Hands To Timorese," *Marine Corps News,* 19 September 2001.

_____. "15th MEU(SOC) Stands Ready," *Marine Corps News,* 11 October 2001.

_____. "Harrier Jets Conduct Airstrikes in Afghanistan," *Marine Corps News,* 4 November 2001.

_____. "Marines Brave Night On The Sea Keeping Harriers In The War," *Marine Corps News,* 8 November 2001.

Clifford, Kenneth J. *Progress and Purpose: A Developmental History of the U.S. Marines Corps, 1900-1970.* Washington: History and Museums Division, HQMC, 1973.

Isely, Jeter A., and Crowl, Philip A. *The U.S. Marines and Amphibious War: Its Theory and Practice in the Pacific.* Princeton, N.J.: Princeton University Press, 1951.

Kelly, Mary Pat, "Rescue: Out of Bosnia," *Naval Institute Proceedings,* No. 1,109, July, 1995.

Kent, Zachary. *The Persian Gulf War.* Hillside, N.J.: Enslow Publishers, Inc., 1994.

King, John. *The Gulf War.* New York: Macmillan Publishing Co., 1991.

Kosnik, Mark E. "The Military Response to Terrorism," *Naval War College Review,* Spring, 2000.

Krulak, Victor H. *First to Fight: An Inside View of the U.S. Marine Corps.* Annapolis: Naval Institute Press, 1984.

Lehrack, Otto J. *No Shining Armor: The Marines at War in Vietnam.* Lawrence, Kan.: University Press of Kansas, 1992.

Lejeune, John A. *The Reminiscences of a Marine.* Philadelphia: Dorrance and Company, 1930.

McClellan, Edwin N. *The United States Marine Corps in the World War.* Washington: Historical Section, HQMC, 1968.

_____. "A Brief History of the Fourth Brigade of Marines," *Marine Corps Gazette,* December, 1919.

McMillan, George. *The Old Breed: A History of the First Marine Division in World War II.* Washington, D.C.: Infantry Journal Press, 1949.

Merrill, W. A. "This Is My Rifle," *Marine Corps Gazette,* December, 1960.

Metcalf, Clyde H. *A History of the United States Marine Corps.* New York: G. P. Putnam's Sons, 1939.

Miller, Francis Trevelyan. *The Complete History of World War II.* Chicago: Progress Research Corporation, 1948.

Miller, Nathan. *Sea of Glory: The Continental Navy Fights for Independence, 1775-1783.* New York: David McKay Company, 1974.

Millet, Allan R. *Semper Fidelis: The History of the United States Marine Corps.* New York: Macmillan Publishing Company, 1980.

Montross, Lynn. *U.S. Marine Corps Operations in Korea, 1950-1953.* 5 vols. Washington, D.C.: Historical Branch, HQMC, 1954-1972.

Morison, Samuel Eliot. *The Two-Ocean War: A Short History of the United States Navy in the Second World War.* Boston: Little Brown and Company, 1963.

Moskin, J. Robert. *The U.S. Marine Corps Story.* Boston: Little, Brown, 1992.

Nash, Howard P., Jr. *The Forgotten Wars.* New York: A.S. Barnes and Company, 1968.

Navy Department. *Naval Documents Related to the United States War with the Barbary Pirates.* Washington, D.C.: Government Printing Office, 1939-45.

_____. *Naval Documents Related to the Quasi-War Between the United States and France.* Washington, D.C.: Government Printing Office, 1935-38.

_____. *Official Records of the Union and Confederate Navies in the War of the Rebellion.* Washington, D.C.: Government Printing Office, 1894-1922.

Newcomb, Richard F. *Iwo Jima.* New York: Holt, Rinehart and Winston, Inc., 1965.

Parker, William D. *A Concise History Of the United States Marine Corps 1775-1969.* Washington, D.C.: Historical Division Headquarters, U. S. Marine Corps, 1970.

Proehl, C. W. *The Fourth Marine Division in World War II.* Washington, D.C.: Infantry Journal Press, 1946.

Quilter, Charles J. *U.S. Marines in the Persian Gulf: With the I Marine Expeditionary Force in Desert Shield and Desert Storm.* Washington, D.C.: History and Museums Division, HQMC, 1993.

Richards, T. A., "Marines in Somalia: 1992," *Naval Institute Proceedings,* No. 1,083, May, 1993.

Russ, Martin. *The Last Parallel.* New York: Rinehart, 1957.

Schwarzkopf, H. Norman, with Peter Petre. *It Doesn't Take a Hero.* New York: Bantam, 1992.

Sherrod, Robert. *History of Marine Corps Aviation in World War II.* Washington, D.C.: Combat Forces Press, 1952.

_____. *On to Westward.* New York: Duell, Sloan and Pierce, 1945.

Simmons, Edwin H. *The United States Marines: The First Two Hundred Years, 1775-1976.* New York: Viking Press, 1974.

Simmons, Edwin H., et al. *The Marines in Vietnam, 1954-1973: An Anthology and Annotated Bibliography.* Washington, D.C.: History and Museums Division, HQMC, 1974.

Sledge, Eugene B. *With the Old Breed at Peleliu and Okinawa.* Annapolis: Naval Institute Press, 1996.

Smith, Charles R. *Marines in the Revolution: A History of the Continental Marines in the American Revolution, 1775-1783.* Washington, D.C.: History and Museums Division, HQMC, 1975.

Smith, Holland M. *Coral and Brass.* New York: Scribner's, 1949.

Smith, S. E., ed. *The United States Marine Corps in World War II.* New York: Random House, 1969.

Stockman, J. R. *The Battle for Tarawa.* Washington, D.C.: Combat Forces Press, 1947.

Sweetman, Jack. *American Naval History: An Illustrated Chronology of the U.S. Navy and Marine Corps 1775-Present.* Annapolis: Naval Institute Press, 1984.

Thomason, John J., Jr. *Fix Bayonets! And Other Stories.* New York: Scribner's, 1926.

Toland, John. *But Not in Shame.* New York: Random House, Inc., 1961.

Twining, Merrill B. *No Bended Knee: The Battle for Guadalcanal.* Novato: Presidio, 1996.

Vandegrift, A. A. *Once a Marine: The Memoirs of a General.* New York: W. W. Norton & Company, 1964.

Westcott, Allan, ed. *American Sea Power Since 1775.* Philadelphia: J. B. Lippincott Company, 1947.

Wolfert, Ira. *Battle for the Solomons.* Boston: Houghton Mifflin Company, 1943.

Zimmerman, John L. *The Guadalcanal Campaign.* Washington, D.C.: Combat Forces Press, 1949.

INDEX

Page numbers in **bold** type indicate references in captions to illustrations.